D1572284

Carolina Christmas

Archibald Rutledge

Carolina Christmas

Archibald Rutledge's Enduring Holiday Stories

Edited by Jim Casada

The University of South Carolina Press

Published by the University of South Carolina Press
Columbia, South Carolina 29208

www.sc.edu/uscpress

Manufactured in the United States of America

19 18 17 16 15 14 13 12 11 10   10 9 8 7 6 5 4 3 2 1

Library of Congress Cataloging-in-Publication Data

Rutledge, Archibald Hamilton, 1883–1973.
   Carolina Christmas : Archibald Rutledge's enduring holiday stories /
edited by Jim Casada.
      p. cm.
   ISBN 978-1-57003-954-6 (cloth : alk. paper)
   1. Christmas stories, American. 2. Christmas—Southern
States—Fiction. I. Casada, Jim. II. Title.
   PS3535.U87C37 2010
   813'.52—dc22

                                                    2010025088

Recipes contained in this book are being published solely because of historical interest and have not been kitchen tested. Neither author nor publisher assumes any responsibility for the reader's application of the material contained herein.

Frontispiece: From the *Mercersburg Academy Karux,* vol. 22. This and all other images are in the possession of Jim Casada unless otherwise stated.

This book was printed on Glatfelter Natures, a recycled paper with 30 percent postconsumer waste content.

To all kindred spirits who share my love of sporting tradition,
admire Archibald Rutledge's enduring literary legacy,
and cherish the joys of Christmas

Contents

❧ Contents ❧

Illustrations

Acknowledgments

Over the course of some three decades involving active study of the life and literary endeavors of Archibald Rutledge, many individuals have helped me or encouraged my efforts. Foremost in their ranks was the late Irvine Rutledge, Old Flintlock's son. Irv was enthusiastic about my plans for a series of anthologies that would once again make some of his father's finest writing readily available to the reading public, and I cherish our extensive exchange of correspondence and the occasion when I met and chatted with Irv and his wife on the steps of Hampton Plantation. Other members of the Rutledge clan, most notably Don Rutledge and Elise Bradford, two of Old Flintlock's grandchildren, have been quite supportive of my work. A few years back they did me a singular honor by asking me to make the acceptance speech for Rutledge's posthumous induction into the South Carolina Academy of Authors.

As always, my wife, Ann, has been my shrewdest critic, sometime typist, proofreader extraordinaire, and helpmate in general. The good folks at the University of South Carolina Press, who have published three previous Rutledge anthologies, have been paragons of patience as I procrastinated in my all too typical fashion. They know how to turn a manuscript into a book, seamlessly making the transition from raw material to a polished finished product, and I have every confidence their past performances will be replicated in the current work.

Although I have now been a recovering professor for a decade and a half, as I originally began accumulating Rutledge information the staff at Winthrop University's Dacus Library was most helpful in obtaining obscure items for me, arranging to procure articles through the wonders of interlibrary loan, and generally doing what fine librarians do while laboring in unappreciated obscurity, making life easier for authors and editors. Similarly Dale Arenz, who has amassed and indexed an incredible holding of outdoor magazines, was of invaluable assistance when it came to obtaining copies of a couple of obscure Rutledge articles.

Finally I would be remiss if I did not thank all those readers who share my enduring pleasure in the works of Archibald Rutledge. He takes all of us down darkening but delightful roads into a world of nature, sport, and life we have largely lost. To those who share my joy in these vicarious experiences and who have evidenced same by buying my previous Rutledge collections, I herewith tender a simple but heartfelt thanks.

A Note on Selection

Unlike my previous Archibald Rutledge anthologies, selection of items for inclusion in the current one has been a relatively simple, straightforward undertaking. The seasonal focus explains this in large measure, but some mention of how the pieces included were located does seem merited.

Rutledge was an incredibly prolific writer, and seldom does a week pass when I do not discover a new story or poem that he wrote. He almost certainly had a few thousand stories published, along with hundreds of poems, in a literary career that spanned portions of eight decades. Many, though by no means all, of these publications subsequently appeared in book form. In fact, with the exception of *My Colonel and His Lady* and the little inspirational books he wrote, virtually all of Rutledge's full-length works comprised previously published magazine features, essays, short stories, or poems.

The selections included in the present work come from a wide variety of sources, and some of them have been published many times over, not only in Rutledge's own books but in various collections and anthologies. Others have not, at least to my knowledge, seen the printed light of day since their original appearance. Virtually without exception, and this is true even for those selections that were reprinted several times, readers would have to have recourse to out-of-print books, some of them quite rare, or difficult-to-find periodicals were they desirous of reading this material. Indeed that consideration, along with the enduring appeal of Rutledge's work, provides a prime underlying justification for the current book.

As a part of introducing each selection, its previous place or places of publication, insofar as they are known to the editor, are cited. Unlike the quartet of Rutledge anthologies I have previously edited and compiled (in chronological order of appearance, with all but the final work being from the University of South Carolina Press, these are *Hunting and Home in the Southern Heartland: The Best of Archibald Rutledge, Tales of Whitetails: Archibald Rutledge's Great Deer Hunting Stories, America's Greatest Game Bird: Archibald Rutledge's Turkey-Hunting Tales,* and *Bird Dog Days, Wingshooting Ways*), the present one contains some poetry. Although I would readily confess that I find his poetry less appealing and less enduring than his prose, in the current instance the subject matter lends itself to inclusion of a few selections of the former genre.

This book differs rather dramatically in one other way. The final section, devoted to culinary matters associated with the Christmas season, contains material that in large measure originates with my wife, Ann, and me. As co-authors of a number of cookbooks, all of which focus on wild game, fish, and nature's bounty, we felt it appropriate to include coverage of one of the highlights of Yuletide at Hampton Plantation—fine and festive fare.

Rutledge frequently mentions the dishes that graced sideboards and the family table during the holidays, and the recipes, food memories, and menus found here make every effort to convey not only the spirit but the gustatory reality of December dining at his beloved home by the Santee River. To that end we have also incorporated recipes that have passed down through generations of folks in the Low Country along with selections from our own cookbooks in an effort to capture culinary memories of a Carolina Christmas.

Introduction

Hampton hunts and wildwood walks are experiences I have shared vicariously with Archibald Rutledge from the days of starry-eyed youth to the present. As a youngster his stories in *Field & Stream* and *Outdoor Life* so entranced me that I carefully timed my visits to the barbershop in order to be sure to face a lengthy wait for a barber's chair. That wait ensured ample opportunity to read and savor his latest contributions to the magazines. Many of the finest of those pieces dealt with the Christmas season, and the passage of two generations and appreciably greater familiarity with his work has merely served to reinforce my enchantment with the writings of this squire of the Santee.

That enchantment, along with realization of just how deeply the celebration of Christmas figured in his love of Hampton Plantation, underlies this work. Only after one reads and ponders the dozens of Yuletide stories he wrote does full realization come of his passion for the season's traditions and the way they had long been celebrated at his cherished home by the river.

Hunting was an integral and important part of the season, a welcome escape and chance to reconnect with the good earth of the Low Country after months of exile in Mercersburg, Pennsylvania, where Rutledge taught for thirty-three years as he endeavored to raise a family and somehow resurrect the faded glory of the familial home. One senses that when the long train ride south ended, a burden lifted from Rutledge's mind, and for three weeks or so, year after year, his spirits soared, and he gained new inspiration for the poetry and prose that flowed from his pen in impressively prolific fashion.

To be sure, Old Flintlock, as he was known to family and friends, hunted in Pennsylvania. It wasn't the same, though, for in his hunter's heart nothing quite matched the hallelujah chorus of a pack of hounds triumphantly coursing a whitetail, an approach to outdoor life that ran like a sparkling thread through the entire fabric of Southern sport. He would enjoy the thrills of the chase virtually every day of the Christmas break, and when he wasn't hunting deer there were always wild turkeys (then hunted in fall and winter rather than spring), quail, waterfowl, rabbits, squirrels, woodcock, snipe, and more. Joyful as the experience was, Rutledge savored it even more thanks to sharing the Hampton hunt with his sons, extended family, and neighbors. In fact once Arch Jr. was gone, dying while still a young man, things were never quite the same.

For decades, though, December provided an annual opportunity to call back distant yesteryears when George Washington had visited Hampton, when a signer of the Declaration of Independence had hunted the same ground, and when what Rutledge described in the title of one of his books as "Santee paradise" was indeed a sportsman's Eden. Most of what is finest and most enduring in the vast corpus of his writing revolves around life at Hampton, and nowhere did he shine more consistently than in his treatment of the Christmas season as it figured in his life and the shared lives of others, black and white, who called the plantation home.

The breadth of Rutledge's knowledge is impressive. He was a gifted teacher, talented gardener, seasoned woodsman, craftsman (today turkey calls he made fetch anywhere from $1,500 to $4,000 in collector circles), devoted friend, raconteur par excellence, outspoken conservationist, staunch patriot, and a writer for the ages. When he deals with the subjects he knew best—whether it is the history of the Low Country; folkways of his beloved black companions whom he called, in the title of another book, "God's children"; deer and turkey hunting; or something else—he has to be reckoned as one of the giants of American literature. Selections from his body of writings have appeared in scores if not hundreds of anthologies (I have identified just shy of one hundred such volumes and suspect my bibliographical meanderings have done little more than scratch the surface). Today, two full generations after his passing, he remains an iconic figure, at least on a regional basis, and some index to this fact is provided by the great interest among bibliophiles in his books. Many of them fetch hundreds of dollars on the out-of-print market; some bring thousands.

Yet these and other hallmarks of Old Flintlock's appeal, while worthy of mention, are tangential to the thrust of this collection. It is intended, quite simply, to be a celebration of all the myriad delights of Christmas as savored by a man totally enamored of tradition. It is in no sense a stretch to suggest that his annual returns to Hampton, stretching from just after the turn of the twentieth century until his retirement from Mercersburg Academy in 1937, laid the groundwork for what many consider his greatest book, *Home by the River*. The same holds true for a Herculean achievement that endures as surely as his words, the resurrection and restoration of Hampton. Today it belongs to us all, for late in life, with two of his three sons having predeceased him and the wolf of economic woe hovering as near as ever, he sold the plantation to the state of South Carolina.

If you find yourself in the Charleston area, particularly deep in December, make a point of visiting the home and walking the grounds. Rest assured that as you wander, full of wonder, ghosts of Hampton Christmases past will greet you at every turn. Mayhap a short warm spell will have induced red blooms amid the green leaves of camellias. Possibly you will spot a deer, a lineal descendant of those whitetails that brought the joys of the chase and culinary delight to the table at Hampton, browsing along a woodland edge at dusk. You will certainly see and hear the "birds of the Southern winter" covered in one of the selections that follows. More than anything, though, particularly if you have read these pages in advance, you will be blessed with some of the inner peace and uplifted spirits that Rutledge always found when he celebrated Christmas at Hampton.

The sweet Southern scribe who was Archibald Rutledge belonged to a time of simpler days and simpler ways, a world that we have in large measure lost. Yet he continues to nurture us with the wit and wisdom of his words, and to share Christmas with this quintessential Southern gentleman, albeit vicariously, is to visit a time and place of wonder.

I

Christmas in Dixie

The hunting experience was part and parcel of the holiday season at Hampton, and the quest rightly holds preeminence in the contents of this anthology. Nonetheless Rutledge was closely attuned to the wider meaning of the season. He delighted in the simple joys of sharing and giving, not merely with his immediate family but with neighbors and, especially, the black residents on the plantation. A great lover of tradition, Old Flintlock looked back with longing to Christmases past, and in the selections offered here the reader gets a solid feel for the manner in which he cherished the way the Rutledge clan had celebrated the season over the generations.

The opening selection, a chapter from the little book in which he paid warm tribute to his parents, My Colonel and His Lady, *especially evokes an easygoing world of gentility and graciousness we have largely lost. Indeed the same can be said of much that Rutledge wrote, and for me at least, therein lies much of the enduring appeal of his work. He vicariously takes his reader to old plantation days and long-lost ways with an unerring compass pointing straight to the human heart. At no time of the year does life hold more romance, more meaning, and a greater sense of spirituality than at Yuletide. Rutledge knew this, and better still, he was able to capture in words what most of us feel but find difficult to express.*

Sixty years after the fact, his youngest son, Irvine, captured much of the excitement and sense of anticipation that underlay the family's return to Hampton Plantation in a short piece he wrote entitled "My Father Takes the Whole Family to Hampton for Christmas." It comes from a little booklet, Tales of Hampton, *he self-published in 1987 and presented to family members and a few others. His recollections merit sharing in full as an introduction to the Christmas in Dixie that was an integral and important part of the family's existence for so many years.*

My earliest memory of going to Hampton goes back to the time when I was five, which puts it in December of 1917. My brother Arch was nine and my brother Mid was seven. Early in October my father, who was teaching at Mercersburg Academy in southern Pennsylvania, announced that he was taking the whole family to his old home for the Christmas holidays. It was before the family had a car and the trip was no minor undertaking.

The excitement of the announcement increased in November, and by December we could hardly wait for the day of departure. For at least a week beforehand Mother and Dad had worked every minute to get ready. The three-week trip for five people required all of the advance planning that my parents could give to it. The day of departure arrived and the five of us, with considerable luggage, boarded the train in Mercersburg. In twenty minutes we changed trains in Marion, Pennsylvania, and in another twenty minutes we were in Hagerstown, Maryland. There we boarded a Baltimore and Ohio train that took us through Weverton on the Potomac River and into the Union Station in Washington, which was, I felt sure, the biggest building in the world. The great high ceiling echoed every sound in it, especially when a train caller began to call the trains. He was a large man with a large voice. His "call" lasted for five minutes or more and he ended with a dramatic flourish, his voice growing especially melodious with "Atlantic Coast Line going South."

We boarded our fourth train, the Atlantic Coast Line, and my father soon herded us into the dining car where shining white table cloths and waiters in white uniforms made an impressive appearance. We sat down to a sumptuous meal, the train got under way, and soon the lights outside began to zip by faster and faster. My father's spirits were rising each mile of the way. After dinner we were permitted to stay up until after we had passed Richmond, the strategic point at which my father was at last certain that we were safely on our way.

The phrase, "South of Richmond," was a poem in itself for my father. A book of poems he wrote that was published in 1923 was called *South of Richmond.* In it he wrote:

> *South of Richmond roars the train;*
> *Subtly o'er my weary brain*
> *Dread delicious languor steals;*
> *Peace my tired spirit heals.*
> *From the struggle of the mart,*
> *Hurrying to the homeland's heart,*
> *Through the deepening night I glide*
> *Into dreamlands sweet and wide.*

When we awakened, a different world greeted me. Instead of ice and snow, we saw wide broom grass fields running back to tall longleaf pines. Cottonfields vied with fields of tobacco, and the trees in the watercourses were festooned with Spanish moss and crowned with bunches of mistletoe.

Arriving in Charleston, we barely had time to eat breakfast and be transported by my Uncle Tom to a dock where the ferryboat *Sappho* awaited us. It was, at that time, I am sure, in its declining years. It carried about six cars per trip. When a car drove onto it, the *Sappho* tilted somewhat fearsomely, but the balancing of it was a marvel. We could see in its hold three giant Negroes, each controlling a large barrel of sand, who effortlessly rolled the barrels to counteract the tilting. Even in midstream my brothers and I watched in fascination as a delicate balance was kept by a gentle rolling of the barrels. After a forty-five minute trip we reached the town of Mt. Pleasant where, waiting with a fine horse and carriage, was my grandfather, Colonel Henry Middleton Rutledge. He seemed quite ancient, but I was five and he was seventy-seven.

The journey from Mt. Pleasant to Hampton was just over forty miles. As I slept most of the time, I recall little of the long ride, except I recall my parents' mentioning the Sixteen Mile House and the Thirty-two Mile House as we passed. Once a flock of wild turkeys crossed the road, and I remember a great hurrying to get guns loaded but not in time to get a shot. I often dozed off when the Colonel was regaling Dad with stories of deer hunts and awakened when still other stories were being told.

It was twilight when we at last saw the lights of Hampton. My grandmother greeted us with a venison, sweet potato, and rice supper, fell on my father's neck, and between kisses called him "Benjamin." (It was explained to me that it was because he was her youngest son.)

The next morning we three boys were turned over to three Negro boys our own age, Prince, Will, and Samuel, for a tour of the grounds and the livestock. They were sternly directed by my father and theirs not to let us tease the plantation bull, climb any tall trees, or wander into the woods with which we were not yet familiar.

The memory is unusually clear and vivid. Perhaps it is because I was very young and all the world was new and strange and beautiful and exciting.

Christmas with My Colonel

⌣∶∾

Rutledge was the youngest child of his parents, and his deep veneration for them stands out clearly in much of his work. Quite possibly as the last child he was spoiled, and indeed he hints as much in some of his writing. He pays glowing tribute to his mother and father in My Colonel and His Lady, *and this material from chapter 5 of that work (pages 59–74) offers ample indication that Christmas was as important to them as it was to him. Selections of the material below also appeared as "Carolina Festival" in* Coronet, *December 1949, 117–19.*

I used to love to see my Colonel at Christmas, surrounded by his friends and by the faithful Negroes who adored him. Perhaps no picture of him would be complete without a reference to the manner in which he used to spend Christmas Day.

On that magic morning, the Negroes do not stay long in the colored settlement, but with a promptness that is hardly a racial characteristic they repair to the Great House, thronging gleefully across the fields, shouting and singing, and exercising that extraordinary power for social affability among themselves that is truly a racial characteristic. They help to make Christmas what it is on the plantation. They are friendly, affectionate, simple-hearted folk, faithful and grateful. In no way do they resemble the curious caricatures that are presented to us in the popular magazines. These people are dusky peasants—dull, perhaps, in some ways, but exceedingly acute in others. For example, as a judge of human character, motive, and behavior, a plantation Negro is, I believe, an expert. He is capable of acute observations on life and manners, and his criticism is sometimes delicately veiled.

Now they are gathering for a share in the plantation's Christmas festival. I find the yard thronged with them when I take a little stroll before breakfast, and I discover the Colonel greeting them. Here I see Henry, the overseer; then Gabriel, a hunter of renown; then Blossom and Dollie, swarthy twins; old Sambo, who remembers the days of slavery, which, he has often told me, he enjoyed far more than the days of desolate freedom that followed; then a score of meek-eyed patient women, and twice as many frolicking little blacks. They are humble, lovable people, these plantation Negroes.

Before breakfast we distribute to the Negroes whatever we have for them in the way of Christmas cheer. Then the family gathers for breakfast. I love to think of it: the ample room from the walls of which gaze down faded portraits of the plantation owners of an earlier generation; there gaze down, too, a whole fringe of deer horns, festooned with Spanish moss. A plantation home without its collection of stag horns is hardly to be found, and in passing I may say that some of the collections, dating back almost to the time of the Revolution, are of remarkable interest. I know of one such collection that contains upward of four hundred racks of the white-tail, every one having been taken on that particular plantation. In some families, there is a custom, rigorously adhered to, that no deer horns must ever leave the place, so that the horns of every buck killed find their way into the home's collection. Such a frieze in a dining-room seems to fill the place with woodland memories, and serves in its own way to recall the hunts, the hunters and the hunted of long ago. Here on the same wall hang the portrait of a famous sportsman and the antlers of many a stag he took in the old days. Gone now are they all. We have only the dim picture and the ancient antlers.

Christmas breakfast on the plantation, over which my Colonel genially presides, makes one think of a wedding breakfast. The table is gay with sprigs of holly, with graceful ropes of smilax. A huge bunch of mistletoe, large enough to warrant the most ardent kissings of whole communities, stands upright in the center of the table, its pale cold berries mysteriously agleam. Then Martha and Sue bring in the breakfast—wholesome, smiling Negroes they are, devoted to the family, and endeared to it by nearly fifty years of continuous loving service. Here the breakfaster may regale himself on plantation fare: snowy hominy, cold wild turkey, brown crumbly corn-breads, venison sausages, beaten biscuits, steaming coffee, homemade orange marmalade. Unless my observation be at fault, the making of coffee on a plantation is a solemn rite not to be trusted to anyone save the mistress of the house. Mother used to love to make it herself before the ruddy fire in the dining-room, its aroma mingling with the fresh fragrances from the greenery hung about the walls. She carried coffee-making to the point of a fine art, and served it out of a massive silver coffee-pot—the same used when a gentleman named General George Washington visited this home during his southern tour in those last years of the eighteenth century.

While we are at breakfast, we have evidence that the day is not to be spent in languorous and ignoble case, for from the yard we can hear the Negro huntsmen tuning up their hunting horns; and in response to the faint mellow blasts we hear the joyous yowling of staghounds. Some of these come to the dining-room door, and there stand the dogs, ranged in the order of their temerity, fixing us with melancholy great eyes, more eager, I really think, to have us finish our repast and join them in the woods than envious of us for our festive board.

On the plantations that I know, deer hunting on Christmas Day is as natural as a Christmas tree, or kissing one's sweetheart under the mistletoe.

After breakfast, we gather on the plantation porch, and I smell the yellow jasmine that hangs in delicate sprays from the tall white columns. In the flower garden two red roses are blooming. In the wild orange trees beside the house myriads of robins, cedar waxwings, and a few wood-thrushes are having their Christmas breakfast. A hale, dewy wind breathes from the mighty pine forest. The whole landscape, though bathed in sunshine, is still fresh with the beauty of the morning. Now the Negro hunters come round the side of the house, leading our horses, and followed by a pack of hounds. A rather motley crew they are, I think, for few plantations can boast of full-blooded staghounds; but they know their business. What they lack in appearance they supply in sagacity.

My father, dressed for the hunt, talks gravely with the drivers. With him, this is one of the most serious things in life.

There is, I suppose, no grander sport in the whole world than riding to hounds after deer; and this is a sport typical of a plantation Christmas. With my Colonel, throughout his long life, it was almost a religious rite, and it never failed to supply the most thrilling entertainment for visitors. Indeed, I do not know exactly what the rural South would be without deer hunting as a diversion. Even in the cities, when distinguished guests arrive, the primary entertainment always provided is a stag hunt. Nor is such a matter at all difficult to arrange. A city like Charleston is full of experts in this fascinating lore, and these Nimrods are ever ready to leave all else to follow the deer. During the Great War, when many notable officials were in Charleston, they were exceedingly diverted by this practice of deer hunting. It seemed to take them centuries back, to the time when the cavaliers of Shakespeare's time rode to hounds in the New Forest, in Sherwood, and in Windsor. In the coastal country, deer are, and have always been, plentiful, and I believe that they are so used to being hunted that they are inured to the surprise and the rigor of it.

Soon we are astride our mounts, turning them down the live oak avenue toward the deep pinelands, with my Colonel in the lead. As we ride down the sandy road, we are on the lookout for deer tracks; and these are seen crossing and recrosssing the damp road. The Negro hunters who have charge of the pack have to use all their powers of elocution to persuade the hounds not to make a break after certain hot trails. The horses seem to know and to enjoy this sport as well as the men and the dogs do. No horse can be started more quickly or stopped more abruptly than one trained to hunt in the woods.

We start a stag in the Crippled Oak Drive, and for miles we race him, now straight through the glimmering pinelands, sun-dappled and still, now through the eerie fringes of the "Ocean," an inviolate sanctuary, made so by the riotous tangle of greenery; now he heads for the river, and we race down the broad road to cut him off—down the very same stretch of road that in Revolutionary days the planters of the neighborhood used as a race track. There is a stretch of three miles, perfectly straight and level, broad, and lying a little high. Down this we course. But the crafty buck doubles and heads northward for the sparkle-berry thickets of the plantation. I race forward to a certain stand, and just as I get there, he almost jumps over me! The dogs are far behind; and the stag gives the appearance of enjoying the race. Away he sails, his stiffly erect snowy tail flashing high above the bay bushes. I await the arrival of the dogs, and soon they come clamoring along. I slip from my horse and lead him into the bushes. I love to watch running hounds when they do not observe me. They always run with more native zest and sagacity when they are going it alone. A rather common dog, of highly doubtful lineage, is in the lead. The aristocrats come last. I am always amused over the manner in which full-blooded hounds perform the rite of trailing. This business is a religion with them. They do not bark, or do anything else so banal and bourgeois; they make deep-chested music, often pausing in the heat of a great race to throw their heads heavenward and vent toward the sky perfect music. Their running is never pell-mell. A good hound is a curious combination of the powers of genius: he is Sherlock Holmes in that he works out infallibly the mazy trail; he is Lord Chesterfield in that he does all things in a manner becoming a gentleman; and he is a grand opera star, full of amazing music. I get a never-failing thrill out of listening to hounds and out of watching them at close hand. To me it appears that the music they make depends much upon their environment for its timbre. And as they course over hills and dip into hollows, as they ramble through bosky water-courses or trail down roads, as the leafy canopies over them deepen or thin, their chorus hushes and swells, affording all the "notes with many a winding bout" that the best melody offers.

Our stalwart buck makes almost a complete circle, outwits us, enters the mysterious depths of the "Ocean," and is lost. But perhaps—at any rate, on Christmas Day—for us to lose his life is better than for him to lose it. Yet his escape by no means ends our sport.

We start two stags next, and then they lead us a mad race toward Wambaw Creek. I catch a far-off glimpse of white tails and glinting horns. We horsemen, taking our lives in our hands, essay to race the two bucks to the water. We manage to overtake the hounds but not the deer. Indeed, after almost a lifetime of following deer, I may truthfully say that I have seldom, in our country, seen deer in distress before hounds. Unless wounded, or unless very fat (as they are in September), or unless cornered against wire, deer play before dogs. They pretend that they are going to run spectacularly, but after a show of gorgeous jumping and running, they skulk in deep thickets, dodge craftily, cross water, and in other ways rest themselves and baffle their pursuers. When the hounds do approach them again, the deer are as fresh as ever.

So all that Christmas Day we roam the sweet greenwood, breasting through aromatic myrtle thickets, passing under huge patriarchal oaks, riding down the solemn aisles and the fabulous naves of the stupendous cathedral of the forest.... Wild things we saw in their beautiful home: shadowy deer, stately wild turkeys, flocks of bluebirds, chickadees, hosts of robins, and one superb illustrious eagle soaring momentously in the far blue sky....

After a few more chases, we return to the plantation house and if there is a sport that whets the appetite more keenly than deer hunting, I do not know it. To the ancient home we turn, to the patriarchal live oaks watching before it, to the red roses, to the yellow jasmine, and within, to the ruddy fires, the rooms festooned with fragrant greenery.

I remember what an old Negro said to my father when he was describing to the old servitor a certain kind of liquor. The Negro, in such matters, had an almost painful imagination. This description was just a little more than he could stand. "Oh, please, boss," he said, "don't tell me about that if you don't have none along with you." His was a sentiment with which I can heartily sympathize. I hate, for example, to describe a plantation Christmas dinner if I cannot offer my readers the dinner itself. And yet I cannot think of it without recalling the snowy pyramids of rice, the brown sweet potatoes with the sugar oozing out of their jackets, the roasted rice-fed mallards, the wild turkey, the venison, the tenderloin of pork fattened on live oak acorns, the pilau, the cardinal pudding!

And this is a dinner by candlelight, even though the daylight lingers outside. Twilight falls as we come to the nuts and raisins. Then we form a great semicircle before the fire, and we rehunt the chases of that day, and my Colonel regales us with many stories of the long ago. One or two of the older hounds have the privilege of the dining-room, and their presence on the firelit rug adds reality to our stories. I often think that, had they the power of speech, what they could tell us would be well worth the hearing.

It is late ere our stories are ended. It has been a glorious day. My Colonel and I wander out now onto the front porch to watch the stars and to listen to the far, sweet singing of the plantation Negroes, breathed to us over the dewy starlit fields. The night is radiant with constellations. They never mean so much to the mortal spirit as at this Holy Time.

The risen moon is casting a silvery glamour over the world. Certain great stars blaze in the velvet void of heaven. We never weary of hearing the Negroes singing their spirituals of Christmas, the sweetest melody, I think, of which the human voice is capable. The live oaks shimmer softly in the moonshine. We hear flights of wild ducks speeding overhead, hastening toward their feeding grounds far down the river. The magic of the night is abroad; now, we know, the deer are coming out of their coverts delicately to roam the dim country of the darkness. Over the old plantation the serenity of joyous peace descends—the peace of human hearts at Christmas time. Beauty and love and home—these are of peace, these make that peace on earth which Christmas in the heart alone can bring.

Christmas Eve on the Plantation

This selection comes from the December 1922 issue of the Outlook, *pages 709–11. Frankly, parts of this story do not ring true. For one thing a horseback ride of better than forty miles is a daunting one for man and beast, even across the level terrain of the Low Country. Also typically the Rutledge family arrived at Hampton Plantation well before Christmas Eve, traveling southward by train, and Rutledge would not have been alone. Perhaps Rutledge had been to Charleston alone on business or for some other reason. Or he could have created a fictional situation simply because it served his storytelling purposes. Certainly he did that on other occasions. Whatever the case, this early story is vintage Rutledge.*

*I*t is Christmas Eve, and I'm on my way home for the holidays. But I'm not on a sleeper with screaming wheels, nor on a vessel whose engines sob and pulse and heave, nor in a motor on a twenty-five-miles-an-hour speed limit highway—skimming along blithely at forty-five. I'm driving that obsolescent creature known as a horse. We've already come forty miles; two more, and we shall be at home.

You might well suppose that my journey has been over prairie; but it has been through wild-woods all the way. From Charleston, the road parallels the coast to Georgetown, sixty miles distant; and the only breaks in the glancing forests are certain starved clearings. It would be hazardous to say that this land is cultivated; for much of it is a mere agricultural shambles, wherein crab-grass and sheep-burrs have fatally assaulted the legitimate crops of cotton, peas, and corn. What a planter of the region once pathetically remarked to me is certainly true: "If we could only get people to eat crab-grass instead of corn, some of us here could make a living." True, one passes a few fine estates, such as the great Horlbeck pecan orchard, containing upward of a thousand acres. But most of the dwelling-houses along this road belong to poor Negroes. Of these cabins a word may be said.

They are in general of two types: either old and smoke-grimed and staggering in posture, or else painfully new, with the sap oozing out of their pine boards; often they may be so new as to be unfinished. I mean that a porch or a set of steps may be begun, but left for months and even for years in the state of hopeful beginning. I have known a family to put a roof on one side of a house, and to move in, and actually not to finish the other part of the roof for a matter of two years. Some people laugh at this sort of thing, and they say that it is just like Negroes to plan and not to execute. My observation leads me to a different feeling and to a different conclusion: I grieve over these cabins; and I know that they are unfinished because their owners are shackled by a dull, uniform, absolute poverty, which is the mother of a fatal inertia. If, for example, a Negro knows a good trade, and can thereby make a little ready money, he will build himself a pretty home, and he will finish it inside and out. But when a man's earthly possessions consist in an acre of barren land, and when he has no market for whatever tiny yields he is able, by weary toil, to scratch out of it, then he exemplifies what Gray meant when he wrote of the power of chill penury to repress noble rage; and what our own Edwin Markham means when he shows us the warblers going to roost in the swaying gray banners of moss. From the stockade where the deerhounds are kept I hear a joyous clamor. They know very well that a hunt is afoot for tomorrow. From the stable yard come the voices of the Negroes, singing, shouting, and breaking into peals of infectious laughter. On the broad steps of home, in the dusk, I talk with many Negroes who have come to see me. Their types are interesting.

Gabriel, the hunter, wants to know how soon I can join him in the pursuit of a buck that he has been "saving" for me all year; and from under his coat he produces a marvelous otter hide as a Christmas present. This wily creature he has trapped with a skill that few even among the ranks of expert woodsmen possess. His knowledge of woodland affairs is in singular contrast to the ignorance of wild life of that great army of people, otherwise intelligent, who really wouldn't know the difference between a drumming grouse and a flying buttress.

Martha, one of the members of an elder race, and for half a century the very soul of fidelity to my family, comes to tell me how Germantown, the name of the village where she lives (it is on the borders of the plantation) has guarded its fair civic name during my absence. A strange Negro, it seems, had come to Germantown, a settlement of Negroes of the very best type. This newcomer had behaved in a very shifty manner; and, as a result, he had been strictly ostracized. Martha put the matter to me most graphically when she said: "He has no principles; so we 'hibit [prohibit] him, and we 'hibit his hog." It would not do merely to punish the man by a show of outraged decency, but he must be given to understand that, since he would not behave himself, his stock should not enjoy free range. Possibly there are several other communities in our country which would be uplifted morally if the attitude of the better people toward any brazen sinner was to "'hibit him and 'hibit his hog." Martha's earnestness gave me a very lively sense of the real depth of her morality.

Prince, the wood ranger and plantation watchman, tells me in his quiet fashion how he has been trying to look out for the place, and how he has had several encounters with poachers and plunderers. He has but one remark to make about all these rapparees and land pirates. "I make them ca' sail." Possibly no expression that the Negroes use is more vivid. The trespassers were made to "crowd their canvas," as Tennyson says. Prince also tells me of the misfortune of old Cudjo, a plantation charge, whose mule had died from the effects of a slip-knot's having been tied about its neck; and Prince has the humor to suggest that creatures more intelligent than mules get into difficulties with slip-knots.

Round the corner of the house there comes now a messenger on horseback. It is a Negro from a neighboring plantation, and he has brought a message from a boyhood chum, who wants to know if I cannot join him on a Christmas deer hunt, and then dine at his place. Appreciating the frailty of human nature, the messenger adds that the mint bed down at his master's place hasn't been frozen.

Suddenly our attention is attracted to the approach of a most massive figure tolling slowly down the avenue. It is a huge Negro.

"Here comes the crowd," mutters Prince, with an infectious chuckle.

Seven miles has he walked, seven sandy ones. It is Hacklus Manigo, a Negro of very singular and admirable type. Like most stout people, he has a keen mind, and he is well read. Until he became so heavy he used to be an engineer on a river steamer; and he belonged to a religious sect known as "the Sanctified Ones." Now, some people will smile at that; but, knowing Hacklus, I have never taken his religion mirthfully. By the light of a dingy lantern, in the oily and grimed cabin of a Santee River steamer, "in the dead vast and middle of the night," I have had him expound to me, with the sad penetration of naïve intelligence, the Gospel of St. John. His tiny Bible was thumbed and stained with oil. Hacklus always carried it with him; and he carried its contents in his heart. And because of that the owner of the steamer has told me that Hacklus was the best engineer on the coast; that, amid a thousand temptations to drink, he was ever sober; that, while the other boat-hands would wander off when the steamer touched at a town, this man was ever at his post. Kipling has hymned his Mc-Andrews; in incomparably minor tones, but with not a whit less admiration, I can hymn this thoughtful black engineer. And now he's come to talk with me a while—not of hunts and of woodcraft, not of the affairs of the day and of the hour, but of the things of the spirit. "It's all in these two things," I hear him say, toward the end of our talk: "'To do justly, to love mercy, and to walk humbly with God'; and, 'I am the resurrection and the life.'" I never hear those tremendous words without thinking of Hacklus Manigo; for his life has helped to teach me what they really mean.

On the plantation dinner is usually served at night; and as I go into the dining-room I can see that every one is waiting for me to hear a story. It happens to be so human and so typical that it will bear telling. Its gentle satire is as harmless as it is delicious.

"Oh, do you know," my raconteur says, launching forth eagerly, "that the old Holbrook Randolph place has been sold? But it has been bought by *such* people! They've made money in fertilizer; they came originally from Oil City. Such hideous materialism! Well, of course they had to alter everything about the fine old place. And even the approach has been changed. The avenue now winds to the *back* door, which has been remodeled and made the entrance! Of course," comes the salient comment, "people of that kind never could get used to going into the Randolphs' *front* door!"

Festive is a plantation dinner table, with a huge haunch of venison, a wild turkey, snowy pyramids of steaming rice, crisp brown corn breads, and Bahama sweet potatoes, the sugar oozing out of their loose jackets. And there's the fellowship. And there are the plans for the morrow. Merrily the firelight plays on the frieze of stags' horns circling the room; it gleams on the faded paintings; warmly it enters and is lost among the lavish festoons of holly, myrtle, cassina, mistletoe, and smilax that deck the room.

When once more I go out on the broad porch, the moon has risen, striking silver lances through the misty river fens. Far off I can hear the Negroes singing their Christmas spirituals. They rise, those humble hymns, to the Creator in his mighty fane. The night has magic about it; I think of Whitman's superb phrase, "the huge and thoughtful night." Over the earth there is the sense of some serene arrival. The stars seem aware; the world is about to commemorate the coming of Love. And here, on this lonely plantation, even the humblest heart can feel that this is God's Holy Night; even the weariest heart can feel that all shall be well for them who love the Christ, and who, like Hacklus Manigo, try to walk humbly with their God.

Christmas Eve on Wicklow

Most readers do not associate Rutledge's name with fiction, although any close perusal of his writing will soon lead to the conviction that he knew and appreciated the Southern adage that suggests "'Tis a poor piece of cloth that can use no embroidery." Yet early in his career, in particular, he produced a lot of fictional pieces. Many involved frightening situations such as narrow escapes from alligators, snakes, sharks, and the like, but other topics were covered as well. This fictional effort appeared on pages 281–95 of one of his early books, Heart of the South.

15

On the bronzed face of Colonel Asher Blake, usually so cheerful and serene, there was the shadow of a frown.

"Mobile," he asked, putting the question casually and hardly waiting for an answer, "did you ever hear of a man by the name of Robert Burns?"

Mobile, the giant Negro paddler, poised for a moment his dripping cypress blade, permitting the yellow Santee water to trickle down it and over his huge black hands.

"Is you mean dat hog-stealin' gen'man what used to live to the Ferry?" Mobile queried seriously, always patiently willing to be accommodating.

"No," Colonel Blake answered gravely, "this gentleman was a Scotch poet; he said something about you and me, Mobile,"

"He cuss we?" asked the Negro, concerned over the Colonel's gravity.

"No, he didn't curse us, and he didn't say this exactly to us, Mobile; but it happens to apply most exactly to our present situation."

"Ain't no Ku Klux?" Mobile asked with some apprehension.

"Oh, no. He has nothing to do with the Klan. But in one of his poems he remarks that the best laid plans of mice and of men often go to smash."

"He had a head," said Mobile, with a decision that bespoke his appreciation.

"You know how we two planned to duck here as usual on this Wicklow tract this winter?"

"You and me and the duck, Cunnel, dat's all gwine be to Wicklow dis season."

"But, Mobile, the plans have jumped track. Wicklow won't see us this year— except for this little last visit today."

"How come?" the Negro questioned in surprise.

"Mobile, Wicklow has been sold. Sold!" Colonel Blake reiterated, "and you and I are sold, Mobile. Pierrepont Billings of Baltimore has bought our hunting-ground. He's a millionaire, and you and I will have to clear out."

"I neber done see a million-man," Mobile commented with a quaint authentic interest.

"Well, he'll probably be as natural and as pleasant as if he had nothing. You needn't look for horns on a millionaire, Mobile."

"He carry haversack wid de money?" asked the Negro, the idea of taking care of a million dollars striking his imagination as something of a problem.

"Oh, no; he leaves most of it in the bank. But I tell you what, Mobile, he will carry some for a certain good paddler I know."

"I like mo' better for paddle you, Cunnel."

"I have it!" Colonel Blake suddenly exclaimed with an emphasis that clearly showed his pleasure. "I'll get these people to make you the Wicklow watchman. Someone will have to stay on the property. Why shouldn't you do it, Mobile, and make some money regularly?"

The Negro for a moment did not answer; but Colonel Blake detected his strong feelings in the manner in which the long slender cypress canoe shot forward through the tops of the tide-drowned lisping marches. The powerful black sank his broad paddle with deft precision, swept it backward until a gliding maelstrom hurried importunately after it, and swung it across the boat with a rhythm as perfect as it was poetic and unconscious.

The two men, Colonel Asher Blake and Mobile Manigo, had been comrades since boyhood. The former owned the melancholy old Daisybank Place on the west bank of the Santee; and he had long since given to Mobile a few acres of the ancestral tract; and in the possession of this land Mobile felt that he shared in the ancient pride of the Blakes. Though the men were both now well over sixty, in neither had abated the love of following, mile after mile, the lonely reed-hung reaches of the delta creeks.

When autumn came, bringing with it to the languorous Riviera of the delta immense flights of wildfowl, the Colonel, having harvested his crops, would renew as a hunter his ancient fellowship with Mobile. With the first tang of autumn in the air, with the first aromas of the declining year fragrantly breathed from thicket and pineland and lonely wasteland of reeds along the mighty river, the two old friends would gravitate toward each other; and many were the plans laid for the coming campaign.

"Is the old boat all ready?" the Colonel would ask.

"She done already ready."

"Have you calked that big hole in the bow with anything better than clay?"

"Oakum and tar, sah."

"Do you have two new paddles? One floated away, I remember, and a bull alligator crunched up another when you prodded him with it."

. "Two new ones—new till he shine."

"Did you fasten that old decoy's head on straight, the one that used to look as if he was cocking his eye at the evening star?"

"She straight, sah."

"If you only had some kind of a gun, Mobile. Are you sure that that old musket of yours is out of commission?"

Colonel Blake had reference to a weapon of ancient days and of fearsome aspect. The last time Mobile had fired it, spurts of flame had been jetted from certain rust-holes in the barrel; the nipple had broken off; and he had been half-blinded by backfire.

"She's past she prime," Mobile admitted sadly; "she can't specify no mo.'"

"There's that gun out at Morris' store; perhaps we can get that for you somehow. But he wants fifty dollars for it. She's a beauty, though: hammerless, twelve gauge, thirty-two inch barrels."

"Cunnel, please, say, don't talk 'bout it. I done already love dat gun, but my hand can't reach so high."

This sort of thing had gone on year after year for a decade; but it was really the sport that took them. But now the ways of Mobile and the Colonel were going to suffer change. Wicklow, the vast delta tract where they had hunted for so many happy and prosperous years, was sold; and immediately it was to be posted as a private game preserve. Such was the contingency which had led the Colonel to his remark to Mobile concerning Robert Burns.

From Mobile's manner as he now paddled along the edge of the river, it was clear that he seemed enthusiastic about the Colonel's suggestion that he become the watchman on Wicklow. After a time he asked: "Will this million-man, what you call Mas' Billin', is he gwine let you hunt same fashion how you always done already hunt?"

"I fancy not," the Colonel replied. "You'll have to admit, Mobile," he added amiably, "that you and I can be classified as disturbers of the peace as far as these wild ducks are concerned."

"We sholy done already jar them," the Negro admitted. "And is this we las' day?" he inquired desolately.

"Well, yes; but if I can get that good position for you, things will turn out mighty well after all. Later, perhaps, you and I can get together on many a hunt back in the swamp, and around the edges of Wicklow, or down near Cane Gap."

"I ain't neber do no reg'lar work," the Negro said ingenuously. "Is you think I can specify for Mas' Billin'?"

"My bet is on you, Mobile. You'll make a very valuable watchman."

"I know you would count on me, Cunnel; ain't you done save my life that time? You wouldn't neber have throw that dollar and sebenty-five cent worth of medicine into me if you didn't count on me. But I dunno 'bout these strange man."

That day, though the number of mallards and black ducks taken by these two old delta-hunters was seventy-two, was a sad day for both men. The change impending affected them; but the Colonel managed to conceal its effect with more success that the Negro. Though at twilight they drew up to the Daisybank landing with almost a record kill, their hearts were heavy.

"To-morrow," said Colonel Blake as he toiled heavily up the slippery bank in his rubber boots, leaving Mobile to take the canoe to his house up the Canal where Dolly his wife would dress the ducks for shipment, "Jubal Haines will be here to look over the Wicklow place and to make certain arrangements concerning it. Mobile, do you want to be watchman? Shall I recommend you to him?"

"You done know best, Cunnel," the big Negro responded, with a kind of trust which is akin to the love which casteth out fear; "if you done say Mobile is for watch Wicklow, Mobile gwine watch him."

The following day Asher Blake was favored with a visit from Jubal Haines, an enterprising young real estate agent from Charleston, through whom the purchase of the Wicklow tract had been made. To the Colonel's surprise, the purchaser himself, the great Pierrepont Billings, was with Haines. The three men sat on the broad veranda of the Colonel's home, gazed out over the wide melancholy reaches of the delta country, and talked the matter over. Both visitors knew that their host was the man who could give them the sort of information of which they stood in need.

"I was over the property last season," Billings said; "as it lies on the delta, the first thing it needs is a good watchman. Don't you think, Colonel, that it should have a man actually living on the place? There's an old Negro cabin over there."

"Your property must have a man on it, Mr. Billings," the Colonel answered with decision. "If there isn't a good watchman on the ground, your ducks will be poached. And there are deer, too, back in the swamp, and turkeys."

"I've always heard," Billings answered, a pleasant smile lighting his face, "that the very best man to watch a hunting preserve is the very worst local poacher."

Haines and Colonel Blake laughed.

"Yet we ought surely to have somebody reliable," Haines put in quickly—Haines who was long in land values but very short on the varied landscape of human nature—"and I'm not at all sure that an expert poacher would be such a man. Wicklow's a valuable place," he added.

"I tell you what I think we ought to do," said Billings with kindly yet crisp decision: "if you will be kind enough, Colonel, to suggest a man, I'm going to take him. Who, in your opinion, would make the best watchman for Wicklow?"

"There's a Negro here who would be my first choice," said the Colonel with quiet certainty; "his name's Mobile Manigo."

Neither Billings nor Haines answered for a moment. In the eyes of each shone a sudden light, which seemed to express either the awakening of a suspicion or else the confirming of a vague doubt.

"You consider him all right, do you?" Haines queried, his eyes narrowing and his tone plainly showing that he did not share Colonel Blake's opinion of Mobile.

Billings, being a man of bluff candor, said with amiable directness:

"To tell you the truth, Colonel, we were making some inquiries of this nature down at the post office, and this Mobile Negro was the very one against whom we were warned. He's rather a redoubtable hunter, is he not?"

"That's the very kind of a man you want to watch your place," the Colonel answered. "Some people don't understand Mobile," he continued; "as for me, if I owned the Kohinoor, I'd give it to him for safe-keeping."

"Ye-es," Haines admitted grudgingly, "he might guard the Kohinoor for you; but would he keep Wicklow for us? That's the real question."

"I'd stake my life on him," Colonel Blake answered quietly.

"I'm going to try him," said Billings. "Haines, you will please make the necessary arrangements." About a week after this conversation, Mobile, duly established in the staggering cabin on the lonely delta, was the official Wicklow watchman.

One day a letter came from the owner to Colonel Blake. Enclosed was a check for one hundred dollars with the request, couched in careful terms, for Billings had sensed something quixotic about the master of Daisybank, that he keep a negligent wary eye on the newly purchased property. This sum the Colonel carefully laid aside. He intended not to spend a cent of it unless he could satisfy himself that he had been of some genuine service to the new owner of the delta tract.

Yet, some days after he had written Colonel Blake, if Pierrepoint Billings could have seen him, he might have had the gravest misgivings concerning the nature of the help that the Colonel was giving the Wicklow cause. There appeared every indication that the Colonel was setting out to cross the river for the purpose of poaching on the property.

Lying along the thwarts of the canoe was his duck-gun; stowed away in the boat were a dozen decoys. The Colonel was wearing a battered sou'wester, and over his shoulders was an old tarpaulin cape. To an understanding eye, he presented a figure of most sinister import as far as the Wicklow wildfowl were concerned.

And it was a fine day for ducks. A fine sleety rain was driving in from the east; there was a big tide, flowing the old rice fields; from afar came the rolling of the surf, telling the ducks plainly enough that conditions were not right for them to put to sea that day. On such a day wildfowl with good sense will stay in the flooded fields, disporting themselves among the submerged beds of wampee, duck-oats, and wild lotus. Off the tawny river-mouth there will be no welcome for them such as there is on fair, warm days. It was a morning for ducks on Wicklow; and as Asher Blake paddled across the Santee he discerned with the eye of a connoisseur that the Billings preserve was alive with wildfowl. Long battalions of mallards came thronging in; Wicklowward seemed to speed all the fleet companies of teal. These flew as if they were bullets out of some mist-hidden machine gun. In one tremendous corps a thousand widgeons wheeled over Bald Eagle Acre on Wicklow, circled lower, and settled with a glad clamor. The sky seethed with ducks. There was no cessation of the thin sweet music of their wings. All this Colonel Blake saw and understood. The blear sky rained ducks.

Had ever a sportsman a chance like the Colonel's? But there was Mobile. Wicklow had a watchman.

Leaving the rain-wreathed river, with a few skilled strokes the Colonel piloted his canoe into Widgeon Creek, the winding waterway which insinuated itself for miles into the lonely Wicklow country. In this creek, somewhat shel-tered from the fine insistent rain, there were many ducks; but their numbers were small compared to the jocund quacking hosts feeding in the old fields beyond either bank. It was just after he had started a flock of widgeons that he came upon Mobile, who, with the eye of an old ducker, had judged that some-one was disturbing the ducks in the creek, and had come out along the solitary rain-soaked bank to investigate.

The Colonel waved his hand genially to Mobile; then, driving the bow of his canoe into the putty-like mud of the bank under a huge old cypress, called to the Negro to join him.

"We better go to the house," the watchman suggested. "We can be in the dry and the warm. I is glad for see you, sah," he added simply.

"If I wanted to keep dry and warm, Mobile, I would have stayed at home on a day like this."

Mobile, who had been leaning easily against the massive bole of the patri-arch cypress, shifted his weight nervously. Down the lone reaches of the creek he looked defensively. To tell the truth, Mobile was desperately uncomfortable. His ancient comradeship with Colonel Blake had suddenly let him understand the purpose of his visitor's coming. An appreciation of the unfortunate design of his old friend's visit caused Mobile a sickness of heart. The Colonel looked at Mobile with a merry twinkle of significance in his eye.

"They're swarming back yonder in Bald Eagle Acre," he said with no attempt to conceal what that swarming meant to him.

"Plenty of ducks this winter," Mobile answered in a general sort of way; yet his tone was pathetically impotent.

Then came the direct question.

"What do you say, Mobile, to letting me slip in back yonder for a shot or two? Haines is in Charleston. Billings is in Baltimore."

The Negro was grievously affected. There was nothing in life he would rather have done than paddle Colonel Blake into the forbidden country. More-over, sensible, of course, of the white man's superior intelligence and of his standing-in with the owner of the property, the Negro was not quite certain of his ground. Yet he thought he saw straight.

"I is the watchman," he answered. "Cunnel, you wouldn't done already ask me to let you shoot. Ain't you done l'arn Mobile different?"

Halting and unskillful were the words; but their import was definite and final.

"I 'member you done tole me," the Negro volunteered, as if trying to justify himself, "dat I must always 'hibit myself and 'hibit my hog from trespass on other people lan'. Ain't you done comin' to the house, Cunnel, fo' a talk? You can get dry and warm. I done save a otter-hide for your Christmas," he ended.

The Negro's voice was almost pathetically pleading. In it was deep affection striving to avert a rupture.

But Colonel Blake did not answer. He merely shook his head in reply to the invitation. Shoving his canoe off so that it rushed back into the creek and spun its bow toward the river, pulling his hat further down over his brows, and with no word of farewell to his dusky comrade of a thousand adventures, he paddled swiftly down the misty creek.

"Fidelity," the Colonel said to himself as he paddled homeward, "thy name is Mobile."

Three days later happened to be Christmas Eve. In the pineland store on Daisybank plantation, the storekeeper Morris, after much laborious counting of silver, was able to cash the check that Billings had mailed to the Colonel. Fifty dollars the Colonel straightway paid on a store-bill of mature standing; the rest of the money he crammed into an old cloth tobacco-bag, which he rammed with decision into his pocket.

Emerging from the store, he cast an appraising eye at the western sun.

"I can go across this afternoon," he muttered.

Hurrying down to his landing on the river, he launched his canoe. In twenty minutes he made the mouth of Widgeon Creek, up whose cypress length he paddled toward the cabin of the watchman. Mobile, setting traps along the creek-edge, saw the Colonel coming and hurried down to meet him.

"How's this watchman business going, Mobile? Has anybody been asking you to let him take a crack at the green-wings and the shovelers?"

Mobile smiled a little uncertainly.

"Ain't nobody done already ax dat but you, sah."

"No poachers, then?"

"T'ree bal' eagle, sah."

Mounting the bank and joining the Negro, Colonel Blake drew a dingy tobacco-bag from his pocket. It looked like a toad mounted by an amateur taxidermist. Bills stuck from it, and it was weighty with silver.

"Mobile, you said your hand couldn't reach that gun at Morris' store. This will give you the reach. This is Christmas Eve, you know," he added as he laid the bag in Mobile's huge hand.

The giant watchman looked utterly bewildered. He wasn't sure that this was not a second bribe.

"It's all right," the Colonel assured him. "It's not for anything you are to do, but for something you have done."

Seeing the presence of a mind moving in a wider and more luminous orbit than his, Mobile looked wonderingly at his old friend. He shook his head, admitting that the business was a mystery to him.

"It's just this way, Mobile. Haines and Billings were doubtful about you. I was not. I knew well enough that you wouldn't let me hunt. I never would have asked you if I had thought I couldn't count on you; and of course I wouldn't hunt here even if you had let me. Besides, Billings sent me a hundred dollars that I had to earn in some way. I had to figure out some kind of work to do. At last I laid this scheme to earn half, giving you the chance to earn the other half. This is your fifty; and you get it for running me off Wicklow the other day."

"I done say it been something like dat; but I couldn't no way onrabble the ponderation."

"Well, now it's unraveled. And if I were you, I'd take this money and reach that gun from Morris. I must be getting home, Mobile. You understand this business, don't you? I tested you, but I never would have betrayed you."

"I done know all along it been all right somehow," Mobile responded, "'caze you neber is ack in no other way but the only way. You jes' done want to make sartin and fo' sho' dat Mobile could specify."

The first stars were wanly waking ere Asher Blake made the passage of the dreamful mighty river. On him they shone benignly, those Christmas stars.

A Plantation Christmas

This story, from pages 290–300 of Plantation Game Trails, *must be reckoned one of Rutledge's most evocative. Careful readers will detect sentences and even paragraphs scattered here and there that are the same as those in "Christmas with My Colonel." Rutledge was a master at recycling his prose, but a sufficient portion of this story is different to justify its inclusion.*

*W*hen to the mystical glamour that naturally belongs to the Christmas season one can add the romance that belongs to the South—especially the old-time South—nothing short of enchantment is the result. I do not think that even in the England of cavalier days was Christmas more picturesquely celebrated than it is to-day on those great plantations of the South which have managed to preserve the integrity of their beauty and their charm. But descriptions in general terms are never very interesting or impressive. Instead, I shall give certain vivid impressions that Christmas on the plantation have afforded me, hoping thereby to convey at least a little of the charm with which, in the Southland, this ancient festival is invested.

At home I have never seen snow at Christmas time. True, it sometimes falls there but never seriously. Instead, we have a green Christmas, made so by the prevalence of pine, holly, myrtle, sweet bay, and smilax that over the top of many a tree weaves emerald crowns. Always when I go home for Christmas (and this has been an unbroken habit for twenty-five years) what first impresses me is the freshness of the forest—the apparent livingness of the trees, the vernal balminess of the air. And next to the green of the woods, what heartens me most is the singing of the birds. A plantation Christmas is one of wildwood fragrances and wildwood lyrics as well as one of roaring open fires and festive boards and ancient carols, consecrated as only the centuries can hallow.

I remember getting a Christmas tree that may be considered typical of the plantation variety. A Negro and I hitched an ox to a cart. In the spirit of the occasion the ox apparently did not share. His aspect was lowering, and his motions were physically mournful. Nevertheless he took us into the plantation pine forest, where dulcet odors were abroad, where the huge pines were choiring dimly, where the mellow sunshine was steeping the coverts in the mute rapture of deep-hearted peace. It was "holly year" that year—that is, the crop of holly berries was unusually good. Under a shadowy canopy of live-oaks we came to a holly tree some thirty feet high, heavy-foliaged, perfect in symmetry, cone-shaped, and ruddily agleam with berries. Its clean bole shone like silver. Out of this tree we flushed a horde of robins that had been feasting on the berries. The scarlet of their breasts blended with the brightness of the berries. The birds were not scared. Many of them, alighting on the immense limbs of the oaks, at once broke into trills of delicate song, of the sort that we hear in the North in early-April twilights.

We cut our Christmas tree and the ox bore it homeward for us. In the old ballroom of the house—a room that, running up two stories, has a prodigious height of ceiling—we set it, directly in front of the vast fireplace, which will accommodate logs seven feet long. There stood the regal tree, all jade and silver and scarlet, dewy and tremulous. It needed no decorations. We didn't have to make a Christmas tree—we just brought one in. I felt sorry to have cut so lovely a thing, but Christmas deserves such a tribute. For decorations of a minor sort we use the red partridge berry, mistletoe, smilax, cedar, pine. He who cares to investigate the Druidical history of the mistletoe will discover that it is a symbol of the plighting of love's troth. As such, nothing could be more appropriate at this festival of joy and human affection.

In the South, as perhaps is the case nowhere else in the world, there are many superstitions associated with Christmas. No doubt this fact is due to the Negroes, without whom no plantation can be exactly natural or picturesque. One of their superstitions, which amounts to a genuine belief, is that "Christmas falls." Possibly long ago some slave heard his master say, "Christmas falls on

Friday this year." But whatever be the origin of the expression, plantation Negroes firmly believe that the coming of this great day is heralded by some mighty convulsion of nature. This belief really has an august source; for we find it in Milton. He describes with what tumult and dismay the powers of darkness fled at the birth of Christ.

On the plantation I used, as a boy, to sit up until midnight on Christmas Eve to hear Christmas "fall." It always fell, somehow or other. True, I never heard it; but the faithful always did. Ears that are attuned to hear something supernatural usually hear it. My hearing was too gross; but I used to be immensely impressed by the spiritual advancement of those of my dusky comrades who declared that they distinctly heard the mystic far-off detonation.

Another superstition that I also used firmly to believe—and it has poetic beauty that the other lacks—is that on the stroke of twelve on Christmas Eve every living thing of the bird and animal world goes down on its knees in adoration of the newborn Master. Convinced that what the Negroes were telling me was true, and not a little impressed by the grandeur of the phenomenon as it was described, I went one Christmas Eve to the stable yard, and there sat drowsily with my Negro comrade Prince, while the stars blazed, and the pines grieved, and the distant surf roared softly on the sea-island beaches. As midnight approached we became restless, and our nervousness was communicated to the various creatures in the ample old barnyard. The roosters crowed with uncommon vigor and assurance, the hogs grunted with unwonted enthusiasm, and the sheep bleated, with strange pathos. After a time, clearly in the moonlight we saw an old ox heave himself for a rise. For a moment he assumed a most singular position: his hind-quarters were up, but his head was quite low—he was actually kneeling. Prince pointed him out in awed triumph. Nor did I raise any question; for deep faith in another human being, even though you may consider it merest superstition, is ever an impressive thing, having about it also a certain sacredness that the heart with unreflecting wisdom and generosity willingly pays obeisance to.

Yes, on a plantation, Christmas *falls;* and likewise, every living thing goes down on its knees in the dust before its Maker.

Awakening one Christmas morning, I remember what a pleasure I experienced from hearing, just outside the window, a Carolina wren caroling like mad. Of course, this bird is not a great singer, but for sheer joyousness and abandonment to gladness I do not know his equal. His ringing call, without a trace of wariness or doubt, carries farther than the note of any other bird of the same size. I have heard it full three hundred yards across a river. Now I heard it coming through my window, the curtains of which were gently stirred by a faint breeze out of the aromatic pinelands. Climbing a pillar under my window was a yellow jasmine vine, and in a festive mood to suit the season it had put forth a few delicious blossoms—golden bells to ring for Christmas, saffron trumpets to sound the Day's welcome. Beyond the window I could see the mighty live-oaks, with their pendulous streamers of moss, waving gently like my white curtains; then the imperial pines, towering momentously. Christmas morning, with birds and sunshine and scented seaweeds! Going to the window, I looked out. All the dim sweet plantation was steeped in faerie light. The far reaches of bowed and brown cottonfield; the golden broomsedge fringing the fields; the misty river rolling softly; the sleeping trees, jeweled with dew, the uncertain pearly sky—all these had a magical look. A silvery silence held the world divinely, in virginal beauty.

But soon that stillness was broken, and by no gentle sound. It did not surprise me, but not many Americans other than plantation dwellers would have expected it. Firecrackers! "What is home without a mother?" queries the old saw. Why, it's like Christmas to the plantation piccaninnies without firecrackers! The Puritan Christmas of New England has something exceedingly snowy and austere about it. In the South it is a day for frolic—at least, on the plantation it is not associated in any way with church services. Nor do I think it less a genuine festival of the hearth and the home because all the little Negroes shoot fireworks, all the plantation belles hang mistletoe (and strangely linger near it), and all the plantation men go deer hunting.

The Negroes do not stay long in the colored settlement, but with a promptness that is hardly a racial characteristic they repair to the Great House, thronging gleefully across the fields, shouting and singing, and exercising that extraordinary power for social affability among themselves that *is* truly a racial characteristic. They help to make Christmas what it is on the plantation. They are friendly, affectionate, simple-hearted folk, faithful and grateful. In no way do they resemble the curious caricatures that are presented to us in the popular magazines. These people are dusky peasants—dull perhaps in some ways, but exceedingly acute in others. For example, as a judge of human character, motive, and behavior, a plantation Negro is I believe, an expert. He is capable of acute observations on life and manners; and his criticism is delicately veiled. Now they are gathering for a share in the plantation's Christmas festival.

I find the yard thronged with them when I take a little stroll before breakfast. Here I see Ahasuerus, the overseer; then Gabriel, a hunter of renown; then Blossom and Dolly, swarthy twins; then old Sambo, who remembers the days of slavery, which, he has often told me, he enjoyed far more than the days of desolate freedom that followed; then a score of meek-eyed patient women, and twice as many frolicking little blacks. They are human, lovable people, these plantation Negroes. And I have found them trustworthy in the highest sense. I remember that when I took my bride to the plantation for a visit, our trunk had to be brought the last ten miles by cart. For the precious trunk containing all sorts of bridal apparel I sent an old Negro named Will Alston, impressing on him the importance of his guarding the trunk with his life.

Twilight of that day fell, and Will did not arrive. Moreover, a rain had set in, and I did not see how, if he had started from the steamer's wharf with the trunk, he could have escaped disaster. Donning a long raincoat, I mounted a horse and rode through the lonely pinelands to meet Will. About three miles from home I saw his cart standing in the middle of the road. Upon it a lively shower was roaring. The driver was not in sight. Dismayed, I rode up quickly to see a sight I shall remember as long as I live. The trunk was in the road *under* the cart; on the cart's bottom, just above the trunk, Will was sprawled, taking all the rain that came, and shunting it away from the precious treasure he was guarding. I was considerably touched by this display of his humble but genuine fealty, yet he appeared to think nothing of it.

"I couldn't let the trunk get wet," he said simply. He was driving an ox, which was, of course, perfectly willing to stand, plantation oxen being somewhat expert in that particular.

Before breakfast we distribute to the Negroes whatever we have for them in the way of Christmas cheer—possibilities in this respect having been of late somewhat diminished by a national law. Then the family gathers for breakfast. I love to think of it: the ample room from the walls of which gaze down faded portraits of the plantation owners of an earlier generation; there gaze down, too, a whole fringe of deer horns, festooned with Spanish moss. A plantation home without its collection of stag horns is hardly to be found; and in passing I may say that some of the collections, dating back almost to the time of the Revolution, are of remarkable interest. I know of one such collection that contains upward of a thousand racks of the white-tail, every one having been taken on that particular plantation. In some families there is a custom, rigorously adhered to, that no deer horns must ever leave the place; so that the horns of every buck killed find their way into the home's collection. Such a frieze in a dining room seems to fill the place with woodland memories, and serves in its own way to recall the hunts and the hunters and the hunted of long ago. Here on the same wall hang the portrait of a famous sportsman and the antlers of many a stag he took in the old days. Gone now are they all. We have only the dim picture and the ancient antlers.

Christmas breakfast on the plantation makes one think of a wedding breakfast. The table is gay with sprigs of holly, with graceful ropes of smilax. A huge bunch of mistletoe, large enough to warrant the most ardent kissings of whole communities, stands upright in the center of the table, its pale cold berries mysteriously agleam. Then Martha and Sue bring in the breakfast—wholesome smiling Negroes they are, devoted to the family, and endeared to it by nearly fifty years of continuous loving service. Here the breakfaster may regale himself on plantation fare: snowy hominy, cold wild turkey, brown crumbly cornbreads, venison sausages, beaten biscuits, steaming coffee, home-made orange marmalade. Unless my observation be at fault, the making of coffee on a plantation is a solemn rite, not to be trusted to anyone save the mistress of the house. She loves to make it herself before the ruddy fire in the dining room, its intriguing aroma mingling with the fresh fragrances from the greenery hung about the walls. She loves to carry coffee-making to the point of a fine art, and to serve it out of a massive silver coffee-pot—the same used when a gentleman named General George Washington visited this home during his Southern tour in those last years of the eighteenth century.

While we are at breakfast we have evidence that the day is not to be spent in languorous and ignoble ease, for from the yard we can hear the Negro huntsmen tuning up their hunting horns; and in response to the faint mellow blasts we hear the joyous yowling of stag-hounds. Some of these come to the dining room door, and there stand, ranged in the order of their temerity, fixing us with melancholy great eyes—more eager, I really think, to have us finish our repast and join them in the woods than envious of us for our festive feast.

On the plantations that I know deer hunting on Christmas Day is as natural as a Christmas tree, or kissing one's sweetheart under the mistletoe.

After breakfast we gather on the plantation porch, and I smell the yellow jasmine that is tossing her saffron showers up the tall white columns. In the flower garden two red roses are blooming. In the wild orange trees beside the house myriads of robins, cedar waxwings, and a few wood-thrushes are having their Christmas breakfast. A hale, dewy wind breathes from the mighty pine forest. The whole landscape, though bathed in sunshine, is still fresh with the beauty of the morning. Now the Negro hunters come 'round the side of the house, leading our horses, and followed by a pack of hounds. A rather motley crew they are, I think, for few plantations can boast of full-blooded staghounds; but they know their business. What they lack in appearance they supply in sagacity.

There is, I suppose, no grander sport in the whole world than riding to hounds after deer; and this is a sport typical of a plantation Christmas. It is almost a religious rite and it never fails to supply the most thrilling entertainment for visitors. Indeed, I do not know exactly what the rural South would do without deer hunting as a diversion. Even in the cities, when distinguished guests arrive, the primary entertainment always provided is a stag hunt. Nor is such a matter at all difficult to arrange. A city like Charleston is full of experts in this fascinating lore; and these nimrods are ever ready to leave all else to follow the deer. During the Great War, when many notable officials were in Charleston, they were exceedingly diverted by this practice of deer hunting. It seemed to take them centuries back, to the time when the cavaliers of Shakespeare's time rode to hounds in the New Forest, in Sherwood, and in Windsor. In the coastal country deer are, and have always been, plentiful; and I believe that they are so used to being hunted that they are inured to the surprise and the rigor of it.

Soon we are astride our mounts, turning them down the live-oak avenue toward the deep pinelands. As we ride down the sandy road, we are on the look-out for deer tracks; and these are crossing and recrossing the damp road. The Negro hunters who have charge of the pack have to use all their powers of elocution to persuade the hounds not to make a break after certain hot trails. The horses seem to know and to enjoy this sport as well as the men and the dogs do. No horse can be started more quickly or stopped more abruptly than one trained to hunt in the woods.

We start a stag in the Crippled Oak Drive, and for miles we race him; now straight through the glimmering pinelands, sun-dappled and still; now through the eerie fringes of the ocean, an inviolate sanctuary, made so by the riotous tangle of greenery; now he heads for the river; and we race down the broad road to cut him off—down the very same stretch of road that in Revolutionary days the planters of the neighborhood used as a racetrack. There is a stretch of three miles, perfectly straight and level, broad, and lying a little high. Down this we course. But the crafty buck doubles and heads northward for the sparkleberry thickets of the plantation. I race forward to a certain stand, and just as I get there, he almost jumps over me! The dogs are far behind; and the stag gives the appearance of enjoying the race. Away he sails, his stiffly-erect snowy tail flushing high above the bay-bushes. I await the arrival of the dogs, and soon they come clamoring along. I slip from my horse and lead him into the bushes. I love to watch running hounds when they do not observe me. They always run with more native zest and sagacity when they are going it alone. A rather common dog, of highly doubtful lineage, is in the lead. The aristocrats come last. I am always amused over the manner in which full-blooded hounds perform the rite of trailing. This business is a religion with them. They do not bark, or do anything else so banal and bourgeois; they make deep-chested music, often pausing in the heat of a great race to throw their heads heavenward and vent toward the sky perfect music. Their running is never pell-mell. A good hound is a curious combination of the powers of genius: he is Sherlock Holmes in that he works out infallibly the mazy trail; he is Lord Chesterfield in that he does all things in a manner becoming a gentleman; and he is a grand opera star, full of amazing music. I get a never-failing thrill out of listening to hounds and out of watching them at close hand. To me it appears that the music they make depends much upon their environment for its timbre. And as they course over hills and dip into hollows, as they ramble through bosky watercourses or trail down roads, as the leafy canopies over them deepen or thin, their chorus hushes and swells, affording all the "notes with many a winding bout" that the best melody offers.

Our stalwart buck makes almost a complete circle, outwits us, enters the mysterious depths of the ocean, and is lost. But perhaps—at any rate on Christmas Day—for us to lose his life is better than for him to lose it. Yet his escape by no means ends our sport. We start two stags next, and they lead us a mad race toward Wambaw Creek. I catch a far-off glimpse of white tails and glinting horns. We horsemen, taking our lives in our hands, essay to race the two bucks to the water. We manage to overtake the hounds but not the deer. Indeed, after almost a lifetime of following deer, I may truthfully say that I have seldom, in our country, seen deer in distress before hounds. Unless wounded, or unless very fat (as they are in September), or unless cornered against wire, deer play before dogs. They pretend that they are going to run spectacularly; but after a show of gorgeous jumping and running, they skulk in deep thickets, dodge craftily, cross water, and in other ways rest themselves and baffle their pursuers. When the hounds do approach them again, the deer are as fresh as ever.

After a few more chases, we return to the plantation house; and if there is a sport that whets the appetite more keenly than deer hunting, I do not know it. To the ancient home we return, to the patriarch live-oaks watching before it, to the red roses, to the yellow jasmine; and within, to the ruddy fires, the rooms festooned with fragrant greenery. As we enter the dining room almost every one begins to smile in a most understanding fashion; for on either side of the huge bunch of mistletoe in the center of the table are two *decanters*—and they are full!

I remember what an old Negro said to my father when he was describing to the old servitor a certain kind of liquor. The Negro, in such matters, had an almost painful imagination. This description was just a little more than he could stand. "Oh, please, boss," he said, "don't tell me about that if you don't have none along with you." His was a sentiment with which I can heartily sympathize. I hate, for example, to describe a plantation Christmas dinner if I cannot offer my readers the dinner itself. And yet I cannot think of it without recalling the snowy pyramids of rice, the brown sweet potatoes with the sugar oozing out of their jackets, the roasted rice-fed mallards, the wild turkey, the venison, the tenderloin of pork fattened on live-oak acorns, the pilau, the cardinal pudding!

And this is a dinner by candlelight, even though the daylight lingers outside. Twilight falls as we come to the nuts and raisins. Then we form a great semicircle before the fire, and we rehunt the chases of that day, and of many of the long ago. One or two of the older hounds have the privilege of the dining room, and their presence on the firelit rug adds reality to our stories. I often think that, had they the power of speech, what they could tell us would be well worth the hearing.

It is late ere our stories are ended. It has been a glorious day. I wander out now on the front porch. The risen moon is casting a silvery glamour over the world. Certain great stars blaze in the velvet void of heaven. Far off I can hear the Negroes singing their spirituals of Christmas—the sweetest melody, I think, of which the human voice is capable. The live-oaks shimmer softly in the moon-shine. I hear flights of wild ducks speeding overhead, hastening toward their feeding grounds far down the river. The magic of the night is abroad; now, I know, the deer are coming out of their coverts delicately to roam the dim country of the darkness. Over the old plantation the serenity of joyous peace descends—the peace of human hearts at Christmas time. Beauty and love and home—these are of peace, these make that peace on earth that Christmas in the heart alone can bring.

Christmas in the Castle

This piece originally appeared on pages 502–3 of the December 17, 1919, issue of the Outlook. *As is the case with so much of Rutledge's work, it mixes fact with what was likely a bit of literary license. Will was a real figure, as were the other individuals mentioned in this story, and the positive traits he associates with these stalwarts of plantation life—faithfulness, endurance, skills in woodscraft, sense of humor, and a rare knack for storytelling—remind us of Old Flintlock's closeness to the simple folks he knew so well. Indeed this delightful story is a poignant example of the fact that Rutledge, in addition to his own abilities in weaving a captivating tale, had a rare knack for capturing the nature and nuances of tales told by others. It also reveals his keen ear for dialect.*

$\mathcal{E}$ very Christmas now for about twenty years I have been able to go home for a brief vacation; and one feature of my visits that has brought me increasing interest and pleasure has been the conversations I have had and the comradeship I have enjoyed with the plantation Negroes in the Castle. This is a small and comfortable outbuilding which, until the innovation of ranges, had served as a kitchen. Since that day it has been given over for the comfort and entertainment of the Negroes who come up to the Great House, as they call the plantation house proper. There are in the Castle two long benches, several chairs and stools, and an ample fireplace. There have I spent hours upon hours talking with Negroes of all kinds, singly and in groups; and there, I believe, I have been admitted to an understanding of the Negro's heart and an appreciation of some of the salient traits of his character.

How few Americans realize that the Negro is the prince of "reminiscers." This I have learned in the Castle, where Joe, Old Isaac, Sambo, Gabriel, Henry Snyder, our foreman for twenty-five years, Ben, and a score of others regale one another and me with their waggish conversation and with their tales pathetic and humorous. Sometimes they tell me stories of my marvelous prowess as a little boy on the plantation—stories so impressive that it is not at all difficult for me to believe that somehow I have deteriorated in power and resourcefulness as I have advanced in years. Then the talk may turn to the recounting of strange happenings of the old days on the various plantations near us: of the great flood which had drowned more than fifty people; of the phantom deer that had warned the colored boy Ogechee of his death; of the burning of the great house at Waterhon, a few miles above us; and of the planter who, when his only daughter died of yellow fever, lost his mind, kept every one from the house, and at dead of night buried his beautiful and only child in a coffin standing upright upon the ground, heaping about it and over it a prodigious mound of earth. This strange grave can be seen today. Out of the sunken top of the moldy mound there has sprung a beautiful young cedar, graceful and symmetrical, a fit memorial to Beauty dead in youth.

During our talks in the Castle there will creep unconsciously into the language of the Negroes strange words whose sound has for me a peculiar fascination; nor do I disclaim that these words are a part of my own vocabulary—though the opportunity to use them is small. There can be no doubt but that some of these are genuine survivals of the original tribal African words. Unmistakably they express by their combination of letters much of the mysterious character of the Dark Continent, which, though fairly well explored, is very far from being understood. In our talk, a dragon-fly is never anything but a "bungiewala." The synonym for small is "machinchie." A common cottontail rabbit is invariably "madindie," while his cousin, the swamp rabbit, is "befemba." Weather that is showery and uncertain is "giffie." Small bushes such as the gallberry are "jubroeroo." Of course "yeddy" is always used for "hear." Is it a wonder that sportsmen from the North who visit our place are staggered when a Negro guide suddenly exclaims: "Ain't you yeddy dat madindie in dem jubroeroo?" or, "Giffie wedder is de time for hunt dem machinchie befemba?"

But more than the use of these words, to which I have since childhood been familiar, I enjoy some of the chaffing and the witty sayings that lightly and ingenuously touch our conversation. Perhaps, "to start something," I may ask Gabriel, a notable backslider, how long it has been since he has been to church.

"I ain't been sick in a long time," he will say. "When I is well," his explanation will continue, "I don't need to go to church; but when I is poorly, I is 'bliged to call on my Captain."

"He has never been to church," Old Isaac will put in accusingly; "I know 'case I have been watching him ever since hatchet was a hammer."

"Cap'n," Henry will say, "you sure should have been here this summer to see that corn that Lisbon done grow."

"Was it fine?"

A general infectious chuckling will pass around the group.

"Fine?" This is with high disdain. "So short, sah, that a baby bumblebee could sit on a clod and suck the tassel."

"Joe," I may ask, "how is it that your brother Ben is out yonder cutting that tough live oak, when we can't get another man on the river to touch it?"

A silence will fall on the group; and it is the pregnant silence of sympathy. They seem well to know why Ben is willing to accept the most arduous task that plantation life offers; for live oak is probably the hardest wood in existence to handle.

"Ben," his brother Joe answers, his voice shading to quiet tones of thoughtfulness and grief, "he lost his wife last month. You know, Cap'n, they been very happy together. Now Ben is trying to work off his grief."

We shall sit silent for a time, looking into the fire and thinking of Ben. The Castle can be a thoughtful place; and that fact is not the least of its charms.

I remember once sitting alone there one Christmas Eve with Old Galboa, a veteran retainer who had been with us throughout his long life. Latterly he had fallen into wretched health. All his family had preceded him to the grave. He was telling me that he would welcome the call for him to go.

"I have prayed to be taken," the old man said; "and the Lord is good enough to do anything for me."

When I think of resignation and simple faith like this, I wonder where in the world today its counterpart is to be found.

It has been in the Castle that I have learned most of what I know of Negro superstitions. For my part, I am a lover of certain varieties of superstitions; for not infrequently they create the atmosphere of romance. They color the fancy. They stimulate the imagination. When life is merely obvious, it is a dreadful thing, and it makes for dullards of soul. Superstitions tinge life with a sense of the abiding mystery of things. Some of the Negro superstitions are very quaint, many are inspired by a religious fervor, few indeed, if any, could be called merely vulgar. It is at the Christmas season, when the world itself is awake to spiritual things, that the Negroes talk most superstitiously; thus it is that I hear in the Castle much talk that is tinged with the marsh light gleams of strange beliefs.

There is a superstition that Christmas "falls"; that at midnight at Christmas Eve a far-off rolling sound, presumably like the crack of doom, can be heard. Few, however, ever are willing to listen for it. It is a fearsome report to fall on mortal ears; and it is altogether safer to be innocently asleep when such things are happening. There is a belief that shortly before daybreak on Christmas morning all animals and birds go down on their knees in adoration of the new-born Master. I distinctly recall being taken as a little boy to the barnyard at dawn on Christmas Day to see the fulfillment of this beautiful superstition. My guide pointed out to me, in the winter morning's mist, several cattle lying down, which he declared, awesomely, had taken the attitude of prayer. This is a belief that I like to ponder, for in it are many elements of beauty and of poetic faith.

Among the other superstitions is one to the effect that a torrential rain invariably follows a death; and its purpose in falling at such time is to put out the tracks of the departing spirit. When I asked Henry Snyder why the tracks should be blotted out, he said:

"That is a road, Cap'n, that every man has to travel alone. Each one has to find his own path. We can't have even a track to guide us."

Superstition or not, Henry's explanation of the reason for it assuredly has in it fundamental truth of something like a universal appeal.

The matter of tokens interests me especially. A token is an apparition foretelling death; but usually, instead of taking some spectral form, it may be some common bird or animal that has acquired extraordinary size, or else some unusual phenomenon in nature, such as a violent hailstorm or a fall of meteors. A common sight in an uncommon place or at an unexpected time is a token. As an example of this last sort of supernatural visitant, I can mention an eagle taking an obscene repast with black vultures; a goat walking along the top rails of a fence and eating poison ivy; a wild turkey standing alone under a great oak near the plantation house. Indeed, anything unusual is to the active and picture-making mind of the Negro an evidence of that Power unseen that is forever communicating, in ways natural and in ways strange, with his children. Of common tokens, these have come under my own observation: a storm; the fall of a mighty yellow pine sound of heart; a nine-foot diamondback rattlesnake; a buck with white spots on its otherwise dun coat; a huge alligator; an albino robin; and a fall of snow. I mentioned the boy Ogechee and the warning he had of his nearing dissolution. He was asleep by the barn when a deer that had just swum across the Santee approached him—certainly without seeing him until quite close. Upon perceiving the boy the buck gave a loud snort, at the same time whirling away. Ogechee awoke to see the creature vanishing; and when he saw by the deer's tracks how close the animal had come, he and all his friends were positive that a true token had appeared; and, though it must be admitted that Ogechee had for some time been sick, he did not survive this experience more than two weeks.

One day in the Castle the conversation turned upon snakes, of which, I remorsefully report, the Santee region is most abundantly supplied. I questioned whether there were any great diamondbacks about. It is well, not only on account of the menace to people, but also the danger to stock, to rid a place of these huge and truculent serpents.

"I don see one last month," Steve said; "he been right by the plantation gate."

"What did you do with him when you had killed him, Steve?" I asked, somewhat shocked to hear of one of the great creatures being seen so close to the house.

Steve laughed; and all the others of the group, knowing his somewhat negative courage, joined in the laughter.

"I 'fraid him," Steve answered; "he look at me just like he was a token."

The snake escaped, but Steve was not to make a getaway.

"I 'member the day," Old Isaac put in, gravely. "I done see a cloud of dust coming down the road, and I say, 'Dat is a storm.' But dat been Steve runnin'."

But I think it not hard to forgive a man for retreating from so formidable a creature as the regal diamondback, especially if to his stately grim maliciousness there was added a sense of his possession of supernatural power.

With many of the Negroes who visit the Castle I have hunted and fished, and from them I have learned something of the ways of the creatures of the wild. Sometimes this knowledge would be imparted in a jesting fashion. For example, one day we were discussing the matter of the escape of a deer. I can hear Gabriel, the hunter, now as, bending over and sketching with a black coal a certain design, he tells how the deer eluded us.

"I follow the tracks," he explains; "and he done made his last high jump this side of the old road. Then he stopped. Right there he done read his guidebook. That tell him to run for the ribber; so there he run. A buck, Cap'n, don't run wild; he always read his guidebook."

With Gabriel and Negroes like him I have ranged almost every swamp in the wide Santee country, have traversed endless miles of those placid pinelands, and have explored the reed-hung, tortuous creeks of the lonely delta. In these trips I learned certain traits of Negro character that I shall never cease to respect. One is that with a decent white man a Negro, even under circumstances that make for roughness, is not vulgar; indeed, he manifests a most commendable reticence. He has, too, wonderful endurance in the woods and on the waters. More than once I have been on the point of abandoning an object of pursuit when my dusky comrade would press me to continue. He has what I call stalking patience; and that is patience to the degree that makes it one of the primal virtues. Of his understanding of the ways of wild life and of his powers of woodcraft too much can hardly be said. When I am hunting with a Negro, although the sport is not new to me, and although my eyesight is good, it is invariably he, and not I, who first sees game. I know that at least twice my escape from being struck by the dread cottonmouth moccasin has been due solely to the keenness of vision of my companion.

It is in the Castle at Christmas that I can return, in some measure, the long faithfulness of these Negroes. They care less for material rewards than one would suppose. Of course we have on the hearth bricks a row of baked sweet potatoes, with sugar oozing out on their brown skins. We have pipes and tobacco—that come as regularly as Christmas and I do. On great days we have coffee and cigars. But in my heart I believe that these plantation Negroes chiefly love conversation and particularly that which has to do with memories. They have an acute sense of the transiency of life. They know much of its illusions. Their understanding of life is, in its way, comprehensive; I mean that, though the vision is narrowed, they see much clearly. I once complimented a Negro for giving another a dollar to help rebuild his house which had been burned. The giver said to me: "Cap'n, we must help one another. I may be in trouble tomorrow. Trouble is common to the race." And by the race I knew he meant humanity. They come to the Castle for comradeship and sympathy and amusement; and while they do enjoy themselves, I am sure that I am more richly rewarded than anyone else. I have learned here how much more blessed it is to give than to receive; especially if one gives, as I must needs do, from gratitude and appreciation.

Of the faithfulness of these Negroes, for which I am so thankful, one typical example will suffice. It concerns Will, and of the manner in which he behaved when he was given charge of my wife's trunk when she, as a bride, was making her first visit to the plantation. In that country the matter of transportation is a critical one. A trunk has to be shipped from Charleston by boat. Then it has to be hauled ten miles in a wagon. With many an admonition Will was dispatched to bring the trunk up from the boat. He went in an ox wagon. It is not difficult to imagine with what anxiety a bride would, under the circumstances mentioned, await the safe arrival of her trousseau.

Darkness fell on that fatal day and Will had not returned. With the coming of night there came a gloomy, interminable downpour. One thing seemed certain: everything in the precious trunk would be soaked through. Toward nine o'clock, with the rain still falling, I mounted a horse and rode out to meet Will. Three miles from home I encountered him, his beasts plodding along stolidly through the plashy sand in the road. Will was quietly singing an old Negro spiritual.

Upon questioning him, I learned that the trunk was safe. I asked him how it could have been kept dry. Then he told me what made me want to weep. On the approach of the storm he had unhitched the oxen. Then he had taken the heavy trunk from the wagon and put it in the road beneath the vehicle, spreading over the trunk his coat. Then he had crawled back in the wagon bed and lain down over the trunk, across certain cracks, so that no water should touch the thing entrusted in his keeping. He had lain there and taken the lashing of the wintry rain for more than an hour. When I came up to him, his coat was still protecting the trunk, to which the fine rain could not penetrate.

Is faithfulness like that a thing to be forgotten? And yet Will had no idea that he had done anything unusual. He had merely carried through his orders. But in reality he had fulfilled a trust; he had kept the faith.

Soon I hope to be again on the plantation; and while there, every rainy day, and many an hour on other days, I shall spend in the Castle. During the greater part of the year it is my strenuous duty to attempt to educate American youth; but during the Christmas season it is my privilege and delight to attend, in a humble classroom known as the Castle, the great School of Humanity.

Prince Alston

God's Special Child

Rutledge once described Prince Alston, his boyhood buddy and staunch hunting companion in adulthood, as a "companion to my heart." The bond between the two transcended the barriers of race, geography, and society's dictates. The two men, so different in circumstances and education, understood one another in a fashion that could only be shaped and molded by countless hours together. One of Rutledge's most powerful and poignant poems, "You Came Out in the Rain," focused on Prince and the conclusion of the last Christmas they shared.

> *You came out in the rain to say goodbye,*
> *And stood beside the car. I did not know*
> *You lingered there beneath that weeping sky*
> *Because you did not want to see me go.*
> *Or wanted to be with me one more minute.*
> *I did not guess that gracious gesture's worth,*
> *The quiet beauty and the wonder in it,*
> *Hinting of all the glory on the earth.*
>
> *So much I have forgotten! So much goes!*
> *The loving things that many lips have said;*
> *Triumph and sorrow, ashes and the rose . . .*
> *Yet by one memory I'm comforted;*
> *It sings to me again and yet again;*
> *To say goodbye, you came out in the rain.*

Rutledge was always convinced that Prince had a premonition of coming death and endured the pouring rain to say a last, loving goodbye to the man with whom he had shared so many adventures. This selection is taken, with some judicious editorial excisions and mixing, from God's Children *(pages 132–150).*

A Negro from whom I learned much about nature was one who is no longer with me, my comrade, Prince Alston. We were of the same age, and for a generation we were inseparable, enjoying a woodland fellowship that brought us very close together. As boys, we shared a thousand adventures in the deep plantation woods, the wide plantation fields, the deep and strange plantation waters. I developed into an amateur naturalist; Prince became a peerless woodsman. He brought to his understanding of birds and animals, wild and tame, a certain occult comprehension that no white man ever attains. He appeared to regard all beasts and birds as his younger brothers and sisters, and he spoke to them and of them as he shared all their hopes and fears. In all this was something of the mystic's fathomless far reach to the heart of God. Nothing in nature appeared too small to escape his notice.

My association with Prince Alston had been lifelong. He was the son of Martha, for forty years our plantation cook, and of Will, for a longer period our wood bringer and fire builder. Prince and I were of the same age. But his infancy, though he was supposed to be relatively unimportant, was far more dramatic than mine. Nature often seems to overlook with the most exasperating candor many of those very distinctions upon which we most fervently insist. One day, while I was sleeping in my carriage in the front yard, Prince was being plunged, in the back yard, into a huge caldron of hot pea soup. He thus early attained over me an ascendancy in point of authentic interest; and, although I was supposed to be the master and he the man, perhaps he has maintained it to this very day. I owe him much. For forty-four years our comradeship lasted, and it was one of deep affection. For my part, I see no reason for the termination of it, either on this or on the other side of the grave.

Prince's affair in the caldron happened quite naturally. His mother reported to mine that the baby had a "spasm." Recognizing at once the child's desperate need, and knowing that an immediate plunge into warm water is the best first-aid remedy, my mother called for hot water. None was forthcoming, but Martha suggested that in the back yard peas were boiling. My mother, with little Prince in her arms, hurried down the back steps. Before her under a huge live oak was the momentous-looking caldron, just beginning to steam gently. After dipping in her finger to determine the temperature of the water, and finding it tepid, she laid the black baby among the steaming pea pods, holding him gently but firmly in place. Almost at once his crying stopped. Prince was saved. Moreover, a certain glamour was shed over his infancy, and for years he went under the strange and distinctive appellation of "the Pea-Soup baby."

Prince's inheritance was a good one, I mean his spiritual inheritance. His mother was possessed of a primeval faithfulness and affection, and his father of an almost heartbreaking humble loyalty. And his son Prince has always had that kind of spirit in him.

Through childhood and boyhood my Black Prince and I were inseparable companions in a thousand plantation escapades: we were thrown from the same woods pony at the same time; we were together pursued by the same infuriated bull; nearly drowned in the same pond when our canoe upset; and in the matter of gleeful butting, the half-wild goat that we had captured made no distinction between us as victims for his sinister jesting. Whenever our frolics came to the attention of the elder generation, we were equally reprimanded. My father repeatedly scolded us as one, especially on the occasion when we knotted together the tails of two semiwild boars that were feeding at a trough, with their backs close to a convenient hole in the fence. And Henry Snyder, the Negro foreman, a very superior person, for whom I early acquired a dreadful respect, used to be very severe with us—chiefly because we delighted in ruffling his oppressive dignity.

Our worst offense occurred on the day when, after borrowing a set of deer horns from the frieze in the hall, and draping two deerskins over us after the manner in which the Seminoles camouflaged themselves while deerstalking, we burst into the barnyard, where scores of Negroes were threshing rice, superintended by Henry. We charged the crowd with wild, weird shouts, scattering madly the gravest and most sedate of them, especially Henry, in whom, as the leader of his clan, a peculiarly high and sensitive kind of superstition had been developed. Henry's ability as a runner, jumper, and general escaper had never been publicly demonstrated before, but he showed on that day the power to lead, in rather magnificent style, a precipitous retreat. We paid dearly for our fun, for to make a man lose an assumed and cherished dignity is of all insults the most deadly.

But mischief did not occupy us wholly. We planted a little garden together; we had scores of curious pets, such as alligators, raccoons, fawns, foxes, and minks; we rode together after the cattle; visited the solitary spacious pinewoods to get lightwood for the fires. We also, from earliest times, hunted and fished a good deal together, though I cannot report that we supplied the plantation table with commendable regularity. Our failure to do so was not due to any lack of fish and game, but rather to our discursive natures, for no sooner were we well started on a hunt, or well settled by some cypress-brown, bass-haunted lagoon to fish, than some new interest of the wildwood or of the wild water would divert us. Thus I remember that we spent a whole half-day trying to see how many deadly cottonmouth moccasins we could catch with our fishing tackle. We did well, but when we presented our catch to Martha, in a somewhat darkened kitchen, her reaction was decidedly volatile and picturesque.

Young as I was, even in those first years of my association with Prince I recognized in him a decided superiority in certain matters. A plantation Negro is as close to nature, I suppose, as any man in the world, and close in an intimate, authentic sense. He is still a child. Folded on that ample bosom, he hears and obeys the voice of the ancient mother; he has with marvelous accuracy what we slangily but felicitously call the "low-down" on all the creatures of nature. The knowledge of them that came to me in some small degree after many years of patient observation and study, Prince appeared to have instinctively. His understanding of wild things was not scientific, but natural. I have always noticed that he spoke of an animal as if it were a human being; he fixed no gulf between the two neighboring kingdoms. His eyes in the woods used to surprise me; now they amaze me. My own eyesight has always been normally good, but it does not clairvoyantly apprehend as does his. As boys together, he was almost invariably the one to warn me when I was about to step on a snake. He could take me to the spot in the sunny wild field of broomsedge where a little fawn lay. He could see, on the topmost tiny spire of a towering yellow pine, that wisp of gray that betrayed the presence of a scared fox squirrel. It was he who took me to the den of a huge bull alligator on a lonely island. He had heard that Minotaur roar, had discounted all the ventriloquistic quality of that weird bellow, had located the singer accurately, and to the formidable monster he guided me, when he was not more than eleven years old. We caught the huge reptile, Prince and I, with a hook and line. We drew out Leviathan with a hook.

Because of our close and genuine comradeship, I used to go to Prince's cabin as often as he came to my home, and as we were together every day and usually until nightfall, the one would go halfway home with the other. The way led through the woods, and along the edges of the melancholy plantation burying ground where, for more than two centuries, the Negroes of the place had been interred. There the mighty pines towered tallest; there the live oaks stood Druidlike; there the jasmines rioted freely over hollies and sweet myrtles, tossing their saffron showers high in air. As children, Prince and I dreaded this place. I can remember going along this dusky road many a time, my love for him taking me farther from home than my reason warranted, his love for me overmastering his fear of the graveyard, so that often he used to come with me all the way to the plantation gate. We used to walk that road holding hands, and even now I can remember how the hands of those children, one black and one white, used to tighten as a dewy strange wind gushed by us, or as an owl would begin his haunting twilight note.

All things human change, and the time came when a temporary parting was inflicted upon Prince and me. I was sent away to school and to college; he remained in his old wild free life. His prospect looked to me as halcyon as mine was foreboding. It was years before we were able to renew our companionship. When opportunity was once more afforded us to be together, we were both grown. Whatever, in a deeper sense, my growth had been, I do not think that essentially it was very far in advance of his, and certainly in physical development he had immeasurably surpassed me.

Whence got he those mighty shoulders? When came that iron grasp? Whence got he that huge and rugged forearm, that splendid depth of chest? Though not of great height, his stature, leonine and massive, would set all the athletic coaches of America agog if they could have seen it. While I had been delicately pursuing French verbs to their dim lairs, and trying with many a headache to determine whether Pragmatism is a true philosophy and Relativity a true scientific theory, Prince had been felling forests, digging canals, driving mule teams, and, with the sun at about 115 degrees, he had been plowing down knee-high crab grass, shouting and singing as he worked. Standing to the thighs in fetid, snake-haunted swamp water, all day long he had sawed huge cypress logs, he and his fellows laughing and joking as they toiled. Or out in the lonely forest of yellow pine, from daylight to dark he had brought thundering to earth the giant trees, tall as masts of brigantines, and full of nameless aerial melodies in their crowns.

Black, rugged, independent, Prince was a man long ere I became one. Years and other matter had parted us, but when we met, we clasped hands with the old affection, and perhaps understood each other as perfectly as two human beings ever do. Death's is not the only veil through which we cannot see; an impalpable arras separates most of us. The human soul seems a shrouded thing, and most solitary. Love alone is capable of destroying isolation and of breaking down every barrier.

That Prince was a real psychological study I have, of late years, come deeply to appreciate. There was, for example, his mastery of animals, which had in it a spiritual legerdemain fascinating to behold. No man who watched this Negro with dogs or mules can be persuaded that magic is dead. On occasions that are literally countless I have shamelessly referred to him dogs that were of the most incorrigible sort, dogs that would not even make up with me. Immediately he would establish a definite relationship with them, partly by firmness, partly by kindness, but chiefly by an occult and complete fathoming of the dog's mentality. I recall how he made Blossom mind him when she would pay me not the slightest attention.

This hound was new and strange, and Prince and I took her into the woods for a ramble. Young, diffident, headstrong, she was prone to race pell-mell after any alluring scent that assailed her delicate nostrils from the damp sandy road. We were in wild country, and to have her escape on a trail would have been serious. I was about to suggest that we put her in a leash when she suddenly left the road on a dead run. A fresh buck track explained her joyous haste.

At thirty yards a shout from Prince brought her to a bickering halt. She was too far away for him to catch her, or even to threaten her effectively with the long lash that he carried. The hound did not want to come back. Yet, while ignoring me, she deigned to give Prince a bright, undetermined look, as if

41

inquiring politely the reason for his impertinent interruption of her urgent business. Knowing that it would be a vain thing for me to try to lure the dog, I left it all to him—I usually left anything to him that was difficult—watching closely to discover by what mental artful sleight he would accomplish the miracle. Clearly, it was to be a spiritual, not a physical, struggle.

"Blossom," he called, "come here, child. Here, Blossom, come here to me. You is the prettiest, fines', most 'bedient houn' I ever did see. That's a good girl. Come on now. Come on, honey Blossom. I know you wouldn't leave me here in the road all by myself. That's a sweet Blossom."

Flattering wiles, couched in tones that reached the hound's very soul, accomplished what force and anger and less delicate deception could never have done. But there was more than that to the performance. Into the immense solitude environing the individual Prince had suavely obtruded himself. All creatures will, I suppose, respond to blandishments, but they must be of the intimate and understanding variety. The hound Blossom was completely taken by Prince's tones. She turned toward us. Then she approached step by step, a little contritely. At last she made a little run, frisked about Prince, leaped up on him affectionately, licked his hand. I had had, in college, a course in Practical Psychology, and one in Animal Psychology. But my knowledge had left me helpless, whereas Prince knew what to do without ever having been taught.

Watching Prince handle the biggest, stubbornest mules in timber camp, I came to believe that the secret of his mastery over them arose from his ability to establish in them a definite conception of their inferiority. He then took it for granted that they would work, his attitude being objective, hale and natural. He talked to them also, as it were, in their own tongue, and to his raillery they responded with astonishing willingness. To manage mules should be accounted something of an artistic tour de force.

I remember the first time I ever saw Prince operate on a stubbornly planted mule. It happened down in a little seacoast village near home. A farmer's mule, hitched to an infirm and staggering wagon, loaded heavily with a Saturday's purchases, had made up his mind that the prospect of seven long sandy miles ahead did not appeal to him. The animal balked in the middle of the village street, right between the post office and the general store, so that the performance created considerable stir. At such a time, all local and loafing celebrities are exceedingly fertile in advice. To this scene of hopeless *status quo* Prince and I arrived after some very heroic measures had been used without the slightest response on the part of the immobile mule. He had been cruelly beaten; his harness had been taken off. The wagon had been rolled back. But there he stood violently rooted, with a certain exasperatingly virtuous expression on his countenance. Curses and shouts left him unmoved. Even a small fire built under him had had no effect at all as a persuader to progress. The city fathers had become less assured of tone as one after another of their solvents for balkiness failed. The affair had come to a state of impasse when Prince stepped quietly forward, while I watched fascinated. He approached the mule with gentle assurance, and insinuated one arm around the stubborn neck. His touch was affectionate. Putting his mouth to the mule's left ear, he said something to the miserable statue. Instantly the creature rigidly relaxed, and almost blithely the mule stepped forward from the position which for more than an hour he had sullenly maintained. When Prince came back to me, I asked him what he had said to his friend. The Negro laughed, for he never seems to take seriously any of his feats with animals. But his must have been the magic words having the exact wave length of the dull creature's obscure and baffled soul.

For many years I had searched in vain for a specimen of the black fox squirrel, a variant in color of the gray. It is in reality a color due to a condition known as melanism. Mentioning to Prince one day my wish, I was surprised to have him say, "I show you one today." Together forthwith we went to the woods. It was mid-March, and the leaves gave the forest an emerald misty look.

Prince took me up a long watercourse through the woods where grow many tupelos, gums, and redbud maples. Ere we had gone a half mile we had seen gray fox squirrels, big handsome fellows. Each one was in a maple tree. At last my companion pointed to what I should have taken for a spray of dead Spanish moss. It hung almost drifting from among the ruby buds of a maple. It was a fox squirrel, black as ebony.

"How did you know it was here?" I asked.

"He been here las' summer," Prince answered, "and the year befo', when he was a baby. A fox squirrel," he added, "this time of the year will come a mile or mo' to get the redbud."

Woodcraft of this kind Prince gathered during those years when he was a worker of turpentine, and no kind of toil is more exacting in the matter of compelling the worker to traverse almost every foot of the forest. He must literally go from tree to tree. Being a keen and accurate observer, and not only seeing but actually entering into the lives of the children of the wild, he had gathered an astonishing amount of firsthand information about nature, and this knowledge, like all information acquired through experience, had become a part of his character. Many men use their knowledge of nature merely as an intellectual decoration. This Negro guided his life by that knowledge and by those ancient laws. Because he did live by those laws, ordinary physical obstacles had for him no substantial existence. Long since he had learned, without any mechanical device, how to annihilate distance.

One afternoon I said to Prince that he and I ought to go deer hunting the next day at daylight. I could see that my request embarrassed him a little. But he said he would join me, adding, "I will be back by then."

"Back?" I asked. "Where are you going?"

"I have to step up to Jamestown," he answered.

This place is twenty-three miles from home, and swamp miles, too, over corduroy roads which are usually inundated. Prince walked the forty-six miles, most of them in the dark; and at daylight the following morning he was in the plantation back yard before I was up. In fact, what woke me was the joyous yowling of the hounds which announced the arrival of their beloved lord and master. Prince thought nothing of walking twenty miles to buy a plug of tobacco, a pound of bacon, a sack of flour. And usually in making his journeys he did not follow roads; as short cuts he knew all the animal paths through the forest. When he needed wood, taking his ax, he went to the pinelands, perhaps a mile or more from his cabin, and would return with a massive section of a lightwood log on his shoulder. He did things directly, quietly, in nature's way. When I read stories of Negroes who are little more than minstrels, I do not recognize in them blood brothers to my Black Prince. Though superstitious in a piquant way, as all elemental human beings are, he was not afraid of the dark. Moreover, without being able to name a single star, he could guide himself by them; and, lacking starlight, he retained an uncanny sense of direction even in the deepest woods at night. Well I remember the time he and I, taking an acetylene lamp, went to the forest to try to discover and to count the deer that we could "shine" with the light.

It was late October, and the dying year was beautiful as only lovely things departing can be beautiful. It had rained that afternoon, and as we set out on our expedition, a sodden yellow evening with sallow lights was faintly gilding the ruined trees. Pale lilac gleams suffused the fading woods. By the time we had left the inner plantation bounds, night had come down, starless, occult, mysterious. Before we had gone a mile farther, our blazing light had disclosed for us five deer, airy shapes of the fabulous darkness, delicately roaming the forest. I was wearing the lamp as a headlight, and it disclosed to us not only the deer but our own surroundings as well. Prince said he knew where we were, though we were in virgin timber a long way from any road. On we went, deeper and deeper into the double night of the forest and of the darkness. I heard the muffled joyous gurgling of a stream; the earth deliciously exhaled dewy odors. Other odors there were too, strange and pungent. Suddenly on my arm the hand of my woodsman closed like a vise.

"Cap'n," his soft voice said, "step back this way."

I obeyed, knowing that he had detected something that I had not.

"I smell a rattlesnake," he said. "I think he is in them huckleberry bushes ahead. We must go around him."

It may be that I owed my life to Prince that night, but I doubt if he even remembered what I so vividly recall. I can still feel his hand, hear his voice. It was a voice I infallibly trusted. It was a human voice that had never deceived me. Its tones were akin to the tones of nature.

Not far from that patch of bushes that we wisely avoided, my light began to sputter. Then something behind the glass flared, blinked, and was gone. In vain I tried to re-kindle the flame. We were in abysmal darkness, there in the far-off silent woods, inhabited by creatures less appealing than deer. I was as lost as if an airplane had dropped me in the Brazilian wilderness. But I did not have the sense of being lost, for I had with me an infallible guide.

"Do you know where we are, Prince?" I asked.

"Yes, sah, I know."

"Can you find the road?"

"Yes, sah."

"How do you know which way to go?"

"My mind done tell me."

By the expression "my mind" a Negro does not mean his thinking capacity, nor yet his knowledge. He seems to mean his prescience. At any rate, in a half hour we were back in the familiar plantation road. It was not that we had been actually delivered from any special peril, for with daylight we could have found our way. It was rather that Prince demonstrated to me that he had a sense of direction that would function even in the profoundest darkness, and there's always something miraculous in one person's doing what a supposed superior cannot. Here, indeed, was a child of nature. And there was no more pretense in Prince than there is in a good black furrow or in a boulder or in a sunrise.

Of him as a spiritual human being, I had no misgivings. I knew his heart too well. But most wives are exceedingly dubious concerning the state of their husbands' souls. It was so with Prince's wife. She unburdened herself to me one day.

"Prince is good," she said in her gentle, compassionate voice, "but he cannot acclaim himself a Christian."

"Why not?" I asked, surprised.

"Because," she said thoughtfully, "he is a deer hunter. With Prince, deer hunting is religion."

But her subdued indictment of her husband was delivered with a faint smile, with a patient delicate tinge of humor, as if the future state of her sinful deer hunter did not seriously alarm her. As a matter of fact, Prince's faith would have put to shame the religion of many a supposed pillar of the church. The faith of this humble Negro was aboriginal, complete. How often have I heard him say simply without a grace of professional unction, things like these: "God is good enough to do anything"; "The weather is so dry that I have a doubt mind, but if we trust in God, He will help us"; "Cap'n, we gwine understand everything when we done reach the Promised Land."

45

About such a human being there is an atmosphere of permanence. He was one of the true inheritors of nature's bounty. When I would go home after all those years and find him there, he always impressed me with his changeless unspoiled quality, like that of a sentinel pine, or of the primal pagan night. Much of life is a matter of waiting, and partly for that reason we yearn toward the things in nature which, like mountains and forest, wait with a lordly patience. Surely for the wild mortal heart to await quietly is an illustrious achievement. Prince had the ancient patience of the pioneer.

Some of the language that Prince used would not be easily apprehended by the ordinary listener. I have made little attempt to give his tones. They were musical and soft. And in addition to the "gullah" of the Carolina coastal Negro, he used a few words as strange as any ever heard in America. These were of genuine African origin, as their sound will connote. For example, when he says, "Cap'n, I yeddy one madindie in dem jubrocroo," he means that he hears a cottontail rabbit in the gallberry bushes. "De wedder giffie" means that the weather is uncertain. "Machinchie" means small; "bungiewala" means a dragon fly; "bofemba" means a swamp rabbit. It would hardly seem credible, and yet it is true, that Prince used often to say to me, when we were boys, "Let we go hunt dem machinchie bofemba an' dem blue bungiewala."

I owe to Prince what I hope is a fair understanding of life's deeper values. I can still hear him say, "When I take a man into my heart, I can't hate him no mo'." I can see him in a freezing drizzle, far from home and at dusk, making easy in the lonely wood the bed of an old cow that is sure to die that night, and I know that such a man's religion is a living thing, prompting him to act. I can hear him going through the ghostly woods at night, whooping in a voice so melodious that it would charm a hardened critic, and I know that his spirit is wild and free and joyous. To get on into middle life retaining a free spirit is a thrilling accomplishment. To range the wildwoods singing, and with the heart singing, is no light thing, for to do this is to be a child of God.

A Wildwood Christmas

This is Rutledge the nature writer with a flair for anthropomorphism blended with fiction at his best. This piece comes from Those Were the Days *(pages 444–62). It appeared earlier under the title "Black Roland" in the January 1942 issue of* Sports Afield *(pages 14–15, 46–48).*

I

*T*he high-bush huckleberries were in bloom. Wild yellow daisies starred the level floor of the great pine forest. But for faint aeolian airs sounding in the lofty crests of the huge yellow pines, the woods were still. Had it been nearer the river, many birds would have been singing on that April day; but this was the wild pinewoods country, and few birds are found there. Between Montgomery Branch and the Green Bay, the country is silent and solitary; one might imagine it almost bare of life.

But life was here in its most wonderful form—life reproducing itself. On that benign Carolina springtime day, a whitetail doe had given birth to a fawn. To a wild creature of her physical perfection and native vigor, birth was natural and unattended by fear or pain.

Seven months ago she had mated with the great ten-point stag from Fox Bay. Now her hour was past, and the burly little buck was surprisingly wide awake. He lay curled in the broomsedge bed under the fragrant myrtles.

The mother stood over him, licking him, cleansing him, loving him. Her whole attitude was a blessing and a caress. Her liquid eyes were tender with affection. They should have been wide with amazement, for the fawn was unlike any she had ever seen before. Her baby was black—a perfect glossy black, strange and beautiful.

Once in the wilds of Wambaw Swamp she had seen a spectral white buck; and a spotted half albino had come across the river the previous summer. But her baby from the tips of his ears to the points of his tiny gleaming hoofs was solid ebony.

With the tall, rocking pines for sentinels, with the bright sunshine warming the dewy wilderness, and the peaceful sky above, it did not seem a baby deer could so soon be in danger. But he was not an hour old before he was in peril of his life. His watchful mother knew what to fear in those lonely woods, and she was alert to every sight or sound or odor that might threaten her fawn.

The first premonition of trouble came to her as an odor. With a start her head lifted, her eyes were set forward, and her body became tense. Her black nostrils widened apprehensively and defiantly. This odor was not unpleasant, but the doe dreaded it; it was animal, yet seemed vegetable also.

Depending as she did on power of smell more than on eyesight to identify anything that approached, the doe now took a step forward in the suspected direction, her nostrils flaring. She knew the character of this ancient enemy, but as yet she had not seen him. She glanced back at her baby; then she moved clear of the bed of grass in which she had given him birth.

The black fawn lay in the dappled sunlight, happily drowsing and blinking. He knew nothing about death. When he was first born, he had been chilly; but now the genial sun was warming him, and he was beginning to feel at home in his new world.

His mother advanced a few yards towards the clump of sweet gum bushes that grew about a huge yellow pine stump. All about the stump the trash and leaves had been strangely cleared away, leaving a circle of clean white sand. Years before a forest fire had burned some of the stump roots deeply into the ground, leaving a cavernous black hole there. And now, coming out to sun himself was the evil creature that the doe had winded, a great diamondback rattlesnake nearly six feet long, the serpent terror of the western world.

Moving with lordly deliberateness up the sandy incline from his den, the banded death came into the sunlight of the sweet springtime world. It was as if a chimera from another and sinister planet was invading the wholesome realm of earth. And for all the horror of his wide-sunken eyes, the sullen droop at the corners of the mouth, the cold pallor of his lips, and the powerful jaws, the huge serpent was beautiful. There was majestic rhythm in his movements, the spirit of power was in him, and the spirit of awe went before him.

As soon as the doe saw the rattler, she stopped, and all her hair stood out slightly so she looked menacing and larger than natural. Mingled emotions of hatred and anger gleamed in her eyes. She had seen many rattlers before, and she had killed some. But none were so large as this. There was but one way in which she could kill him: that was by springing on him with her forefeet drawn tightly together like a sheaf of spears. Her polished, sharp hoofs made deadly lances. But to kill a rattler a deer has to have his enemy fairly in the open.

The fawn's mother now waited. Restlessly she stamped one forefoot. She looked back to where her baby lay. And when she turned her head, the monster saw her. Only about a yard of dread length had cleared his hole; only his great spade-shaped head and the extreme forepart of his heavy body lay on the white sand—that circle he had cleared about the old stump.

The rattler saw the doe and he was afraid. He lay there looking at her with his cold, basilisk like eyes. Then he swung his head slowly, turning back into his darksome den.

When he disappeared the doe knew that, for the moment, the danger had passed; but she knew also she could not leave her baby where he was. It was not, of course, that the reptile would have considered the fawn his prey; but such a serpent is extremely irritable and considers anything that moves near his den an enemy. Yet the mother would have to stay with her baby until he could walk.

Still trembling a little, she nibbled at the tender green shoots of grass. Then, with head low, she returned to her strange little black fawn.

The mother, bending above him, now pushed him with her nose, now moved him with one of her front feet. She was trying to see whether she could get him to stand up. At last he did, but his legs were very wobbly, and they seemed much too long and slender. The doe now stepped forward, bleating softly, until her full breast was directly above her baby. He began to nurse, indifferently and uncertainly at first; but when he found how good the milk tasted, he spread his legs, sank his tiny hoofs into the sand, and went to work in real earnest.

When he had had all he could hold, he took a few teetery steps then lay down, and his mother lay beside him. Little Roland slept; but his mother kept untiring watch.

After the black fawn had slept three hours, he awoke. Already he was stronger, was growing, and developing an air of naïve intelligence. If she had not seen an enemy coming from under the old pine stump the doe would now have left her baby, and have gone to the lush savannas and the misty green watercourses to feed. But she would not leave him near the den of a diamondback. It was not that this dreaded serpent would deliberately attack the fawn. But he might be attracted by its odors; the monster might approach; the fawn, in moving from him, might touch or alarm him. Then he would strike. Perhaps the mother did not think of all that. Perhaps she knew only that the diamondback means death, and that she must get her baby out of danger.

Standing up, she gently nuzzled the fawn until he swayingly took his feet. Then with her black nose she pushed him forward slowly, step by step. Sometimes she would go a little way ahead to make certain all was well; then she would coax him forward through the grass and ferns.

When they reached a dense clump of gall berries on the edge of a savanna, she let him lie down. They had come a safe distance. She tucked him into his wildwood cradle. And the fawn slept; that is, as much as a deer ever really sleeps—more daydreaming than slumber, drowsing and blinking, relaxing and resting. It is perhaps worth noticing that all herbivorous creatures sleep lightly whereas the carnivora slumber profoundly.

The doe, satisfied now that her baby was safe and happy, stole swiftly away from him and began to feed on the tender grass of the savanna. At any other time of the year she would not have fed until twilight, then on through the night; but now, partly because the woods were thick with greenery, and chiefly because her baby had to have his milk regularly, she ventured abroad in the daylight, in the retired security of the wild forest. She knew her fawn would not stir from where she had left him; and there was now no danger near.

Especially did she feel safe from men; they rarely came into the springtime and summer woods. Not until the beginning of autumn would the forest be clamorous with their shouting, the blare of their guns, and with the tumult of hounds and horns. But men, she knew, were strange creatures, of uncertain habits and disconcerting irregularly of behavior, and sometimes they appeared when they were least expected.

II

"Maisie, if there is going to be preaching on Sunday, we ought to have some flowers for the church and our own ain't nothin'! Where did you find those white wild lilies last year? Maybe you might find some more. But if you go a-lookin' for 'em, you must watch out for snakes. A day like this will bring the rattlers outen their dens. I would like to go with you, but I can't go into the woods like I used to."

Maybelle Mayhew regarded her daughter, tall and slender and boyish at sixteen years of age. She was beautiful to an unusual degree, blooming like a wildflower in her pineland home.

"I know where them flowers is," said Maisie, in a voice that had bird notes in it. "I just go down the road a piece; then I cross Montgomery Branch as you are headin' for Boggy Bay, where we used to pick all them high-bush huckleberries. There's lots of lilies there, and they would sure look pretty in the church Sunday."

"Well, child, be careful. Take a stick with you and beat on the bushes ahead of you as you go along. That's the best way to tell if a snake is there. And keep on the path if you can. And don't be too long a-waitin' to look at a lot of other flowers and at birds' nests same as you allus do."

Bareheaded and barelegged, Maisie ran across the sandy yard of her home, and out into the woodland road that passed the Mayhew farm. She paused for a moment to break a chinaberry shoot. She would use this to investigate the snake situation. Then she sped on down the road, her feet making clear imprints in the damp sand.

Having a woodsman's uncanny sense of direction, from the road she presently turned into a dim game trail, just a narrow path strewn with pine needles, and overhung by a careless disarray of little bushes, huckleberries, gall berries, and tiny sweet bays, now in bloom, their snowy chalices gleaming.

Maisie tapped the bushes ahead with her stick. Once she heard it give a strange klink, and then she laughed to see the glossy back of a land terrapin. Once something scuttled away at lightning speed, and she heard it run up a pine. She knew it was a wild skink, a lizard of gaudy, almost poisonous, colors, and gifted with truly amazing speed.

Into the hushed and fragrant twilight she went, into the dimness and the dewiness of Montgomery Branch, where wampees shed the water like quicksilver, and where were fan palmettos and great purple flags. Wading the stream, she started suddenly when a patriarch bullfrog plunged from the grassy bank into his favorite pool.

From the cool shadows of the watercourse Maisie climbed the low hill to the level pineland floor. She did not know it, but when she paused there, she was standing within twenty feet of the diamondback's den. But he lay hushed and hidden in his ashen coil, and she tripped gaily onward toward the savanna. The white wood lilies always grew in a damp place, and this was the place she had found them the year before.

"Those same ones will be blooming again this year," she said. "They don't seem to mind if I take their flowers. They just keep blooming away. I wish I could be like a wood lily," she went on idly to herself—"always pretty and white and clean."

Searching the pathway ahead with wary eyes, she came to a heavy clump of gall berries, and struck it sharply with her stick. Then she thrust it into the green privacy of the shadows.

Something stirred there; and Maisie, whose eyes were keen as those of any other wild thing, saw a black shape, not much bigger than a coiled rattler.

"Laws-a-massy!" she exclaimed. "Now ain't that som'thin'! And I nigh stepped on him. I hain't never seen one so black before!"

With the end of the stick she separated thick, low branches. The sunlight flooded through the aperture, and there before her wondering eyes lay the tiny black fawn.

"Great Christmas!" she exclaimed. "Hit's a baby deer, and he's as black as the inside of a chimbley! How come he here?" she asked herself. "I wonder where his ma is. His pa, he don't ever mind him; but his ma, she ought to be about. And she might fight me on occasion of him."

Maisie could hardly take her eyes off this dusky woodland elf. When she did look up, there was the doe, only a few yards away; and it was amazing what emotions her mien and her attitude expressed: dread, courage, anger, terror for herself and her baby, boundless affection for her little black fawn, and what looked to Maisie like a pathetic appeal from one woman to another.

"Don't you mind me," Maisie said to her gently. "I wouldn't hurt your baby. . . . But ain't it funny," she added to herself, "that he's black all over? He hain't got nary a spot. Iffen you ask me, that is something I never hoped to see."

The doe kept stepping nearer, hesitatingly, menacingly. The scent of man was of all scents the most dreaded, much more than that of a deerhound, an alligator, or a rattlesnake. A doe will not actually fight a human being in defense of her young; the most she will do is to come near, perhaps feign to threaten, and certainly to look imploringly at the intruder.

"I wish he was mine," said Maisie. "I sure would like to carry him home. But the doe, she wouldn't have no more this year, because deer have a baby only once a year. And she would grieve mighty hard if I took this one. My, but he did look cuddly and cute!"

She had almost forgotten about the lilies. Softly now she stepped away from the doe and the fawn. As soon as she had gone a few yards into the green savanna, the wild mother stole up to her black elf, carefully investigating him to make sure he was safe.

Maisie found her lilies; and with a bouquet as large as she could carry, she set out to return home. But she made a wide circuit about the doe and fawn.

"I know just how she feels," she kept saying to herself. "I'd feel that way if I had a little youngun, and me scared it might come to some hurt. Won't Rodney be surprised when I tell him! And I guess he'll tease me and say it ain't so, same as he allus does. Maybe I won't tell him at all," she reasoned with girlish craft. "As sure as I do, he'll be for hunting him. A little black deer! Rodney won't believe it. He'll be for saying I saw a coon or a cooter, I know him."

When she came to the open road she dropped her stick. "I don't mind snakes when I can see 'em plain like and open. It's steppin' on 'em unbeknown that I don't hanker after."

Soon she was within sight of the clearing in the pinelands that was the home of the Mayhews. She saw her father plowing in the cornfield, her mother sitting on the porch where she had left her. Standing near her in the yard was a third figure. Maisie's eyes brightened at sight of him.

"Hit's Rod," she said, and instinctively she touched her hair with her free hand and smoothed down her dress. "Shall I tell him or no?"

As she came up to the gate, looking at her flushed, excited face, Rodney Magwood, a lean young giant, black-browed and handsome in a backwoods way, said in his drawling, bantering fashion:

"You seed more than flowers where you been. Is you been findin' bird nests again?"

Maisie gave the lilies to her mother. Then she took a womanly moment to compose herself.

"Rod Magwood," she said gravely, "what I seed you ain't never seed before."

Rodney laughed. "Maisie, you see plenty what I don't see, and you see plenty what ain't here to see."

"All right then," said Maisie, sitting down on the top step. "I won't tell you; but and iffen I tole you, you'd be s'prised."

"Uh-huh," Rodney grunted indulgently.

"What did you see, child?" asked her mother.

"A black deer," Maisie announced boldly.

Rodney threw back his head and laughed loudly. Then as suddenly he became silent and thoughtful.

"Look here, Maze," he said, "is you sure it warn't one of them wild black hogs out of the Big Ocean Bay, or maybe a b'ar from outen Hellhole Swamp? They git over this a-way every so and again."

"It was a baby deer, and as black as your houn' dog Bugle; and you know that houn' ain't nothin' but black, same as midnight."

"War you close to him—a little fawn?"

"I was up on him, and his ma, she war right there lookin' at me. I war right sorry for her, she was that worried."

"Did they run from you?"

"He couldn't, and she wouldn't. He is little and weak but awful purty."

"Do tell," muttered Maisie's mother.

"I do remember," Rodney said, "come to think about it, Ned Parler, he tole me he seed a black buck onct. And he didn't shoot at him. It was a thick place and he thought it was an Augus steer what had got away from some place. But when it hit the hill, he saw the horns, and it was a deer."

His tone was changed. People of the back country of the pinelands are superstitious.

"Do you all reckon hit could mean anything—Maisie seein' that black deer, and the moon comin' full tonight? You know the likes of such things are sometimes tokens."

The mother looked at her only daughter with a light of strange fear in her deep-set eyes.

"Like as not it was just a plain deer what Maisie thought was black. Yet I seed a white one onct."

Both Rod and Maisie remembered also; for it was hardly a month after she had seen the albino buck that her only son had died.

"I hope this one is a buck," said Rodney. "I sure would like to kill him when his horns get growed."

"I hopes you never seen him," said Maisie with a maternal protective instinct. "Maybe," she added with a child's strange cunning, "maybe he is a token, and then it would be bad luck to kill him. He might bring us all bad luck, Rod, if we trouble him. The likes of him should be let alone."

"Child, how you talk!" said her mother. Rodney laughed softly, but there was a faint uneasiness in his merriment. Although he could not have defined it, he had a premonition of danger, all the more disturbing because it was vague.

III

Eight years had passed since that sunny April day when Maisie Mayhew had come upon little Black Roland. Time had brought its changes. Maisie and Rod Magwood had now been married five years; they had their little home in the wilderness, and two babies had been born to them, little Rodney and Lucy.

As for Black Roland, he was now a huge twelve-point stag, hero of many an adventure. So hard had he been hunted by the Nimrods of the backwoods that he had crossed the Santee River and for more than three years had lived in the moldering solitude of a huge swamp in the heart of the wilderness.

He lived on Mound Ridge, which is near the western end of the great Santee Delta in Coastal Carolina, a place probably as primeval as any left in North America. Magwood did not live on the Ridge, but he spent much time there, his chief reason being Black Roland. With ordinary white-tail bucks he had an intimate and life-long acquaintance; but this deer was unlike any he had ever seen.

Roland was so very different that the first time Rodney saw him the backwoods hunter was not sure what the creature might be. For this great swamp stag was coal black. It was not only his color that made him remarkable, but he carried a rack of palmated antlers that Magwood knew to be a record, even for that famous deer country. And they were as black as Roland's glistening hide.

For three seasons Rodney had followed him; each season he had seen the buck; once he had picked up one of his dropped antlers. But the hunter's chance to kill this wary king did not come until the time of the great flood. Those wild waters which were to inundate hundreds of thousands of acres of land, began to rise during the first days of the week before Christmas.

For several days Rodney, whose little home was over in the Cedar Hill country on the mainland west of the river, had been reading in the daily paper of the coming of big water. As it had a long way to come, nearly three hundred miles, it took some days to reach his place.

When the swollen river strikes tidewater, the whole delta is deeply submerged—a region sixteen miles long and from two to three miles wide; and at such a time all wildlife in that vast wilderness of bog, marsh, and swamp has a precarious time. Deer and turkeys, snakes and alligators, rabbits and king rails, wild hogs and cattle—all gather on the high timbered ridges; and if these ridges are submerged, the refugees have a swim to safety elsewhere.

"Maisie," said Rod to his little blue-eyed wife that December morning, "the river is up, and I aim to go acrost to the Ridge. First thing you know, Christmas will be here, and we don't have no venison. I can't let that happen to us. I might even see that old black buck we call Roland. John Souther seen him last month. He thought he was a black steer! I know whereabouts he lives." He almost whispered, afraid of betraying the secret even to his wife.

"Don't you take no chances in a freshet," cautioned Maisie. "Mound Ridge is a bad place, even without a big water. That's where you had trouble with that wounded buck—him what made me spend a week mendin' your clothes what he plum tore off. And that's where the Parler boy got struck with that big diamondback rattlesnake what kilt him."

"You ought to see that buck what I mean," said Rodney, ignoring his wife's calling up, none too rosily, the reputation of Mound Ridge. "I've done seen all the big deer horns in this country, but none like his."

"Well, don't you take no chances with him, either. I don't trust no big wild thing, especially if he's got horns."

Rodney laughed at her fears.

"And what would you think of me if I stayed home because I was scared?"

Maisie smiled.

"We do need the venison," she confessed.

"I'll be home afore sundown," he said. "Don't you worry. Ain't nothing on Mound Ridge worse than what I am."

Magwood's two hounds, Check and Mate, howled dismally because he did not take them.

"I don't need you dogs," he drawled. "You ain't no 'count in a freshet. All you'd do would be to get drowned."

Making his way down to the river, Rod shivered and turned up his coat collar. It was a raw day, misty and close to freezing. The wind off the river was bleak. Coming to his dug-out cypress canoe, he got into the frail craft, laid his gun carefully beside him, steadied himself, and then pushed off.

Now he could see the freshet waters creeping up, flooding the land. Soon he was on the great river itself, wide and stormy, rushing to the sea.

As the flood had already engulfed the vast delta lying between the North and South Santees, the whole expanse of wild water now before him was almost three miles wide. With stormy strength the huge tide rushed oceanward, bearing upon its tawny bosom rafts of dislodged sedge, swimming wild creatures, old logs, and tons of natural refuse. All about the hunter was an atmosphere of lonely danger.

"Maisie knowed when she tole me to be careful," he muttered. "This here river sure is gettin' wild. But it ain't so far to Mound Ridge," he comforted himself. "Right yonder at them tall pines on the delta—that's her. If ole Roland ain't already swum to the mainland, he'll have to be on the Ridge. He's a marshy deer; but you can't see no marsh now. He couldn't stay where he generally stays—'less he's a submarine."

As he paddled, he noticed the many fugitives swimming by, heading for high ground: swamp rabbits, razor-back hogs, a huge bull alligator that must have been washed out of hibernation; a burly wildcat, tawny as the flood itself, swimming for life; and once an otter, alone of all the wild things undismayed by the flood, heading gracefully upstream, as if the gloomy might of the down-rushing river were merely a challenge to his sporting instinct.

A hard paddle brought Magwood across the river, and he entered the comparatively hushed country of the drowned delta. All the wooded river banks were deeply submerged. The great marshes were covered, though here and there tall spears of yellow duck oats showed. Out of a moss-shrouded cypress the hunter flushed an old wild gobbler. Huge and black, he beat his way powerfully across the stormy waters toward the mainland.

"If I don't kill a deer," Magwood said, "I might come on him yonder where he's goin'. Maisie would like him for Christmas dinner."

A mile away, across the comparatively open water of the inundated delta, towered the dark pines of Mound Ridge, the only dry place left in that exceedingly wet country. The intervening water was not nearly so rough as the river had been, but Rodney had his troubles: constantly he had to be on the lookout for half-submerged logs. A canoe such as his could easily be tipped over by the heavy momentum of these pieces of flotsam.

Before long he neared Mound Ridge, and when his paddle could touch bottom, he pushed his canoe very quietly up to the Ridge and ran her nose on shore. Sitting perfectly still, he scanned the land ahead of him. Fugitives great and small crowded it. He saw a wild cow; myriads of swamp rabbits; several razorbacks; king rails that kept stepping on and over cottonmouth moccasins; he saw a doe and her twin yearling fawns.

Then, far on the western end, he saw a strange black shape, glistening in the sleety drizzle. He saw the turn of a regal head; he saw the noble antlers, faintly glinting. It was Black Roland!

"I got him at last," he whispered to himself. "If I work it the way I ought to work it, he ain't got no chanct to get away this time. Lawsy, can this boat carry him and me?"

Southward the waters stretched sixteen miles to the ocean; northward the country was widely flooded for an almost equal distance. Both to the east and to the west lay a mile and a half of open water. Rodney opened his gun; he carefully examined his shells. On the inside of his coat he wiped both his gun and his hands.

"This here," he said, "is one shot I mustn't miss. I got a chanct I have waited four years for. But I got to be careful. A deer is a deer. The old buck that gets away is generally the one you cornered. Sometimes he knows a trick worth two of any a man has."

"I know I can't walk up to him," he continued. "I must come up on his right-hand side, and maybe get up to him that way. If he takes the water, I got a boat. I done tole the boys I seed a black buck, and they laughed at me. Now I'm going to show 'em."

Very cautiously he pushed his canoe along the eastern side of the Ridge. Many of the fugitives moved ahead of him, but some turned back. All seemed disinclined to take the water. Familiar with the wildlife of that country, Rodney marveled at nothing but the great black stag, still standing warily on the far end of the Ridge. As he came near the doe and her fawns, they plunged in and struck eastward toward the faint outline of the distant mainland. He knew they would have no trouble reaching it; deer are lithe and powerful swimmers.

True to his buck nature, Black Roland carefully weighed his chances. In time of peril, a doe and her young will go anywhere just to get out of trouble. But it is not so with a buck. He fixes a certain sanctuary in mind; and when he has made his decision, he heads for it with all speed.

Magwood remembered the time he had tried to get a Negro to drive a buck to him; instead, the buck, having another plan in mind, almost ran over and trampled the would-be driver. When Rodney had protested about the Negro's failure to carry the scheme through, the wise man said:

"Ain't you know a buck? He gwine where he gwine."

The wilderness hunter was now within very long gunshot of the black buck. Some deer, often shot at and long-experienced, seem to know what that vital distance is. Roland had seen the doe and fawns head eastward. He would go west. Almost deliberately, even while Magwood was beginning to lay a strangely trembling hand on the grip of his gun, Roland waded out into the water, and in a moment was swimming evenly and strongly for the western mainland, mile and a half distant. And he had to go on; for there was no place between the Ridge and the mainland where he could stop. For a short way, a deer can often distance a man in a boat; but in a light canoe, if a man is a good paddler, he can always overtake a swimming deer in a long pull.

As soon as the black buck was in the water, Rodney threw off all reserve. Pushing and paddling desperately, he rounded the north end of the Ridge before Roland was out of sight. But the deer was some two hundred yards ahead, only his great antlers visible. Behind him the hunter settled down to grim effort; yet he could not paddle as if he were on open water. Roland was swimming through the flooded swamp; and both he and Magwood had to maneuver among the trees that stood in the water.

In this maneuvering, the buck had the advantage, since he merely had to swim through the best openings. If it had been a race over open water, there would have been no doubt of the outcome, but under these conditions the black stag had a chance. Rodney's main hope was to keep in sight and fairly near until they reached the clear water of the river.

Once when his canoe became momentarily wedged between two tupelo trees, Magwood stood up, gun in hand, to take a better look. There was Roland, eighty yards ahead. And far beyond the hunter could see a brightening of the dim swamp, and he knew it was the wide and open river.

Magwood now made his plan. "I'll follow him across the river, keeping up right clost; then I'll shoot him as soon as ever he touches the mainland. If I shoot him in the river, I couldn't manage him in this boat. He might get swept down and clear out to sea like that buck I shot in the river five years ago. The way he is swimming, he is coming ashore right by my landing. Maisie will be surprised when she sees what kind of buck I got this time."

The sweeping tide became swifter as it was less obstructed by trees; the light ahead increased, the river, tawny and wild, came within sight. Roland cleared the swamp a hundred yards ahead of the hunter; but soon Magwood had gained fifty yards, then twenty more. The deer was now at the hunter's mercy. Oblivious of the waves breaking into the canoe, of the driving sleet, the hunter concentrated on Black Roland, swimming valiantly just ahead, his mighty crown of antlers huge above the yellow flood.

"Ain't no deer like this been killed in this country since a hatchet was a hammer," muttered Rodney. He could count the points of the craggy antlers. He was sure there were twelve, perhaps more.

"Maisie, she laughed when I told her about this buck; but she won't laugh when I get him home. And Check and Mate, their feelings is going to be hurt for not being in on a hunt like this."

The black stag and the man were now near the middle of the river; Magwood had paddled within a few yards of him, and was so intent on watching him that he was not watching anything else. This was a very deep and dangerous part of the river. The mainland lay three hundred yards ahead, misty and wild. Both Black Roland and the man, hunted and hunter, longed to reach it.

"If nothin' happens," said Rodney, with melting sleet running off his cap and into his eyes, blurring his vision, "it will all be over in a few minutes."

But something did happen.

Swept from an ancient mooring by the mighty flood, a huge cypress, branches, monstrous bole, and scraggly clutching roots, all half submerged, swept down the middle of the shrouded river. A massive root caught and partly turned the swimming deer. Another, lifting from the water as the tree rocked upward on the flood, caught the frail canoe, and over it went.

Magwood's gun shot downward to the bottom of the river. The canoe, half its side torn away, drifted swiftly off. Rodney, baffled, hemmed by the root, turned and began to swim around the obstruction, clutching frantically for anything that was near. He saw something. Grimly he caught and hung on. For a moment he thought he had hold of the floating cypress. But, recovering from his shock, he was in for an almost equal one; he had Black Roland by the horns; but his position was precarious and awkward. He turned in the water, righting himself. He lay flat on the deer's back, both hands gripping the great bases of the buck's horns. And Black Roland was swimming for his life toward the mainland.

When he felt a little more sure of himself, Rodney let his left hand slip for a moment to his belt. His long-bladed hunting knife was still in its sheath.

"Ain't like I planned it," he muttered darkly, "but since my gun is gone, my knife will do."

In the countless ages during which that great river has rolled to the sea, no doubt many strange sights have been seen on its bosom: naked Indians, picturesque Spanish sailors, French Huguenot refugees, Negro slaves, Tarleton's men hunting vainly for Francis Marion in this gross wilderness. And many a strange scene of wild life this river must have witnessed; but perhaps no stranger sight than Rodney Magwood, the pineland hunter, minus his gun and canoe, riding toward the shore on a great black stag he had set out to kill.

"The hide on the neck of a buck like this," thought Rodney, "is about as tough as a bull alligator's hide. I got a knife; but maybe a good knife ain't enough. Howsoever, it's all I got, and I'll give him what I has."

Valiantly but laboriously swimming with his heavy burden, Black Roland was now within fifty yards of the coveted shore. Just ahead of him, and leaning far over the water, was a huge holly tree, its leaves glistening and its scarlet berries gleaming in the sleety rain. The old buck saw a little strip of white sand beach just below the holly. There he could land.

Gripping Black Roland's left antler with his left hand, Rodney cautiously loosed the grip of his right hand; then he began to open and close it to get rid of the stiffness. He wiped the rain and water out of his eyes, then he softly reached round to his belt, got hold of the hilt of his knife, and drew the blade from its sheath.

As he brought the knife round on the right-hand side, it gleamed dully under the water. Such a feat as he contemplated depended largely for its success on proper timing. It would not be long now—merely a matter of seconds. The man himself had been brought so near the shore he was practically safe; and Black Roland was closer to death than he had ever been in his life.

Curiously, for the first time, as the noble buck, blowing now from weariness, his splendid stamina nearly exhausted by his double effort of saving both himself and his enemy, Rodney saw Roland's left eye as the stag turned his head slightly; and the buck seemed to be glancing back at him.

Beneath him Magwood could feel the heaving of the deer's flanks. With the extra weight of the man, and perhaps from fear of the burden he carried, he was having a real struggle to make the short distance.

Again Rodney saw that attentive black eye, wary, wild, pitiful. . . . He thought of Maisie waiting for him, and little Rodney and Lucy. He even thought of his hounds, and of what a clamor they would set up if he could bring a buck like this home. He thought of the emptiness of that Christmas Eve if he returned with nothing—with indeed less than nothing since his boat and his gun were lost. He looked toward the shore, and the huge holly caught his sight. . . . Holly and Christmas and peace on earth and good-will to every living thing.

In the last few yards before they gained the shore Rodney's feeling toward Roland changed. To reach shore meant life to him; but it meant death to the black stag, after his dauntless battle. Rodney was a hunter of the wilderness, and he had killed many bucks. But no deer had ever before saved his life.

He had a desperate moment of mental struggle; if he did one thing he would go home in triumph, and he would have a story his friends would ask him to retell as long as he lived; he would make Maisie happy, and the children, and they would have plenty of fresh venison for Christmas. If he did the other thing, he would have nothing except the feeling that he had been merciful and generous.

Black Roland was very tired now. His feet were about to touch the sandy bottom of the river shore. As soon as he struck land, the deer, Rodney knew, would break out of the water and race into the forest.

More slowly than he had drawn it forth, but with equal determination, Magwood thrust the knife back into its sheath.

Black Roland's feet struck a sandbar. Rodney slid easily from his back, and as the great buck sprang forward, the hunter gave him a friendly slap.

"Go on, you old rascal," he said, "and don't you let me catch up on you no mo'."

As he waded slowly out of the water, Rodney stopped to break a bough of the brilliant holly; and this was all he carried homeward.

Hatless, and without his gun, but with a strange new light in his eyes, Rodney Magwood appeared at his home.

"Why Rod," said Maisie, as he handed her the holly, "you have been overboard. Where is your gun? I was afraid you might get into trouble. But nothin' matters so you got back safe. I got your hot coffee ready."

Drying off before his open fire, Rodney told his wife and his two wide-eyed children the whole story.

"Now what ever come over me to act like that?" he asked.

Maisie's eyes were bright. Pineland people are not demonstrative. But she came over to his chair and her hand stole to his shoulder.

"You done all right," she said. "To let him live was a real nice Christmas present for that old black buck. I reckon, too, he growed from that same little black fawn I seed when you was a'courtin' me, Rod. I never did want him kilt. Some of the boys, they was a-huntin' this morning, and they done brung us venison and a wild turkey. We'll have a fine Christmas . . ." Then her shy and loving heart spoke openly as she said, "Rod, ain't many hunters would have been man enough to do what you done."

December Doings

This selection comes from pages 32–41 of a book that deserves to be better known, It Will Be Daybreak Soon. *The volume is devoted to Low Country black people. Rutledge knew African Americans of his day as few white people did, and he reached across tightly drawn racial lines with ease. Some of his terms may grate on the nerves of the politically correct in today's world, but to criticize him on this score is to ignore the realities of a far different world. Suffice it to say that he cherished those he sometimes calls his "dark companions" or "black huntermen," and this story of the "doings" of one such individual is as joyous as it is revealing.*

One December day I was hunting on Bull's Island, a superb game preserve off the Carolina coast. With me at the time was a very humble Negro named Richard. Early in the morning we took up the trail of a great stag, whose track indicated that his head would be a prize trophy. All day, through marshes, palmetto thickets, and jungles of pine and oak, we followed him. Just at sundown he left his wary meanderings in the forest and went out on the sand dunes. When we reached the verge of the woods, there he was, a superb creature, poised in the twilight on the crest of a tawny dune. At last our long labor was rewarded. At last I was within range of this old hero of the wilds. I got ready for the shot while Richard squatted by me in excited silence.

But the full moon rose over the ocean, tinging the dark momentous pines, fringing with light the maned sea breakers. It illumined the rolling dunes and the dark clusters of myrtles in their hollows. It touched the statuesque stag, and he became a silver stag with silver horns. The world went argentine, and the presence of Beauty was everywhere manifest. The sight of my rifle, which had been leveled on the deer's heart, was lowered. I took my gun down from my shoulder. I couldn't kill amid that song and hush of beauty. But I fully expected my humble Richard to be dismayed and disgusted over my decision.

"Richard," I said, feeling that my words would sound fantastic to him, "I don't want to shoot him. The world is too beautiful."

My tone was apologetic and conciliatory.

*Archibald Rutledge with his Parker shotgun,
1915. From the* Mercersburg Academy Karux,
vol. 22, p. 4

"Cap'n, I understand," came Richard's gentle voice, "you know, sah, *angels walk in the moonlight.*"

To comment on the loveliness of that idea is sacrilege; as it would be to speak of its poetic adequacy to the occasion. Nevertheless, I must not fail to point out that it illustrates how dangerous it is to assume a spiritual superiority over the Negro. I find that his sensitiveness in the realms of mystery usually anticipates mine. And I have heard that certain missionaries to Africa have owed all their troubles to a brash assumption that primitives are naturally spiritually inferior. They, like children, have visions that to them are real, and they live in a world that is in more direct and vital touch with Another World than ours is. Aboriginal in thought and feeling, plantation Negroes are among the most authentic and interesting of human beings. They may be as yet far from what we proudly call civilization; but to me they seem very close to God. Their religious attitude is as unfeigned as that of children. To them the rain, the wind, the thunder, the stars, sunset, and sunrise are matters of great moment. I have many a treasured recollection of what I have heard Negroes say of these unfailingly recurrent waves in the vast sea of nature's symphony.

Sam Singleton and I left home at one o'clock one winter morning to paddle down the Santee River in South Carolina to a place appropriately called "Tranquillity," since it is as solitary as being in the heart of a wild delta can make it. Our plan was to drop down ten miles or so with the ebb tide, designing to reach at dawn the lonely hummock in the huge wasteland that stretches mistily between the two sea-reaching arms of the mighty river. We were to spend a few days duck shooting at Tranquillity, and we started at a time which would afford us sport with the morning flight.

A Southern river at night is a haunting thing, with great stars hanging like spangles in the dark pines and the ancient water oaks fringing the river shores. Wider flows the dim stream as it moves through the last reaches of the immense coastal plain. Baffling to navigate by broad daylight, the Santee at night is mysterious. And the peril of it undoubtedly was heightened by the kind of craft in which we were traveling. A dugout cypress canoe, it had as certain a tendency to roll as had its parent log, utterly lacking that virtue of stability that one relishes in a boat, especially when one is voyaging through the darkness of a huge river that seems to be wandering toward eternity.

But the stars that had been shining when we left home were soon obscured by a fog so dense that we could hardly see beyond the bow of our little boat. As we were going with the tide, we felt sure of our general direction, but when once or twice we came near looming shores, neither of us recognized the landscape as familiar. Then for an hour there was no land visible. I knew that we ought to be near our goal. But the waves that began to roll our canoe were suspiciously like sea waves. The roar of the surf that we had heard for a long time now became almost clamorous. Attempts to reach either shore were vain. The fact that the tide had now turned, or was about to turn, confused us still further. The canoe shipped water, gallons of it. The mist blinded us. There was no use blinking the truth: we were in immediate danger. I told Sam mildly that in case the canoe was swamped we must turn it over and cling to it. How can I ever forget what he said?

"Never mind, Cap'n," the humble boatman told me; "*it will be daybreak soon.*"

What was there in that plight of ours on which we could certainly count? Only one thing there was: the coming of light—daybreak, sunrise! It came in time to save us, though we were really on the brink of the sea when the rosy radiance over the delta disclosed our position to us. Yet it was not alone the coming of sunrise that rescued us; it was Sam's reminding me that it was *sure* to come, restoring thus my courage. And even now, after all these years, whenever the shadows are deepest and most impenetrable, I seem to hear, out of the dim celestial past, the quiet voice of Sam Singleton, saying to my doubting and besieged heart, "*Never mind, Cap'n: it will be daybreak soon.*"

This psychic power never manifests itself so plainly in the Negro as in his judgment, often immediate and always instinctive, of human worth, of social grace, of the strange enigma of personality. The Negro is not a severe judge, but he is often devastatingly revealing. And his estimate is likely to be put in quaint and forest-bred language. Of a rather vulgar and blustering white woman, I once heard a Negro say simply, "She ain't reg'lar." Of two white men, one very crude in appearance and manner and the other correspondingly suave, I heard this comment: "Mr. A. is rough outside but smooth inside." There is perhaps no more infallible judge of breeding in the world than the plantation Negro. Pomp and display are wasted upon him. Gifted spiritually to a profound degree, to him the spirit of another is transparent. Social climbers and impostors, who sometimes make considerable headway in the cities, never deceive him in his lonely wildwoods. He is too close to the real to be beguiled by the artificial; too naïve to be impressed by the magnificent. Quaint rustic phrases give a native homebred savor to his speech. To him an illegitimate child is a "woods colt," or a "little volunteer." Anything important is "town news." A long time is expressed as "ever since a hatchet was a hammer." Heaven is always the Promised Land.

On one occasion I told Charlie Lesane that he was to have the honor of acting as duck guide to a millionaire. This gentleman, who had made his wealth in shoe polish or in clothespins, was an exceedingly rough diamond. Even I was shocked by his crudity and his profanity, and I knew that Charlie would be impressed in somewhat the same manner. Amid the creeks and marshes the Negro spent the day with the millionaire. On their return to our ducking camp, when I had Charlie aside, I said, "Well, you paddled a millionaire today."

"But he ain't had dat money long," was his significant and coolly appraising rejoinder.

Plantation Christmases

Originally published in Santee Paradise *(pages 102–11), this comes fairly late in Rutledge's career, long after the heyday of the Hampton hunt had come and gone. It finds him looking back with fondness, more than a bit of longing, and perhaps a hint of sadness to the joyous holidays he and his family had known through the years. Discerning readers will notice the occasional sentence or phrase they have already encountered, but then Rutledge turns to a sort of Low Country version of the original Christmas story. Possibly his tale of Dr. Norwood's feat is fiction, but it carries the ring of truth.*

M ost of my boyhood Christmases were celebrated in the tradition of the great plantations. Though the day's pleasures would have seemed bizarre to a stranger, we enjoyed them down to the last firecracker, and all contributed to the Christmas spirit.

When to the mystical glamour that naturally belongs to the Christmas season one can add the romance that belongs to the old-time South, nothing short of enchantment is the result. I do not think that even in the England of Cavalier days was Christmas more picturesquely celebrated than it was in my boyhood on those great plantations of the South which have managed to preserve the integrity of their beauty and charm.

At home I have never seen snow at Christmastime. Instead, we have a green Christmas, made so by the pine, holly, myrtle, sweet bay, and smilax that over the top of many a tree weave emerald crowns. A plantation Christmas is one of wildwood fragrances as well as one of roaring, open fires and festive boards and ancient carols.

I remember what a pleasure I experienced from hearing, upon awaking one Christmas morning, a Carolina wren caroling like mad just outside the window. Climbing a pillar under my window was a yellow jasmine vine, and in a festive mood to suit the season it had put forth a few delicious blossoms—golden bells to ring for Christmas.

Beyond the window I could see the mighty live oaks, their streamers of moss waving gently like my white curtains, then the imperial, towering pines. Christmas morning, with birds and sunshine and scented sea winds!

I went to the window and looked out. All the dim, sweet plantation was steeped in faery light. The far reaches of bowed and brown cotton fields, the golden broomsedge fringing the fields, the misty river rolling softly, the sleeping trees jeweled with dew—all these had a magical look. A silvery silence held the world in virginal beauty.

But soon the stillness was broken, and by no gentle sound. It did not surprise me, but not many Americans other than plantation dwellers would have expected it. Firecrackers! The Puritan Christmas of New England has something exceedingly snowy and austere about it. In the South it is a day for frolic; on the plantation, at least, it is not associated in any way with church services. Nor do I think it less a genuine festival of the hearth and home because all the little Negroes shoot fireworks, all the plantation belles hang mistletoe (and strangely linger near it), and all the plantation men go deer hunting.

The Negroes start the day by coming over to the Great House, thronging gleefully across the fields, shouting, and singing. I find the yard crowded with them when I take an early morning stroll.

Before breakfast we distribute to them our gifts of Christmas cheer. Then the family gathers for breakfast. I love to think of it—the ample room from the walls of which gaze down faded portraits of the plantation owners of an earlier generation, and a whole fringe of deer horns festooned with Spanish moss.

Christmas breakfast makes one think of a wedding breakfast. The table is gay with sprigs of holly, with graceful ropes of smilax. A huge bunch of mistletoe, large enough to warrant the most ardent kissings of whole communities, stands upright in the center of the table, its pale, cold berries agleam.

While we are at breakfast we have evidence that the day is not to be spent in languorous ease, for from the yard we can hear the huntsmen tuning up their hunting horns, and in response to the faint, mellow blasts comes the joyous yowling of staghounds. Some of these come to the dining-room door and there stand, fixing us with melancholy great eyes, more in eagerness, I really think, to have us finish our repast and join them in the woods, than in envy of our feast.

Soon we are astride our mounts, turning them down the live-oak avenue toward the deep pinelands. As we ride down the sandy road we are on the lookout for deer tracks.

Nearly a year's care went into the planning of one particular Yuletide chase. All summer we had known of two magnificent old stags that "used" in the Briar Bed and in Johnson Corner. Their tracks we had seen scores of times, and Prince reported that he had sighted the bucks themselves. We were saving them for a Christmas hunt.

One day in November my Colonel and I met in the big road two acquaintances, Tillman Bunch and Sheriff Lawton. They had guns and a dog, and they were even then examining the fresh tracks of the two stags going into Johnson Corner. What a predicament! We couldn't very well refuse them a hunt, yet the Christmas bucks were in peril. What could we do?

My Colonel did some fast thinking, so that when they opened fire with their fatal question, he was ready.

Could they drive out the Corner? They hadn't had a piece of venison this season. The tracks were large and fresh. . . . It would be easy to corner these deer.

Father said, "Surely, gentlemen. Let me put you on the stands, and then let me drive them to you. But don't forget that a cornered deer is one that usually gets away."

He got the men expectantly posted. Then he took their hound and went back into the Corner. Oh, yes, he drove those stags—but he drove them the *wrong way*! "Was not that nobly done? Aye, and wisely too. . . ." The stags were with us at Christmas, and we found that venison goes very well with wild turkey.

At last we return to the plantation house—to the red roses, to the yellow jasmine outside, and within, to the ruddy fires, the rooms festooned with fragrant greenery.

For dinner we have snowy pyramids of rice, browned sweet potatoes with sugar oozing out of the jackets, roasted rice-fed mallards, wild turkey, venison, tenderloin of pork fattened on live-oak acorns, pilau, and cardinal pudding.

Twilight falls as we come to the nuts and raisins. Then we form a great semicircle before the fire, and we rehunt the chases of that day and of many of long ago.

It is late ere our tales are ended. It has been a glorious day. I wander out now on the front porch. The risen moon is casting a silvery glamour over the world. Far off I can hear the Negroes singing their spirituals of Christmas—the sweetest melody, I think, of which the human voice is capable.

The live oaks shimmer softly in the moonshine. I hear flights of wild ducks speeding overhead, hastening toward their feeding grounds far down the river. Over the old plantation the serenity of joyous peace descends, the peace of human hearts at Christmastime.

The Christmas I remember best in my boyhood departed entirely from our own traditional celebration. A doctor who used to hunt in our neighborhood and often visited Hampton shared the day with us and made Christmas what Christmas really should be. In one way the happening was a simple thing; but in another you could find nearly all the noble instincts at work through love and faith. Some people have the grace of heart to suffuse all life with light. Such a man was Dr. James Norwood.

That autumn a hurricane had destroyed the rice crop, the one source of cash income on our plantation, and it had so damaged the corn and peas and potatoes that our main food supply was almost depleted. Hence it was not with our customary feeling of well-being and happiness that we approached the Christmas season. Everything seemed to point toward a bleak holiday.

Yet all of us, I think, expected some miracle to happen just before Christmas, and my brother and I were downcast when nothing happened, except that Father sent a Negro in an oxcart to the village ten miles away to buy a few oranges for our Christmas cheer. We were too young to understand that Christmas is not a date on the calendar, but a festival of love in the heart.

About nine o'clock on Christmas Eve while we were sitting quietly before the fire, there arose a sudden hubbub outside. My brother and I ran to the door. There stood a tall, muffled form laden with guns and a string of mallard ducks. Behind him was a Negro carrying two suitcases.

"Hello, boys!" cried a cheery voice. "I'm Santa Claus."

By this time Father was with us, helping us to welcome Dr. Jim Norwood, a young physician from New Rochelle, New York, who had hunted ducks with us on the Santee River delta the winter before.

Dr. Norwood was a fine figure of a man as he stood before the fireplace: tall, ruddy, with sparkling blue eyes. In his genial, boyish way he had talked to us previously of his graduation from Harvard Medical School and of his postgraduate work abroad. We also knew of his eccentric millionaire patient, Martin Langdon, who demanded a good deal of Dr. Norwood's time.

"Langdon's going to take me abroad with him next week," Dr. Norwood said. "He doesn't like to travel alone. I am keen on going. It should be a great trip. I go back home on Friday, and we sail on Monday." This was on the Thursday before.

He apologized to Mother for coming on us so suddenly. "I would have written to you," he said, standing with his back to the fire and drinking a steaming cup of tea, "but the little mail steamer has broken down. Well, I've had good sport on the delta, but I didn't want to spend Christmas there alone. You know you told me I could come again," he ended, smiling.

Mother assured him he was welcome and then asked him about a girl named Cerelle of whom he had spoken the year before. "Our engagement is to be announced Saturday night," he replied. "There's to be a big party, and I must be there."

Just then we heard a knock on the door. It was 'Ralgia, a seven-year-old Negro girl. "Please, sah," she said, "Sis Betty's baby got de spasms."

The child had come a mile across the dark plantation fields and was obviously frightened. Such an incident was a frequent thing in our lives, but to Jim Norwood it was vastly appealing, and at the mention of sickness the doctor in him awoke at once.

"Why, poor child," he said, leading her over to the fire. "Tell me what's the matter with the baby."

'Ralgia's bare toes worked convulsively, and finally she repeated, "Spasms, sah."

He went over to one of his traveling bags and drew out a medicine case.

"You aren't going out yourself?" Father asked. "It's probably just a case of colic."

Jim Norwood laughed. "I never let a patient escape me." He said he needed one of us to show him the way back, so I offered to go along.

As we approached Betty's cabin she heard us coming and opened the door wide. She held the sick child in her arms.

"Betty, here's a fine doctor to see your baby," I said. "This is Dr. Norwood."

"Yes, sah," she said gently.

Dr. Norwood looked at the baby keenly. "Bring me the baby here to the fire," he said.

The mother laid the tiny form on a mattress on the floor in front of the hearth. The doctor deftly felt the pulse, applied his stethoscope and listened to the painful breathing. He turned to Betty and said, "Your baby has had pneumonia for some days. It's late to try to turn the tide."

"Can you help her?" I asked.

"I have some medicine with me that may help," he answered. "About the chief thing I can give is constant attention. You go home and tell your mother I will be over in the morning for breakfast, but I can't leave this child tonight."

As I left I heard him say to Betty, "Pull that little bench under the window and lay a folded blanket on it. I want the baby to have fresh air. Then get another cover for her so she won't feel a draft. You can lie down and rest. I will keep the watch."

As I recrossed the plantation fields those last words kept echoing in my heart: "I will keep the watch." There was something simple and powerful about that. There came to me a feeling that Christmas has to do with things even better than roast turkey and plum pudding. It has to do with love and sacrifice.

When I reached home and told my family what had happened, all thought of our own meager Christmas was forgotten in our concern over the stricken child. We were touched, too, by Dr. Norwood's self-forgetfulness, and I overheard Mother saying something about a Christmas angel.

By daylight the next morning all of us were up, and I had started for Betty's cabin when I met Dr. Norwood coming over. His eyes were heavy with sleep.

"I may be able to pull the baby through if I stick close to her. We had something of a fight last night."

While we were eating our Christmas breakfast of hominy, venison sausages, and corn bread, a man came to the door and held out a yellow envelope. "I bring this from Georgetown," he said, "for Dr. Norwood."

The doctor read the message. "Langdon has changed our sailing date. He wants me Sunday morning," he said. "That means I would have to catch the four-fifty from Georgetown this afternoon."

"We could drive you over," Father said.

Dr. Norwood said, "I should go today to be there in time for Cerelle's party tomorrow night. But I kept the baby alive last night only by giving her special attention every hour, and today will tell the story. Is there another doctor within call?"

"Not anywhere near," Father said.

"Then Langdon will either have to go without me or wait until I come," Dr. Norwood said. He then turned to Mother. "Do you think Cerelle will understand if I miss that party?"

Mother's eyes were full of light as she answered, "I know she will."

He wrote two wires for the messenger to take to Georgetown—one to Langdon and one to Cerelle. Then he prepared to return to Betty's cabin.

He spent Christmas Day there. We sent his dinner over to him. He would not leave. And in saving the life of that tiny brown baby he transfigured that Christmas Day for us by his self-sacrifice and changed it into a day of wonderful peace and joy.

A year later Dr. and Mrs. Jim Norwood spent Christmas with us on the plantation. I thought I had never seen anyone else so lovely as Cerelle.

"Old Langdon waited for me," Dr. Norwood said, "and so did Cerelle."

"You ought to see your little patient now," said Mother. "She's a fine, strong girl. Making her well was the work of a master."

"It was Christmas Day," he answered. "The work of a master, yes, the Master. I can only claim to be one of His many servants."

II

A Natural Christmas

Today's readers tend to remember Rutledge primarily as a hunting writer, and un-questionably he was a master of the genre. Yet during his lifetime he was at least as well known as a nature writer. The selections in this section offer solid evidence of why this was the case. He was an astute observer who spent untold hours in the natural world, watching and listening while savoring every sight and sound the inhabitants of his beloved woods provided. Similarly he was keenly interested in flora, as the piece "My Winter Woods" reveals, and as a pioneering conservationist he should be recognized as belonging to the same ranks as Nash Buckingham, Aldo Leopold, Ben Hur Lampman, and Theodore Roosevelt.

My Christmas Birds and Trees

ᵕ:ᵕ

Originally published in the December 1928 issue of Country Life *magazine (volume 55, pages 67–68), this short piece reflects the ever-returning delight Rutledge had in observing the world around Hampton each year during his Christmas holiday there.*

Since childhood I have spent a part of each December at home, in the plantation region of South Carolina, in that glamorous hinterland that lies mysterious behind mysterious Charleston. There the woods in winter are like the New England woods of October—hale, aromatic, suffused with the orient lights of a thousand colors flaming and fading. When at home I love nothing better, during the Christmas season, than to wander out into my woods just at day-dawn. I remember many such mornings, but one there is that lingers. Does not the mortal loss of something beautiful always create an immortal memory?

Leaving the house before the pale career of moon and stars was over, as I neared the ancient plantation gateway I heard the first note of the winter's morning; a timid phoebe bird, always fairylike and eerie, from a shadowy myrtle copse beside the road, a copse greenly veiled with jasmine vines, gave a delicate plaintive call, a glimmering elfin choral of the misty daybreak. I paused to listen; then looked behind me across the cottonfields, now bowed and brown, that stretched backward toward the house. In the east, over the tall beauty of the momentous pines, in a space breathed clear by the dewy wind that awakes before the dawn, throbbed and glittered the great morning star. The note of the phoebe, the shy woodland fragrances waft from the darksome avenue before me, the mantle of mist on the cotton, the blazing star, the bulk and blackness of the mighty like-oak grove—all these haunted me with their spiritual beauty; with a sense of the drowsing yet superb elemental strength of nature, unwearied, constant as a fountainhead, sane, continuous, virtuous, wise.

Into the dewy darkness of the avenue I went. But it was bright enough for me to see the virginal chill dew slip sparkling from the tips of the needles of the young yellow pines. Overhead, the vast tops of the great oaks shut out the sky, while far and wide their deep-foliaged limbs extended. In the cool vaulted space of this old roadway there is ever an ancient sequestered peace. This place is a sanctuary. From the titan trees, great limbs, larger than the bodies of ordinary trees, extend outward and upward, until, passing the boughs of the neighboring oaks, they lose themselves in the shadowy merging and melting of gray moss and silvery-green foliage. Sometimes over their monumental frames vast networks of vines have clambered, lowering down heavy tapestries of smilax and jasmine. In the tropical atmosphere of such a woodland cathedral many kinds of ferns, mosses, and lichens grow; and often the limbs of the live-oaks will be green or gray or brown, the color of the delicate plants that cling to and clothe the burly limbs of these tolerant giants. Under such a canopy of moss and foliage both barred owls and great horned owls find a congenial home. Amid ordinary woodland surroundings owls hoot at twilight and at night only; but in a live-oak avenue they can be heard giving their weird chorus when the sun is high overhead. These strange occult birds seem the veritable oracles of these dim old trees.

As I come out of the avenue, the sun is rising, and the wide pinelands lie before me. All the copses of huckleberry, bay, gallberry, and myrtle are shimmering. The dewdrops glint. With nature's inimitable charm of disarray, the wildwood has all the luring beauty of naïve grace. Here in this mighty forest of pine are fabulous cathedral aisles, solemn transepts, with blue windows looking out on eternity, and with a rolling organ in the towering trees. Despite the prevalence of the greenery everywhere of vines and bushes, despite the live-oaks in the avenue, and the gums and tupelos of the swamp, this is a pine forest, and through it one can travel more than fifty miles in all directions save that which leads southward to the sea; and even then, the pines march down in dark thoughtful ranks to the very beach.

The prevalence of these magnificent trees in my Christmas woods as a standard element of every view, as a noble background for every scene, renders the aspect of the December forest living and green. Yet if there were no evergreens save the pines, there might be a beautiful monotony to them; but the variety of verdure on other evergreens, and the naked strength of the leafless trees, always redeem the view. The foliage of the live-oak, throughout the winter, varies in the tints of its emerald, as is generally true of all evergreens. It is reserved for the water-oak to be the real artist of amazing color. Throughout the long mild winter this stately tree burns gloriously, as maples and beeches do in the North in the autumn; and the saffron, scarlet, bronze, and topaz leaves smolder for months with the slow fires of decay. I know of few wildwood sights more lovely than a long thicket of sweetbay and myrtle tufted and plumed gorgeously by these brilliant water-oaks.

Nor are my Christmas woods as silent as are the snow-steeped forests of colder climes. Indeed, bird life seems more abundant in winter than in summer;

for not only is it far more readily observed, but in addition to the native birds there are the migrated hosts, come like sensible people to this Riviera to spend the winter. Over my head in the sweet air of early morning, in flocks of fifty or more, bluebirds are warbling sunnily, like aerial rivulets. Small flocks of mourning doves flit through the pines on their way to the plantation pea fields to feed. The broomsedge in the woods harbors many meadow larks. Here in the sandy road, damp with dew, are the tracks of a covey of quail. Along the edges of a bay thicket I flush several woodcock that go whirling off in their enigmatic glimmering flight, their wings faintly whistling. Here is the wood-thrush, feasting on the black berries of the wild orange. Here the ruby-crowned and the golden-crowned kinglet are examining, upside down, the economic worth of the great banners of Spanish moss that hang swayingly from the bald cypresses in the woodland ponds. The flicker, the black pileated woodpecker, the downy woodpecker, the nuthatches, are calling, hammering, flying hither and thither—a gay gang of roving carpenters.

Now I come to Jones Pond, a circular lagoon in the airy pine forest, a lake about a half mile in circumference. Here and there on tiny islets in it grow splendid old cypresses, standing like Druids above those mystic waters. Now the tide is like Lethe's in its stillness, a fit image of the reflective mind that at Christmas thinks of sacred things. The tops of the cypresses open and spread like those of sequoias, giving the impression that, after the trees had ascended to a certain level, no farther growth save in a lateral direction was permissible. Such trees have a peculiar and venerable majesty that makes one feel in their presence that he has come upon the guardians of a shrine.

The waters of this wildwood pond remain at an almost constant level. I never knew them to overflow; and in a dry season, wild life comes for miles to assuage its thirst here.

Turning homeward now, I purposely take a path that I know may lead me past a thrilling sight. In a sunny glade not far from the avenue there stands a gigantic holly, fully sixty feet in height; and as there are no other large trees near it, its growth is as arresting in its symmetry as in its height. I always call it the "Robins' Christmas tree," for it is a favorite with these birds; and when the berries are plentiful they crowd into it, not by dozens only, but by hundreds; and in their revelry and feasting they are joined by flitting wood-thrushes, and by crowds of cedar waxwings. Yes, here they are, already making merry, while the mellow sunshine of December floods the scene. I think it not irreverent to say that this tree looks as perhaps a Christmas tree might appear in paradise. The tree, a massive cone, rises superbly in the fragrant air, its gleaming foliage starred with myriads of twinkling scarlet berries. Then the redbreasts, roaming joyously the wide woods, come upon this place, they are as Christmas-hearted as children. I see them now, crowding into the green foliage, their ruddy breasts flashing back and forth against the dark green of the leaves and the shadowy snow of the trunk and branches, or blending in glistening beauty with the color the berries. In the sheer delight from such feasting a robin will often resort to a shady alcove in the tree or to some retired limb near by, thence to give droll and thoughtful utterance to some half-forgotten notes of spring song. Hundreds of robins are feasting now in this tree, calling loudly and gaily, fluttering before the scarlet fruit, darting in and out of the tremulous foliage. There is not perhaps in all nature a more communal and Christmaslike spirit than that of a great concourse of robins banqueting in a big holly tree.

Of all the birds of my Christmas woods, I love best the Carolina wren; nor do I know another bird that has a carol that rings more clearly and more joyously. As I approach the house, I hear, from a thicket beyond the river, a full half mile away, the piercing sweet call of this tiny bird—this rollicking minstrel, always gay, always debonair. In its power to awake the human heart to the beauty and the joy of life, the thrilling song of the Carolina wren is incomparable.

After the Christmas celebration within doors is over, I come out on the porch of the plantation house, my heart turning again toward the woods that I love. The sun has already foundered in the sea of the sky, leaving a golden vortex. The pines stand dark against the west, remote in red magnificence. I hear the white-throated sparrows, the thrashers, and the blackbirds calling as they go to roost in the shrubberies behind the house and in the marshes beside the river. Far beyond the plantation fields the Negroes are singing their spirituals. Surely, at Christmas, "All God's chillun got wings." Flocks of wild ducks, speeding for the delta, pass above me. I hear a fox barking in the moldering fastness of Romney graveyard. Stars emerge, in dewy-silver solitude; and their celestial light gleams softly on my Christmas forest.

Birds of the Southern Winter

Birds of all kinds fascinated Rutledge. Although he wrote more on deer than on any other type of game, he penned at least a hundred turkey-hunting tales along with articles on quail, waterfowl, grouse, and other game birds. Yet he was equally interested in songbirds, and that comes to light in telling fashion in this selection. It originally appeared on pages 370–75 of volume 97 of the Outlook *(1911) and was later included in* Days Off in Dixie, *pages 218–32.*

To the blizzard-bound Northerner there is no more fascinating form of imagination than to picture to himself the sunny homes that have been found by his bird friends that have migrated southward. Yet few bird-lovers can have an accurate idea of the winter surroundings of their summer favorites unless they have observed them in the South.

It is a well-known fact that the robin changes his disposition with his location; when on the lawn he may be the most confiding and friendly companion, but at any distance from a house he is apt to develop traits of wildness and suspicion. The characteristic of wariness is always found among robins in the South. In general, the robin is songless in his winter quarters, his only notes being his liquid word of alarm and his shrill flight call. Occasionally, however, a flock will give voice to a subdued chorus, audible at a considerable distance through the hollow-echoing piney woods. These great pineries of the Southland, together with the swamps that drain—or more often do not drain—them, harbor robins in vast numbers. Near the mouth of the Santee River in southeastern South Carolina the writer recently tried to estimate the number of robins in a flight that was changing swamps. How wide the flight was is not known, but the portion upon which the estimate was based passed over an open field, completely surrounded by tall pines, a quarter of a mile long by a half-mile wide. Over this space the robins flew from noon until dusk—about five hours. At any fixed period there must have been a thousand robins in sight; so, estimating that it took a robin a minute and a half to fly across the field, the total number seen could not run far short of two hundred thousand. Probably the number was greater. During this hurried passage the birds were silent except for an occasional flight call, which would be answered by a score of similar cries.

In the liberal semi-tropical woods of the South the robins have a "continual feast of nectared sweets." They feed chiefly on the black berries of the gum tree, on those of the tupelo, on the scarlet ones of the holly, the cassena, and the bay-brier, and on those of that peculiar hybrid the wild orange. They are also very fond of the faintly sweet crumpled yellow berries of the Pride-of-India tree. The swamps and thickets are full of berry-laden vines, while every watercourse is lined with growths bearing succulent fruits. It is a fact not generally known that the fruit of the wild orange—a semi-domesticated evergreen, bearing small black berries, not edible, about the size of gooseberries—contains an acid that is intoxicant; and the writer has seen robins, gorged on this rich food, become silly and dazed, and actually fall to the ground in what was apparently a drunken stupor. It has been suggested that this unfortunate state was brought about by the birds' gluttony; and while this theory may be correct, the other seems nearer right, since robins are not known to suffer ill effects from overeating other kinds of foods. One of the most beautiful sights in all the pine woods of the South is that of a flock of robins feasting in a holly tree. The bark of the tree is a grayish white, and the leaves, of course, are those of a typical evergreen. The holly often attains—especially near water—a height of fifty or sixty feet, and is usually cone-shaped, like many varieties of cedar; and when its glossy foliage is starred with myriads of twinkling scarlet berries, its beauty is supreme. It looks as, perhaps, a Christmas tree would look in paradise. When the red-breasts, roaming the wide woods, come upon such a glorious find, they are as happy as little children are over the beneficence of Santa Claus. They crowd into the green foliage, their bright breasts flashing back and forth against the dark green of the leaves and the shadowy snow of the trunk and branches, or blending in glistening beauty with the color of the berries. In the delight of such feasting a robin will occasionally resort to a shady alcove in the tree or on some retired limb near by, there to give rather droll and thoughtful utterance to some half-forgotten notes of spring song. Other robins, on near-by perches, will preen their feathers until their turn for berries comes, when they will fly into the tree, whence will instantly emerge those that have had their share of feasting. There seems always to be much good fellowship manifest, and there is little quarrelling except on the part of a few male birds that doubtless have begun to feel the significance of crabbed age. The belief of those who hold that a flock of robins in a berry tree is continually "scrapping" doubtless arises from the habit that the birds have of fluttering before the fruit they intend taking; and when flocks do this, and myriads flutter about a tree, calling in delight and excitement, the casual impression given is one of woodland warfare. As the winter advances, robins draw in from the pine woods and the swamps to cities, villages, and plantations, where they find winter-mellowed fruit awaiting them. In such environments the robins lose much of their wild and wary nature and become the friendly, confiding birds of the Northern spring and early summer.

Among the sweet-voiced lurkers in thickets and in coverts that Milton has called "bosky bournes" the catbird and the brown thrasher are worthy of most notice. The veery, that superb mysterious voice of the woodland, winters in South America, as does the wood-thrush, else these had glorified the winter in the Southern States, would they, indeed, deign to sing at such a season. When the first breath of autumn tinges the Southern woods, the catbirds arrive and immediately begin their foraging for pokeberries. This luscious bird fruit is commonly found along fencerows, in grown-up cleared ground, and on the borders of thickets; and there our querulous arrival is to be seen whisking from pokeberry bush to rail fence, where he will fluff up his feathers, then smooth them—actually flatten them—and, flirting his red-tinged tail, will peer inquisitively from side to side, giving his cautious, questioning call. It may be a fancy, or it may be that this is true only of certain birds that have been observed, but the catbird in the South appears to have more red in his plumage than the same bird in the North; but he has little enough in either home. All winter long cat-birds are to be found in thickety growths that afford them shelter and food. The brown thrashers, as a rule, inhabit the denser copses, where their favorite occupation seems to be scratching—literally shuffling—among the dead leaves for whatever gain such capers afford. They are more frequent singers during the winter than catbirds, though their exquisite lyrics of the dawn and the twilight are heard only with the coming of love in the springtime.

Cedar waxwings are welcome visitors to the South in the winter, for, while they are shy and silent, their manners are attractively demure and their plumage rivals in delicate tints the exquisite blending of shades usually found only on game birds. They are late nesters in the North, being, in fact, rather negligent about the performance of this essential duty; for it is often as late as August before a brood is reared. When their scattered bands wander southward, they unite; so frequently they may be observed in flocks of several hundred. The food they enjoy most is the waxen berry of the mistletoe, though in general they eat just what robins eat, and the two species are often found associated together.

Mourning doves range from Cuba to Ontario, and nest almost throughout their range, though most of them are migrants. Their movements, however, are slow, and are regulated chiefly by the amount of grain that can be gleaned from the stubble fields. By the first of September they are well in flight, and by November the South is overrun with them. There they are to be differentiated from the little rosy-breasted ground dove—known locally as the "mourning dove"—whose note is as crooning as that of its soberer-hued relative is grieving. Doves in the South during the winter feed in open fields much as they do in the North, and roost in great numbers in pine or myrtle thickets, sheltered from the wind. In the daytime, during their resting or siesta periods they resort to cypress or willow-bordered streams, and to the murmuring spires of lofty pines, where they sun themselves and drowse in the high aromatic air. In peafields or cotton-fields of any size it is no unusual things to flush a thousand doves or more; and birds disturbed in this manner invariably fly toward the nearest dry-topped tree. This habit has well-nigh proved fatal to the species, for, by posting them-selves under such trees and by sending out riders over the fields, hunters can kill incredible numbers of doves. A recent report from a branch of the Audubon Society in Alabama stated that a half-dozen hunters in a single day had killed several thousand doves in one cottonfield by the method just described. For-tunately, the Southern states have awakened to the importance of protecting their birds, and wise laws have put a stop to such slaughter.

It was while pursuing a flock of doves in a Southern cornfield that the writer proved the excellent saying of John Burroughs, that in bird study "what no man ever saw before may at any moment be revealed."

Hampton Plantation is one of those vast old rice estates along the lower Santee River in South Carolina. It has always been remarkably rich in bird life. One eventful day in November, 1896, while in a field adjacent to the river, my attention was attracted by the sight of a dove twice the size of those in the flock; its tail was longer and more pointed, and the sheen on its neck glistened and gleamed in the soft autumn sunlight. The difference in its plumage from that of the ordinary dove was visible at a considerable distance. The bird was excessively wary, and, though it was difficult to approach, it would not fly far. It seemed tired, as if it had just completed a long migratory flight. After following it for more than an hour, I succeeded in shooting it. Upon close examination it proved to be a genuine passenger pigeon. This conclusion was confirmed by my father, who as a boy, had seen many thousands of these beautiful birds feeding in the oak trees on the slopes of the mountains in North Carolina. This was the last wild pigeon ever taken in South Carolina, and one of the last observed in America. Arthur Wayne, the well-known Southern ornithologist, the author of *The Birds of South Carolina,* saw a pair of wild pigeons in Greenville County of that state in 1886; but, expert as he is in observation, and tireless as he is in pursuit, he has since that time seen no member of this splendid species. And that excellent bird-lover Frank M. Chapman reports that in eighteen years of field work he has seen but two specimens of the passenger pigeon.

Among the bird sights that have the power to impress through sheer wonder and astonishment none is greater or more beautiful than a vast concourse of red-winged blackbirds, either covering long aisles of cypresses as with a sable mantle or "balling" in inky clouds over the rice stubble. It is estimated that in such flocks the number runs close on half a million. Sometimes they light in some favorite feeding-place—as where a stack of rice has stood—in such countless numbers that they actually swarm on one another's backs, seeming to be two or three tiers deep. The record shot for such a target is 168 birds with two barrels. Blackbirds in the winter resort to the river marshes and the waste thickets of delta lands both to feed and to roost. In company with the redwings there are often boat-tailed grackles, Florida grackles, and rusty blackbirds. Occasionally, too, there will be seen an albino of one of these species, and a most odd and surprising sight it is.

Blackbirds are very destructive to rice, both while it is in the field and after it has been stacked. The tops of the stacks are soon shredded of their grain; but birds forage along the sides all winter. Some kinds of birds, particularly blackbirds and several varieties of the sparrow family, beleaguer the rice all day; but it is at dawn or at twilight that the stacks are gathering-places for all the birds on the plantation. There flames the cardinal, his haughty crest rising and falling with every change in his subtle and various emotions; there the blue jay, ceasing his endless pranks and his noisy clamoring in the live-oaks, will sail out of the top of a tall tree to find his supper at a common table among humbler companions; sometimes the tufted titmouse will feed on rice, as also will flickers; most remarkable of all, perhaps, is the appearance of a hermit thrush among the motley concourse of birds.

In general, the birds of the Southern winter are not singers; and the absence of the lyric strain is a serious defect in a character whose chief charm, as in the case of song birds, is romantic. But probably we should not love their songs half so well if we could hear them all the time. During the winter months even the glorious mocking-bird is a harsh-mannered, harsh-voiced neighbor, though a balmy, bright hour is apt to melt his heart and to lure him into song. Probably the cheeriest, bonniest, of all the winter birds is the intrepid, the dauntless, the deliciously pert and inquisitive Carolina wren, whose carol rings merrily from the faded garden or from the windswept woodpile. During all the months of bare trees and north winds he is singing jauntily, investigating outhouses and cellars, always with his busy air of absurd importance.

No migrant changes its nature so completely during different periods of the year as does the bobolink. In the North, where this sportive songster is found in grassy meadows and along reed-grown streams in the summer, he is the personification of blithe joy and abandon. Bryant's poem to him is an excellent and accurate description of his summer nature; but during his stay in the South he is an entirely different creature. While he is not really a resident of the Southern States during the winter—he winters as far south as Paraguay and southern Brazil—his stay at the end of the summer is often six weeks in length—ample time in which to study a bird in a "stop-over" environment. In the rice fields of the South he is a most interesting as well as a most destructive bird, and his presence adds to the picturesqueness of the great rice harvest. The bobolinks arrive about August 20th, and sometimes linger, if there is good feeding in grassy corn-fields, until the first of October. When the birds first come, they are rather thin and shy, and their only note is a metallic monotonous "pinkpank." But as the season progresses they become very fat and very tame, often sitting on the coffee-grass that lines the margins of the rice field banks until the observer can almost catch them. The plumage of both sexes at the time is softly ochreous, with tints of brown and black on the back and wings.

To the rice-planter these "rice birds" are a veritable plague, so much so that one of the regular expenses of the plantation is that occasioned by "bird-minding." There are various ways in which to combat these pests. One is by posting Negroes on platforms along the banks, from which eminences they bawl their long, hand-woven "wahwoo" lashes. The crack of these whips sounds like the report of a gun and early in the season is rather effective in keeping the birds restless. But after a while they become used to the harmless din, and more strenuous methods have to be resorted to. On a heavy charge of coarse-grained powder a flattened buckshot is rammed tightly. When this shot leaves a musket, it sings above the feeding birds, and its sound is said to resemble the rush of the wings of a sharp-shinned hawk, a dread enemy of rice-birds. At any rate, it has a wonderful effect in making the feeding hosts rise and scatter far. But the only way to keep birds from ruining a crop is to send Negro bird-hunters into the rice after them. The fields at this stage of growth are flooded, and the water is about two feet deep. It is stagnant, muddy, and infested with all manner of water-loving insects and reptiles. Yet the Negro hunter, slouching his battered cap over his eyes, will sink out of sight under the golden canopy of the rice, appearing next far out in the field, enveloped in smoke and shadowed by myriads of birds that he has roused from their banquet. In order to make a telling shot, the gunner is obliged to keep below the level of the rice; and the distance of the stalk is sometimes half a mile. Through tangled growths of saw-grass, over blind ditches and bog-holes, always up to his knees in water and always under the rice, the bird-minder creeps warily. Nor is his anxiety confined to a fear that he may flush the birds out of range; for in the water through which he crawls there lurk the deadly cotton-mouth moccasin, the water-rattler, and even the alligator—though an alligator seldom attacks man unless he mistakes him for some defenseless and legitimate object of prey. When the Negro comes upon the birds, he makes sure of their exact location—which is not an easy matter because of the bewildering sound made by the chirring of thousands of bills on the rough rice hulls—levels his musket over the drooping heads of the grain, and utters a long, rolling whoop. As the feasters clear the level his musket roars out; and, if conditions be favorable, the gunner frequently picks up more than a hundred birds. Other hunters prefer to go into the field and wait until a great cloud of birds, disturbed, yet seeking a place to light, "balls" near enough to shoot.

But while the chief interest occasioned by this late summer visitor is rather expensive and rather unpleasant, there are at such a time observations possible which to the student of bird life are highly valuable. Undoubtedly the most impressive of these is the fact of the rice-bird's gluttony. He grows so corpulent that he grows unwary, he loses his grace of flight, his voice changes from a tenor to a lugubrious bass, and he is actually so fat that if, when shot, he falls on a hard rice field bank, he will literally burst open. Rice-birds roost in the marshes that border the rivers and in tall reeds that have taken possession of waste rice lands. Even there they are pursued by hunters, who, blinding them with a lightwood torch, pick them off their perches. And, even though the birds are a nuisance to the South, for the sake of others who love them for their songs of the summer, laws should be passed forbidding the capture of birds at night.

The bobolinks pay the South another visit in the spring, when they are known as May-birds. At that time they feed on the rice that is being sown. The males are then in full summer plumage and in full song. They precede the females in migration by a week or more, and appear far more joyous than their soberer-hued helpmates. This spring visit to the South is very short, and the true bobolink as he is at this time is not so well known there as the rice-bird is in the late summer.

A drive through the Southern woods in winter is a source of great delight to the bird lover. The level roads, smooth as white sand can make them and fragrantly carpeted with pine-needles, lead from dewy swamp to airy ridges, and by tiny farms of Negroes and poor whites—farms that have been desperately wrested from the engulfing growth of the monstrous woods. In the native growths of pine and tupelo the birds most frequently met, and seldom found anywhere else, are the pine-warbler, the brown-headed nuthatch, and the downy woodpecker. Occasionally, swinging far through the tinted vistas of the purple forest, there will be a magnificent black pileated woodpecker, which, with his flaming scarlet cockade, looks at a distance much as the lost ivory-billed woodpecker must have looked before encroachments of men drove him out of his native haunts. From the grassy roadside flickers bound up startlingly, hurtle to near-by trees, and there hang, their heads peering over their shoulders. On passing through gallberry thickets or along water-courses with heavy undergrowth, jolly towhees, with their striking red and black plumage, will rustle in the dead leaves or startle one by their abrupt "fluff-fluff" rise out of the brush. Perched on a dry twig, they will eye the intruder amiably, though they sometimes seem to express a personal opinion in their baffling incredulous whistle. Or, again, from the depths of some shadowy thicket their clear call, comparable in resonance to that of the bobwhite, will sound far through the woods, "Towhee! Towhee!" In sunny spaces along the road small flocks of doves will be seen, and frequently brown coveys of quail will troop gracefully over the sandy driveway or will huddle together until one passes. Through the sunlit woods large flocks of bluebirds can be seen, warbling that delightful note that in the North heralds the spring. Meadow larks, while usually found in grain fields and cottonfields, are often met with in the pine woods, where they find excellent cover in the tall yellow broomsedge. Traveling together in small flocks, the Carolina chickadee and the tufted titmouse are frequently seen, as are also goldfinches, brown creepers, ruby-crowned kinglets, and blue-gray gnat-catchers. If the observer be fortunate, it is quite likely that he may catch a glimpse of a blue-headed or white-eyed vireo, an orange-crowned, a yellow-throated, or a palm warbler, or even a Southern yellowthroat or a golden-crowned thrush. Most of the members of the sparrow family winter in fields rather than in woods; and so, if the road leads through cultivated lands, one may see vesper sparrows, savanna sparrows—along ditch banks—chipping sparrows, white-throated sparrows, and, most welcome of all, song sparrows, that sing throughout the entire winter.

My Winter Woods

Rutledge's use of the possessive my *offers a telling indication of just how much he cherished the family lands around Hampton Plantation. He literally devoted his life to his family's ancestral home and the surrounding acreage and did so at great personal sacrifice. The need to earn a living and support a family found him in exile in Pennsylvania for well over three decades, but you sense his heart lightening and his outlook brightening when holidays once more found him in the comforting embrace of the wilds and woodlands he loved. This piece originally appeared on pages 57–59 of volume 37 (1919) of* Country Life *magazine.*

*A*s I reached the plantation gate I heard the first note of the winter's morning: a timid phoebe bird, always fairy-like and eerie, from a shadowy copse beside the road gave a plaintive call. I looked behind me, across the misty cotton-fields, now brown and bowed, that stretched back toward the house. In the east there was a whitening of the sky's arch; and set in it, in a space breathed clear by the wind that blows before the dawn, throbbed and glittered the morning star. The note of the phoebe, the shy woodland fragrances awaft from the great avenue before me, the mantle of mist on the cotton, the blazing star, and even the bulk and blackness of the live-oak grove were elements of a type of beauty that I had loved since boyhood. But for the delicate bird-note there was silence. It was the witching hour; and I was on the threshold of my winter woods.

These are the woods in which I was born and where the greater part of my life has been spent. As I go through the gate, with the glimmer of morning resting with mystical beauty on all things, I am at home, even in the dark and solitary live-oak avenue into which I now pass.

Overhead the vast tops of these great trees shut out the sky, while far and wide their deep-foliaged limbs extend. In the cool, vaulted space under the oaks of this avenue there is ever an ancient, sequestered peace. From such old titans great limbs, larger than the bodies of ordinary trees, extend outward and upward, until, passing the limbs of the neighboring oaks, they lose themselves in the shadowy merging and melting of gray moss and silvery foliage. Sometimes, over their monumental frames, vast networks of vines have clambered, lowering down, even in the winter, heavy tapestries of jasmine foliage starred with yellow blooms. In the dampness and the fecund atmosphere of these woodland cathedrals, many kinds of mosses and lichens grow; and often the limbs of the live-oaks will be green or gray or brown—the color of the delicate plants which cling to and clothe the vast dimensions of these tolerant giants. Under such a canopy of moss and foliage both barred and great horned owls find a congenial home. Amid ordinary woodland surroundings owls hoot at twilight and at night only; but in a live-oak avenue they can be heard giving their weird chorus when the sun is high overhead. These strange birds interpret well one aspect of live-oaks: they seem the veritable oracles of these dim old trees.

As I come out of the avenue the sun is rising and the wide pine-lands lie before me. All the copses are shimmering; the dewdrops glint on the tips of the pine-needles; from the thickets of myrtle and bay come fragrances that mingle with the spiceries from the pines. The most characteristic feature of these woods is the prevalence of the evergreens. Everywhere, forming glimmering vistas, fairy outlooks on the far and the alluring, fabulous cathedral aisles, solemn transepts, the pines prevail. After all, despite the undergrowth and despite the live-oaks behind or the water-courses grown with gum and tupelo before, this is a pine forest, and through it one can travel more than fifty miles in all directions save that which leads to the sea; and even then the pines march down to the very beach.

I do not go far into the pine-land on this winter's morning before I come to a turpentine still, where the work of the day is beginning. I hear the songs of the Negroes as they roll barrels or cram the little wood-burning engine with fuel. The spiciest of scents are exhaled from the shining vats. I know the cooper at the still; so I approach his little shed, which stands under a small, gnarled live-oak. There is no more incorrigible optimist in the world than such a man. All day long the sturdy chopping of his broad-axe and the tuneful tattoo of his mallet can be heard above the shouts of the mule-drivers and the creaking roll of the full barrels as they are shoved up the gangway of the still. This Negro cooper makes all his own staves and shapes his own barrel-heads; then, with the help of a frame-vise of his own design, he puts the staves together until the rondure of their arrangement makes a barrel. Forthwith, then, he hammers on the hoops with surprising skill and dispatch. His shop is always littered with snowy strips of pine, with slabs of dry bark, with defective staves; and the air is aromatic and resinous there. It is said that a pine-woods cooper lives longer than any of his fellows; and he might well be immortal, with his wholesome, clean work to do, and such delicious air to breathe. His profession must affect his character, for I never knew a cooper who was not merry. He is always singing and whistling, keeping time with his axe, his hammer, or his mallet. And he interprets very well the liberty, the airiness, the joyous freedom that abide in spacious forests of yellow pine.

The prevalence of these pines as a standard element of every woodland view, and as a regular background or setting for every scene, renders the aspect of the winter forest here living and green. Yet if there were no evergreens save the pines there might be a beautiful monotony to them; but there are many live-oaks and water-oaks, which are never actually bare, but which on the coming of spring reclothe themselves. The foliage of the live-oak varies only in the tints of its green; but throughout the winter the water-oak wears its red and gold autumn foliage. Then there are cedars and hollies, which in that climate and soil often attain stately heights. Sometimes long, level thickets of sweet-bay and myrtle will be tufted and plumed at intervals by these trees and by brilliant water-oaks. Along the river, where there are sere reeds to rustle and dry marsh and canebrakes to whisper, and immense flights of migrated wild fowl to be seen, the presence of the season is more surely felt, and the minor tones of its voice are more distinctly heard. But afar off in the forest, where myriads of robins are holding festivals of feasting in huge bunches of mistletoe and in tall holly-trees, there seems nothing wintry save the red and white berries and the happy and excited tones of the birds.

Most of these birds are haunters of evergreen trees and bushes—those which prevail sufficiently to darken the water-course and to supply dewy retreats and fragrant sanctuaries are the myrtles, the three varieties of bay, the cabbage palmettos, the gall berries, and the wild-tea bushes. With the pines, hollies, oaks, and cedars above, and with these small evergreens below, the woods resemble the summer woods of the North.

And in this pine forest wild life is everywhere abundant and active; more abundant, I think, than in summer, for in addition to the native wild things there are the migrant visitors. Birds are seen and heard everywhere; some singing and some silent, but all of them busy. Warbling sunnily, in flocks of many hundreds, there are bluebirds; think of a flock of five hundred bluebirds flitting among the pines! There are small groups of mourning doves, which feed in the pinelands upon grass-weeds and upon pine-mast. There are meadow-larks, which find ample shelter in the yellow broomsedge. Along the edges of a bay-branch I flush several woodcock that go whirling off in a glimmering flight, their wings faintly whistling. The purple finches are already eating the buds of the sweet gum and the red maple, and the ruby-crowned and golden-crowned kinglets are examining food chances of two great banners of gray moss that swing from a pond cypress.

All these birds are either watchers or the watched. The watchers that I see are somewhat savage of mien: a sharp-shinned hawk darting like lightning through the forest; a Cooper's hawk perched bodefully on a low pine-stump; a marsh-harrier, flying high over the forest, beating his way to the delta where he hunts; a red-tailed hawk circling high over the trees; a great bald eagle, somewhat out of place here, but not far from his home on the wild seacoast, pursuing a lone and splendid course above the forest.

Of this great and varied family of birds none form a more interesting group than the woodpeckers. These are naturally companionable birds, with little in their nature that is shy or subtle; and, depending as they do for a living on making a noise, they do not hesitate to announce their presence by a scraping of bark, a vehement tattoo on a dead limb, or by doughty blows on the reverberant shaft of a dry pine. The greatest of these birds, the ivory-bill, has, within the past twenty years, become extinct in South Carolina, through no known cause; but there remains the black pileated woodpecker, which is the largest and handsomest of the surviving birds of this family. For nesting purposes it makes a new hole each year; and often one tree will have four or five holes that the same woodpeckers have made. The abandoned holes are soon occupied by other birds and animals. A friend of mine found a huge dead pine which contained three pileated holes: in the first, at fifty-four feet from the ground, one of these woodpeckers was nesting; in the second, seventy feet up, there was a family of fox squirrels; and in the third, ninety feet up, a pair of sparrow hawks had built—and all were living in harmony!

Our familiar friend, the flicker, is everywhere to be seen in these woods; and his handsomer relative, the red-cockaded woodpecker, brightens with his presence the open stretches of pinewoods.

Among the other woodpeckers that are here to be observed are the red-headed, the downy, the Southern downy, and the red-bellied. Their close cousins, the nuthatches, are here also—the white-breasted, the brown-headed, the red-breasted. Restlessness with them is a family trait shared by all the woodpecker tribe. And a cheery race they are—calling, hammering, flying hither and thither, restless, energetic, optimistic!

Turkeys and deer are the "big game" of these woods. Deer are the most interesting of all the living things of the pine-lands, but they are the most difficult to observe. At least, this is true of observation under natural conditions. Unless disturbed, they do most of their moving about at night, or in those eerie half-lights which precede dawn and darkness. But sometimes the haunting charm which is conferred on woodlands by the known presence there of essentially wild life is much the same whether the life by observed or unobserved. If it be there, the forest has a mysterious allurement that is readily sensed by the lover of nature's wilder aspects and wilder creatures. That deer are very plentiful in my winter woods is attested by the innumerable deer tracks which can be seen.

I take my place beside a pine, for I have a mind to watch for fox squirrels. I do not have to wait long, for on balmy winter days they are as restless as woodpeckers. I see a big gray one sitting on his haunches on a fallen log, thoughtfully mastering the mysterious convolutions of a pine-cone; another one is coming slowly, watchfully, head-foremost down a tall tupelo. As I can see no black squirrels from this point of vantage, I leave my log and go quietly among a dim water-course, grown with giant short-leaf pines, maples, and sweet gums.

Along the clumps of gray moss on a dwarfed gum I see what I take to be a wisp of dead moss, for it is black. But then the black object takes shape. I see the rather slender tail, the delicately shaped feet a shade darker than the coat, and the telltale white ears and nose. The moment the squirrel sees me approaching he leaps to the ground. Scurrying away, the dusky fugitive chooses the largest yellow pine in the vicinity as a place of refuge. Eighty feet it soars without a limb, and it spires forty feet above the initial branches. Up the slippery bark of this the black squirrel climbs, shrewdly keeping the immense bole of the pine between us. I time his ascent. The climb to the first limb was made in a minute and a half; and he has paused several times, not to rest, but to locate me and to set his bearings accordingly. But even the lofty refuge thus reached does not satisfy his ideas of safety. I see him ascending still, past crutches of the highest desirability, until at last he has reached the very top-most frond of the pine, the slender green spire beyond which there is naught but space and blue sky. There, 120 feet from the ground, the fugitive clings craftily. What his feeling is it is easy to imagine: elemental fear possesses him. But the emotions of the man watching him are more complex. I admire the climber's Excelsior determination; but I regret that so beautiful a creature's attitude toward me is expressed by his swiftly putting between us the height of the loftiest object on the landscape!

Continuing my walk, I come to a woodland pond. It is several acres in extent; and even to me, to whom the sight of it is familiar, the peculiar attribute of motionlessness is strikingly noticeable. And it is in the winter that this is chiefly so. In summer in this pond, black bass can be seen jumping for dragonflies; alligators will swim with indolent strength on the surface or will bellow grimly from its dim borders; and patriarchal frogs will encircle the edges as if holding some mysterious council. But now all these are asleep. And the waters sleep with them. The wind that is swaying the pines has small effect upon this pond; for the many trees densely bordering its edge and standing here and there in the water are draped in gray moss that affords a delicate but effective barrier. Of these trees the "bald" cypresses are at once striking in their appearance. Their tops open and spread like the sequoias, giving the appearance that they had grown to a certain level of ascent, above which no farther growth save the lateral was permissible. These cypresses usually have the outer layers of bark stripped off, which gives the trees a yellowish color. This is the work of raccoons and fox squirrels that use this particular soft bark almost exclusively for bedding their holes. In seasons of great drought these ponds do not go dry. Nor have I ever known one to overflow. But they are constant in loftier things than the level of their waters: for they change neither in their beauty nor in their peace. A spirit broods here that is autumnal; it is rich and sad, full of haunting pathos and romantic charm. It has a tranquility that seems entirely detached from life; and I can never look over the spiritual serenity of this place without imaging, out of the remote and mysterious vistas between the mourning cypresses, the figure of Swinburne's Proserpine:

> *Pale, beyond porch and portal,*
> *Crowned with calm leaves she stands,*
> *Who gathers all things mortal*
> *With cold immortal hands.*

I am now within a mile of home, and the sun is not a half-hour high. For my twilight watching I choose the top of a sandy ridge that falls to a deep water-course on one side and toward level woods on the other. While I love the dawn in these woods, with the dew-hung bay-bushes, the rainy fragrances, and the happy activity of the birds, I love the twilight better; and some of the best hours of my life have been spent sitting alone on a pine-log as the evening falls. I say alone; but all about me there is life.

As the sun sinks behind the dark-tressed pines there is movement everywhere in the forest about me and in the skies above me. One half of the life of the forest is looking for a place to sleep; another, the craftier and wilder, is coming forth. Everywhere birds are flying, with those subdued comrade calls that tell of the approach of darkness. Far above the pines there is a faint, sweet whistle of wild ducks' wings; they are hurrying, I know, to their night haunts in the waste marches of the Santee delta. The sky is suddenly darkened by a vast flock of birds; they are Florida grackles, boat-tailed grackles, red-winged blackbirds, cowbirds, and rusty blackbirds. They are going to roost in the marshes along the river. Now, in a funereal line, pass the black vultures; their powerful flight is very impressive. A covey of quail that has been scattered by some enemy begins to call together, the sweet, querulous note of the old female having in it a human quality. Great flights of robins pass overhead, "changing swamps," or migrating from one feeding-ground to another. Befitting this hour of mystery, from the depths of a gray swamp that has been moldering in misty silence a great horned owl gives his far and melancholy note.

The light in the west is fading. The voices of the day give place to the voices of the night. In a lone pine standing on the edge of a pond a wild turkey has gone to roost, though I neither saw nor heard him fly to his perch. He is rather dubious over something, for he will not settle on the limb, but stands there rocking awkwardly, his long neck craned. There is a noise in the sandy road; it is the creaking buggy of an old rice planter driving homeward in the dusk. Far off I hear the melodious whooping of a Negro. He does it partly from sheer love of music, and partly because "haints" fear such music as he can make. He, too, is going home. Now from the shadowy water-course below me, above whose shimmering copses a wraithlike mist is rising, two forms emerge. I thought they would come, yet I feared it might be too dark for me to see them. They are graceful beyond belief. Their movements are as fairy-like as they are silent. In a little misty glade they frolic and caper. Are they the spirits of this Southern solitude? They are; for they are deer coming out of the thickets to roam the glimmering woods of night.

Their coming is the signal for my going; for now I know that there will be nothing more for me to see, save a great owl dimly brushing past on a silent wing, or a crafty fox pausing spectrally for an instant in the road to snarl secretly at me ere he vanishes into the black woods. The old planter is now out of sight and sound. The Negro has stopped his whooping, indicating that he is either at home or that the "haints" have him. The deer have vanished. The roses have faded from the great gateway of the west. The day in my winter woods is done.

Woodcock in the Snow

This delightful little selection offers a fine example of Rutledge's observational powers and telling testament to the fact that he was a man who reveled in watching nature. He once erected a platform in an ancient live oak at Hampton Plantation so he could spend moonlit nights aloft watching deer, and the strange, unpredictable woodcock was sure to capture his fancy. He likely hunted "timberdoodles," although I don't recall ever having read a story by him devoted to the sport, but this is just a report on their behavior amidst winter's cold. The story comes from Wild Life of the South *(1935), pages 106–8.*

I believe it is not generally known that woodcock have a decided habit of flying by night. Many a time, while crossing a plantation field or an old pasture just at dark, I have heard and seen woodcock fleet by on faintly whistling wings, their speedy and enigmatic flight in no way baffled by darkness and by all those obstructions that the night conceals. Judging by the ease and alacrity of their movements, and by the way in which their low flight takes them through difficult thickety country, I am sure that their eyesight must be exceedingly good in the dark. Indeed, the woodcock's eye is a wonderful organ, both in appearance and in power. Set oddly in the side of the bird's head, it affords him hindsight as well as foresight.

The most impressive flight of woodcock I ever saw came at night; I heard many more in the darkness than could be seen; but the next morning revealed what a great number the storm of the night before had literally blown in. The afternoon had been bleak; a keen wind set in from the north at dusk; and the trees were soon creaking with sleet. At such a time I used always to be abroad to care for the stock, and incidentally to observe how the wild things were taking care of themselves. In the late twilight I was crossing a big cornfield on an elevation above the river when I heard several woodcock pass me, and dimly discerned their hurtling forms speeding southward toward the pine forests on the far side of the plantation. Northward from us, thousands of these fine birds winter; and a spell like this one brings them down. Cold freezes the ground, in which they are obliged to probe for food, and when a cold wave comes they simply fly southward until they clear the freezing area. On the bare hill-top I had excellent chance to see this remarkable flight of woodcock. Scores and scores passed me. Silent they were, save for the whistling of their wings. Good barometers are they, warning the stock-raiser of bad weather.

That night the sleet turned to snow, and the next morning the world was white. I found the woodcock in a rather pathetic plight, many of them so benumbed that they were easily caught. I got some Negro children to help me, and together we gathered in a great many. These we put in a bare room in the house, the warmth of which thawed them out. A fire was kindled in the chimney; a couple of big holly trees were stood in corners to make the birds feel more at home; and ere long they were strutting about like tiny turkey-gobblers, lowering their gorgeous buff wings and spreading their fantails. By another day the snow was gone, and these captives were released.

A Winter Home for Wildfowl

Carrying overtones of a conservationist's conscience, this selection is detailed and insightful, sort of a backyard birder's approach writ large. It was originally published in the February 1920 issue of Forest and Stream *magazine, pages 60–61, 82–83.*

*A*mong those happenings of nature that are calculated peculiarly to impress the thoughtful mind none is more interesting and picturesque than the annual southward migration of our wild waterfowl. I mention this rather than the northward migration in the spring because I wish to give as accurate a picture as possible of one of the southern resorts to which these swift-winged, wise-headed folk repair when the autumn sets in. What they have done for centuries untold the American people are now beginning to do. Call it instinct in the wildfowl if you will, but it is an instinct pregnant with fundamental sagacity.

The southward movement of game birds begins with the flight of the upland plover in mid-summer. But these birds have a long journey, for they spend the winter on the pampas of the Argentine and on some of the plains of Patagonia. Woodcock often begin to move slowly southward as the summer wanes. But the first striking migration is the flight of the reed-birds. They answer also to the names of bobolinks, rice-birds, and ortolans. Toward the end of August these yellow-clad hosts begin to march down toward the ripening rice fields of the South. Many linger in the North and East during September and even to early October, but the migration proper comes earlier. After these birds follow the coots, various shore-birds, the several species of the rails, and then the ducks and geese. How fast and how far they follow depends chiefly on the weather, but in ordinary seasons the migration has been completed by the first of December. By that time the winter haven of which I speak has gathered to its warm and ample bosom its wild children.

One home to which they gather is the region which is embraced by the delta of the Santee River on the South Carolina coast. Its coastal width is roughly from Cape Romain on the south to the mouth of Winyah Bay on the north— a distance of about sixteen miles. Such is, in large, the fronting of the delta on the ocean. Its hinterland penetrates to a depth of about fifteen miles, though northwest of this arbitrary limit are swamps and endless watercourses whereto the ducks of the delta occasionally repair. At about fifteen miles back from its mouth the river divides into a north and south branch, which flow almost parallel to each other to the coast. The land between these two branches, which varies in width from one to three miles, is the delta proper, although the marshes and lowlands bordering both sides of the two rivers are considered as parts of the same region. At the end of the delta proper is Cedar Island, a heavily wooded stretch of shore land, remote and wild. On it are brackish marshes and ponds where wildfowl gather in myriads. These ponds are shallow and sheltered, and I know of no place to which ducks more constantly resort. Southward across the south branch of the Santee and cut off from the mainland at Alligator Creek is Murphy's Island, a typical coastal island of the South Atlantic seaboard. It is several square miles in area, is wooded like the other island mentioned, and contains brackish ponds and sloughs frequented by wildfowl. The woods of this island contain herds of wild cattle and wild goats, as well as white-tail deer.

Offshore from the mouths of the river is Bird Bank, a long, low sandbar, covered by high tides. To this singular place, when the sun is bright and the sea calm, the ducks flock by thousands. Observers who have hidden in barrels in the sand to watch the coming of the quacking hosts have told me that the bar is literally covered, while the warm salt waters about it are dotted with "rafts" of mallards, teal, widgeon, and black duck. If the day is stormy the ducks stay in the sheltered ponds of the islands or in the thousands of miniature sanctuaries in the delta.

This whole stretch of the delta country was once planted to rice, and had an intricate and admirable system of canals and ditches for controlling the water on the rice fields. Rice-planting has practically been abandoned in that section of the country, and the fields have gone to waste and are now grown to wampee, duck-cats, wild rice, and other aquatic plants. The ditches, through the constant dredging of the tides, have in many cases not only remained, but have been widened and deepened until some of them are more like small creeks than ditches. Sheltered by overhanging marsh and jutting mud-banks, they are ideal day resorts for ducks. When the tide is high the wide fields are flooded and the savannah-like depressions between the clumps of marsh are filled with ducks of many kinds. If the weather is windy and cold they remain all day in the ditches and fields; otherwise they go to the islands or out to sea. Invariably they return to the fields to spend the night. The time of their return depends on the stage of the tide. They come in at twilight if the tide is high then; if not, they come in when they know that their night haunts will have the proper depth of water.

While the ducks thus move about over the delta, traveling fifteen or twenty miles in as many minutes to get a meal or a lazy place in which to drowse, the wide marsh fields are full of life of a less restless sort. There are melancholy great blue herons, making the day silent with their immovability—their watchful waiting—and the night hideous with their raucous, guttural calls. There are Worthington marsh-wrens, flitting about with gay impudence. Purple gallinules are there, and Wayne's small clapper rails. The King rail is perhaps the most interesting bird of these marshes, found here in the winter in great numbers. If a man wishes to see Wilson snipe he should visit this place, for he will never forget the sight of flocks of these swift-winged game birds with their darting speed and incisive calls. There is a high sandy mound in the delta, not more than an acre in area. Once in a time of flood, when all the surrounding region was submerged, I found that myriads of wild creatures flocked to this refuge. The rails, the rabbits of the lowlands, and the raccoons took care of themselves in the tops of bushes, in low trees, and on floating masses of sedge on the borders of the island; but the Wilson snipe came to the high-land. I do not wish to be classed with Ananias, but I know there were thousands of snipe on that little space. They rose like the largest flocks of shore-birds, but with that indescribable alertness in springing and surety of choosing their zigzag direction of flight that is so characteristic of this species. As I sat by a fire in a shack on the tiny hummock I heard for a long while the sharp cries from thousands of long-billed wanderers seeking a place on which to alight. All through the next day I watched this extraordinary congregation of snipe, and I am sure that before the waters began to subside the following night the hummock must have been visited by many thousands of these birds.

The most characteristic bird of the marshes is the red-winged blackbird. During the winter, when the native birds are joined by the hosts which have migrated from the North, it is no uncommon thing to see flocks of several thousand individuals. Rusty blackbirds consort with the red-wings, and occasionally purple grackles and boat-tailed grackles are found with them. The planters along the delta who have a little rice stacked in the open will be sure to have black clouds of these birds descending to their very doors and over their fields.

Certain species of ducks winter in this region, and these are some that have been observed in the Santee delta: Mallard, black duck, baldpate, or widgeon, canvas-back, wood-duck, blue-winged teal, green-winged teal, shoveller, hooded merganser, American merganser, bufflehead, ruddy duck, black-head, American golden-eye, scaup duck, redhead, pintail, ring-necked, old squaw, and the surf scoter.

Of these the mallard, the black duck, and the two kinds of teal are the most common. The canvas back is rare, as is also the American merganser. The ruddy duck is seldom seen, and whenever seen, is killed. It is a singularly foolish or a strangely trustful little creature, for it seldom takes wing until a boat has approached within forty yards of it.

The only duck mentioned that nests here is the wood duck. Occasionally, to be sure, other ducks that have not migrated, because of wounds or temporary sickness, mate and rear broods on the marshlands of the delta. But in the fresh-water ponds and lagoons in the pinewoods adjacent to the river, there are ideal nesting-sites for the wood-duck. The bird sometimes makes its nest in the crotch of a tree growing in the water, usually a cypress or a black gum. Occasionally it nests in a hollow, in deserted holes of the pileated woodpecker. From nine to sixteen eggs are laid, and the young, almost as soon as hatched, are hustled into the water, where, when only a few days old, they disport themselves with a sort of elfin surety that is beautiful to watch. In this region the wood-duck is increasing. Lately I have seen a flock of forty in a small pond. One afternoon I counted upward of three hundred passing above the delta to feeding grounds in the swamps. There really should be a close season everywhere on this most exquisite of American game birds.

Occasionally wild geese and swans come to the Santee delta, but their migration route lies to the westward, and those that winter on the lower Santee are stragglers. They are rather common in the Carolinas and in Georgia. During the winter of 1918 I had the privilege of observing at close range what was probably the largest flock of Canada geese that ever stopped on the delta. I was duck-shooting, with a Negro paddling me through the marshes. As we neared the river, which at that point is half a mile wide, we heard the loud honking across the delta. Looking back, we saw the geese coming, flying very low. They passed within one hundred yards, cleared the marsh-tops, and alighted in a stately squadron on the river in front of us. We were not observed, as we had pulled the canoe under a canopy of marsh. Both of us were curious to see the behavior of the big birds. There were fifty-six in the flock, and all seemed of one size save a very old gander that kept by himself and seldom ceased his strident honking. Once on the water the geese segregated themselves into small flocks, numbering about fifteen each; and I could not help wondering if these divisions did not represent families that naturally hung together. For the most part these geese busied themselves with a very ardent preening that they seemed thoroughly to enjoy, there in the wintry sunshine. When at last I told my paddler to push out on the river, the old gander rose first; and soon the inevitable V-shaped battalion formed itself. The geese rose very high, taking a northward direction. Had it been spring I should have said that they were heading for Saskatchewan; but as it was only January I knew that they would go but a few miles up the river. There are depths of the great Santee Swamp north of us that have never been penetrated by man; and wild creatures can live and die there without ever being molested by human enemies.

This delta is a very pleasant resort for wildfowl, but nowhere under natural surroundings are wild creatures freed from enemies. Most wild life belongs either to the pursuer class or to the class pursued. In nature might makes right; or at least might triumphs. The enemies that these wildfowl of the Santee delta encounter are many, and of these, formerly, the worst was the Negro hunter. Pushing about in his dugout cypress canoe, which was hardly visible, he took heavy toll of ducks. White men, also, make it their business to kill ducks for the market. But legislation, and the passing of most of the lands on the delta into the hands of a good sportsman's club, have stopped this kind of pot-hunting. While sportsmen bag many duck, they do not follow the game constantly as does the market hunter.

After man, the enemy of which wildfowl stand most in dread is the bald eagle. This great bird is found in numbers on the wide delta and on the lonely coastal islands and, during the winter, appears to prefer wild duck to any other food. Being indolent of disposition, he catches a crippled duck if there is one to be had; and will take every dead duck that a hunter leaves in the marsh. But when occasion demands, he can exert his majestic self. I have seen no more impressive sight than the spectacle of a full-grown eagle taking his toll of a mighty concourse of mallards.

At daybreak one December morning I was at a blind near Cane Gap, two miles from the mouth of the North Santee. Between my stretch of the river and the mouth of the same, between Cedar Island on the South and Ford's Point on the North, the "big ducks"—mallards and black ducks—were rafted. All were not in one flock; but in all the flocks there must have been fifty thousand ducks, and in single rafts there were several thousand. Just before the sun rose a great bald eagle launched himself out in flight from a lonely pine on Cedar Island, where he had spent the night. Three times he wheeled above the woods on the island; then he turned his course northward. The ducks, I am sure, saw him sooner than I did, and began to rise as soon as they were aware of his approach. The roar of their wings was so loud and continuous that it drowned the low booming of the surf. With a mastery of flight and an entire indifference to the consternation that he was causing, the huge eagle beat his way onward. He was looking for the mallard he wanted. Finally, from a small flock that was hurrying westward up the river he seemed to select one—an old mallard drake. The doomed bird was coming up toward Cane Gap. The eagle, always keeping above him, was hot on the track. The duck was flying wildly; but the eagle, with indolent ease, gained steadily. When about a hundred yards from me, the eagle, then almost above the duck, suddenly swerved downward, turning over in its descent, until it was under its prey. By a movement so quick that my eye could not follow it the talons of the great bird had been buried in the breast of the mallard. A moment later, by a masterly maneuver, the eagle had regained his poise and, rising slowly, beat his burdened way off over the marsh. Far, far through the rosy morning I watched the lone and lordly eagle pursue his flight, until lost to my limited vision in his larger liberty. Wildcats, raccoons, and minks take but few birds. The delta of the Santee is a favorite winter resort of these aquatic birds; and they appear to be increasing there. Nor are they eager to leave when the mystic premonition of the approach of spring comes to them. Sometimes I have started big flocks of mallards in the delta even in late March, when all the cypresses are in a mist of tender green. I believe that a mallard can travel from the mouth of the Santee to the mouth of the St. Lawrence in a single night. Such speed seems prodigious but the speed and the endurance of a wild creature depend generally on what is after it; and in the case of the wildfowl we are considering, grim Winter is after them when they go southward; and love and mating are before them when they journey northward. They are, we may say, driven to the South, and are lured back to the North.

III

The Hampton Hunt
Whitetail Tales

Christmas vacations at Hampton were filled with activity. They included joyous reunions with the black people resident on the plantation, who had not seen the Rutledge family since late summer, and a constant stream of visitors as family and friends from surrounding plantations, nearby McClellanville, and the Charleston area came to the stately old home; and there were all the festivities associated with the season. Yet nothing—not the simple pleasures of decorating Hampton, the festive meals associated with Christmas Day and New Year's, or the opening of presents on Christmas morning—matched the Hampton Hunt. Old Flintlock and his sons, along with Prince and other black huntermen, might have some deals with ducks and doves, turkey and quail, but primacy of place belonged to the whitetail. Rutledge's devotion to deer hunting ran so deep, was so much an integral part of his life, that even after health and advancing years had robbed him of the ability to be afield, nothing gave him greater pleasure than to relive hunts or hold the antlers of a lordly buck in his hands.

Rutledge wrote scores, indeed hundreds, of stories relating to deer hunting in one way or another. Almost all describe an approach to the sport that today belongs, increasingly, to a world we have lost; namely hunting deer with dogs. It was, for practical purposes, the only approach to the sport he knew. That may post a bit of a mental obstacle to most of today's deer hunters, given the fact that modern techniques typically involve watching and waiting from a stand (which should be called a sit, since that is what hunters normally do in these lofty perches). Yet once one gets into the meat of a Rutledge deer-hunting tale, the reader will realize that old-fashioned hunting with dogs has a special appeal all its own. No one has ever written about hunting deer with dogs better than Rutledge.

The deer season in the Low Country in yesteryear was a long one, as it is today. Yet through the prime of his manhood, Old Flintlock could only participate in this sporting love of his life during the Christmas season. Fortunately the three or four weeks available to him were ideal for the type of hunting he pursued. The humidity and humming mosquitoes of the early season were long gone, and brisk weather made for fine scenting and running conditions for the pack of hounds that were used to move deer.

Rutledge wrote many deer-hunting stories set in the Yuletide season, and the sampling offered here merely skims the cream off what is available in this genre. Yet the twelve selections that are offered unquestionably represent some of the finest work of his entire career. Many have appeared in previous anthologies, and tales such as "The Lady in Green" and "Steve's Masterpiece" have to be reckoned some of the finest outdoor pieces ever produced by an American sporting scribe.

A Hunt with the Oakland Pack

Published in one of Rutledge's rarest books, Bolio and Other Dogs *(pages 187–98), this piece covers a hunt that probably occurred before Rutledge's sons were old enough to participate. It conveys two messages with sparkling clarity—the importance holiday hunts had for Rutledge and the special camaraderie that is peculiar to the dog-driving approach to the sport.*

"When you dress on the train on Friday morning, be sure to put on your hunting-suit, for we are going straight from the station to the Oakland Cub, twenty miles across New Bridge."

This sentence in a letter from my brother down in Carolina sounded good to me; wherefore, when the porter bawled me out at Lanes, I packed away my Sunday suit and climbed into my old field equipment. Then, while the A. C. L. train, running an hour late, tried to make up that time between Lanes and Charleston, I had some breakfast, and while so doing looked out at a type of landscape familiar to me and loved by me since boyhood. Moreover, we were running through country which I knew well: by Mount Holly, Otranto, over the Santee River, by Ten Mile Hill, and so at length across the marshes and into the city.

My brother met me with his car, and within fifteen minutes after my arrival we two—boys again, and that's a good thing—were speeding out of the city's western limits. An invitation had come to us to hunt on the lands of the Charleston Mining Company, which controls thousands of acres of land beneath the surface soil of which lie rich deposits of phosphate rock. The Oakland Club leases a very large tract of this land, most of which lies between the A. C. L. tracks and the coast. My brother told me that likely the hunt would have started before we arrived, for an early start is the kind of start to make in Southern deer-hunting.

In leaving Pennsylvania the day before, I had had a blizzard hard at my heels; therefore to me that twenty-mile drive through fragrance and sunshine, along a level road overarched with huge live-oaks and massive pines, was like a trip into an entirely different world. Several times along the road we stopped to notice where deer had crossed in the sand; and once we saw the tracks of an old gobbler that wore No. 10's.

Turning into Bear Swamp Road, we ran for about a mile toward the coast; then a little to our left we saw the hunting party, gathered in the quiet sunshine under the pines, waiting for our arrival. They had taken one drive, and had killed two deer, which were hanging nearby on oak saplings. The hunters had decided not to hunt further until we joined them. In this group of men were some who during the past twenty years have added a great deal to the sport lore of Charleston, and have given to deer-hunting in that region a great deal of high distinction. Such hunters as James Davis and E. H. Hutchinson were there— men whose association with the hunting-game confers on it intelligence, dignity, and the best of fellowship. There were, to manage the great Oakland Pack with which we were to hunt, three Negro drivers, who were mounted. The chief of these dusky scouts was one Henry Washington, a Negro who knows horses, dogs, and deer; who has a voice that carries miles; and who would rather hunt than sleep in the sun—the utmost compliment for activity that can be paid a Negro.

The pack of hounds, which immediately held my admiration, was in some respects a motley crew; they varied in size, in shape, in color, and in disposition. From plain dogs they ranged upward until I saw there a pair of the finest English deerhounds on this side of the Atlantic. These dogs my father had purchased for the Club in the mountains of western North Carolina, where a very fine type of fox-hound and deerhound is bred. The pack, some eighteen in number, was exceedingly restless, for it had already tasted the fruits of sport. My brother pointed out to me several of the more famous dogs: Hammer and Trigger made a great pair, and Check and Mate likewise. There was Old Sked, a dog that had just recovered from a terrible ordeal. His owner, E. H. Hutchinson, missed him one day on a hunt, and for twelve days thereafter the hound did not appear. Finally a Negro came to him to say that strange noises, which he did not care about investigating, were coming from a certain very lonely part of the swamp. Upon going to the place, the hunter discovered his lost dog. The poor creature had fallen into an abandoned well and had been there for twelve days. His condition was pitiful; but after careful feeding and nursing, he came around all right; and now he can bounce a buck out of his bed and make him show his stride the same as he always did.

When we were ready to start for our drive, the Negro Henry, mounted on a sure-footed red pony, whirled a lash of dazzling length and made it crack startlingly above the heads of the dogs. At once they began to throng toward him, heavy-eared, intelligent heads lifted, long tails waving joyously. The drivers and the dogs took one course; we took another, knowing well that when we again should meet we ought to have something interesting to report.

In going to the stands, I had as my companion "Judge" Hutchinson, as he is affectionately called; and while my many years of deer-hunting in the South have made me feel that I fairly well understand the business, I surely learned something that day. As we passed down an old bank overarched by sweet myrtles, he paused to point out several places where bucks had rubbed, and where the old boys had pawed the ground, and where, shielded by night and this remote solitude, they had met the does. There is something mysterious about a trysting-place of this kind; and I was quite fascinated by it and by my comrade's talk.

"Right ahead there," he said, "where the bank makes that bend around to the left, I saw the funniest thing happen that I ever knew to happen in the woods. That Negro, Henry, and I were following the track of a fine buck. He was walking and I was mounted. We had two dogs with us, and we were right up with them. As we came out of the hollow there on the right and reached this path on the bank, the two dogs got right up to the deer—they got in the bed with him. He was lying in a clump of bushes right on the edge of the bank. Well, the first thing I knew, the big buck had jumped right square on Henry. He had to go somewhere, and as the dogs were reaching for his tail, he was not so particular. The Negro was knocked flat, and the buck, too, fell headlong over the side of the bank. The only thing that kept the stag from being laid out unconscious was that his head didn't meet Henry's fairly. For a minute or two I could see nothing on the bank but a scramble of Henrys and bucks. My horse turned around as if it had a fit, I meanwhile trying to get my gun on the deer. But the wise old fellow cleared himself, and my shot went wild. Henry was none the worse for having been run over. I think he probably holds the record for having been jumped on in this way by an unwounded buck."

During our progress we had been dropping off the standers one by one. It now came my turn to be left.

"Right here," said "Judge"; "this is their rialto. Henry will come with the dogs straight through here; and the old buck ahead of them will either run this old path on your left, or will come out through that little clump of pines yonder. I killed a big one here last week. There are the dogs now."

In an instant this good hunter had left me and had returned to a stand down the bank.

The scene about me was wonderful in its wild and fragrant beauty, but with twenty hounds making music in front of me, I had small time to take in the scenery. My object was to locate myself, and then to keep my eye on the two runways that the "Judge" had pointed out to me. Standing under a small rosemary pine, whose limbs were some seven feet from the ground, I awaited developments. Immediately to my right were some tall dead weeds. Several of these I broke off so that an unobstructed view would be afforded of the crossing on that side. By this time the hounds were beginning to warm up. Their voices were remarkably varied; there were deep baritones, grieving tenors, and just plain barks. Above the rising tumult, and controlling it, I distinguished the voice of the Negro Henry. He cajoled, admonished, encouraged, berated, and all in a far-carrying melodious voice. To control a big pack of hounds in woodlands so wild that even an old buck is sometimes embarrassed in breaking through is a high art; but the necessary skill for this Henry possessed. He could ride in the whirl-wind, and direct the storm.

The ever-increasing volume of music lacked as yet that assured and confident tone that means that the deer are up. But I knew that the dogs were close to the bedded animals. From me the hounds were now distant only about three hundred yards.

I opened my gun and for a last time looked at the shells. I was, of course, using buckshot, as rifles are taboo in the level woods of the South. I had some shells in which I had the greatest confidence. They were high-base Arrows, with three and three-fourths Ballistite under a charge of sixteen medium-heavy buckshot, chambering four to a layer. Even while my gun was open, I heard a sudden warning shout from Henry. The deer were up, and unless some miracle turned them, I knew from the direction immediately taken by the pack that my stand would soon be the scene of their crossing. I was in strange woods and having left a long train journey not two hours before, I was conscious of nervousness. Besides, my shot, if the chance offered, would have to be very quick, taken while the deer was jumping over the old bank; for he would emerge from the pine thicket to enter forthwith the tall myrtles beyond. I waited in quiet excitement, marveling the while over the wonderfully sweet chiming of the dogs' voices. They were no longer tuning up now; they were making woodland melodies to which the hunter's heart can listen long after the music is stilled.

I was looking for a shape; I was waiting to hear some movement which would indicate on which side the deer would run. Suddenly I both saw and heard it. A fine whitetail was coming through the pine thicket. In the second necessary for the maneuver I had thrown my gun into the opening which guarded the crossing. If the "Judge," in posting me there, had pointed my gun for me and said, "Hold it for that spot," he could not have given me clearer directions. I pulled on him and over he rolled into the myrtles and soft grasses that fringed the bank. Almost as soon as I reached the deer the dogs were upon the scene, and as I was a stranger to them, I had somewhat of a picnic keeping them off the fallen quarry until Henry, riding like a wild Indian, broke through the heavy thicket and began to crack his long whip over the excited pack.

This was a fine deer that had been shot; and, despite the objections that many hunters raise to the use of buckshot, I here found, and have always found, that a proper buckshot charge is sometimes a lifesaver for a hunter who has to shoot very quickly. Nor have I any quarrel with the nature of the work accomplished by buckshot when the range is not excessive. To support this, I may say that my brother has a record of fifteen straight shots at deer, all killed with buckshot. A little later on this same trip that I am describing, I had the good fortune to walk up at twilight, one day, an old, old stag. He crashed out of a bay-branch far ahead of me, and I gave him the choke-barrel at a distance that appeared to me hopeless. The buck, a very fine animal, was stopped dead by two buckshot that entered the small of his back just forward of the haunches and ranged clear up through his body, through his neck, and finally lodged behind his jaws. The distance, carefully measured, was eighty-nine steps, not under eighty yards. The gun was a twelve-gauge Parker, with thirty-inch barrels. The shell was of the type already described. Of course, my hitting the deer in a vital place was the purest chance, but certainly no rifle could have done more completely the work required.

While I was examining the deer I had just shot, the other standers came up, and one of them remarked that twenty-four hours before that whitetail and I had been nearly a thousand miles apart. It did seem rather remarkable that good luck should have come to me so quickly and so directly after that long journey.

Within a few minutes the drivers had called off the dogs and we were being posted for another drive. My stand was on the edge of a forlorn cotton-patch, an acre in area, surrounded by the wildest forest imaginable. However, not far off the Mining Company had a railroad, and the freights were constantly passing. It was told by two of our party that the deer did not seem to mind the trains, not even the hectic shrieking of the whistles nor the shrill grinding of the brakes and flanges against the rails. Mr. James Davis said that on two occasions, when he had been riding a freight to attend to some business in a remote section of the Company's holdings, he had seen deer lying down near the railroad track, and that the passing train in no way disturbed them. Of course, a railroad running through a hunting-preserve is a nuisance in that it disturbs the hunters by shutting off, by long freights, some of the best crossings at those times when deer are headed for them, and also by making a place more or less public. On this stand, as the dogs were far off when they were put in, I had a chance to look for signs, and I found the cotton-field full of them. The place was tracked from end to end. To such a haunt, deer love to resort at night. They appear to like the free sky over them. In summer they like a cotton-field for a far less romantic reason. In a thicket near my stand, I found in my quiet little prowling the skeleton of an old buck that probably had died or had been killed the year before. Only one antler remained on the skull, the other having in some manner been broken away.

I was not allowed much time for further inspection of these interesting premises; for, far away, echoing high over the great pines that towered dreamily in that lone Carolina forest, the great Oakland Pack was again making overtures that meant a prelude to a grand march. This time, however, the hounds, after jumping, ran a long way to my left, so that I did not see them. But I had a good opportunity to hear them broadside, and to distinguish in their varying voices about a dozen different kinds of eagerness. About a half a mile away I heard a single shot. Several minutes later, before the hushing of the pack would have indicated to me the import of the matter, one of the Negro drivers, circling the thicket through which the dogs had run, rode near me. He was talking joyously to himself, and the mixed metaphors are his own.

"Go on hyar, you fool mule. Ain't you done hear dat shooting? Git out ob dis hyar place, you swinged-tail rabbit. Put on de pot, mule; de 'Judge' done shoot."

Such a compliment, paid to a man who deserves it, was of a type that a Negro knows well enough how to pay; nor do you ever find one of these dusky hunters handing out such unfeigned eulogies to the wrong man.

As we gathered in a broom-grass field, which a deer had foolishly attempted to cross, since that route lay across the stand of the "Judge," we found the successful hunter standing modestly by his deer, while a few yards off, Henry was lecturing to the hounds in a certain violently affectionate way peculiar to him. He was telling them that they had done their part well; and their happy yowling and pleased whining showed that the driver had put across to them his meaning.

Steve's Masterpiece

❤∴❧

This piece from the March 1935 issue of Field & Stream *(pages 34–35, 71–72), accompanied by Lynn Bogue Hunt artwork (as are so many other Rutledge articles in this magazine), gives full and due credit to one of the "huntermen" who, along with his wife, Amnesia, frequently figures in Rutledge's stories. In this case Steve is triumphant, and the hunt concludes with venison for the holiday feast.*

A gray December rain was sifting down through the tall rocking pines. An eerie east wind, insistent and now and then sharp and gusty, made shelter from the storm impossible. Beside a great yellow pine in the Carolina woods Steve, my good good-for-nothing Negro, and I awaited the possible arrival of a buck out of the misty deep woods ahead of us, through which my drivers were shiveringly coming. But because of the wind in the pines and the length of the drive, I could not yet hear my drivers' voices.

"Dis here am a good day for ducks to enjoy," muttered Steve, his tattered hat streaming with cold rain. "God never meant for a man to fight weather."

"But we are out for some Christmas venison," I reminded him. "If an old buck comes along, you'll forget all about being cold. Besides, you know that Amnesia isn't going to welcome you home unless you bring some dinner with you."

"Dat's de trufe," Steve admitted; "but it might be better to be hungry dan to freeze and to drown."

Suddenly Steve laid his hand on my arm. He did not speak; he did not point. But I felt the thrilling warning of his touch. And in a moment I saw what he saw.

When a man has hunted deer for more than forty years, the chances are that he has seen a good many, and of various kinds. I believe I have seen between two and three hundred. Of these I have neither shot at nor killed a great many. On New Year's Day of 1933, I killed my hundredth buck.

Of all the deer I have ever seen, dead or alive, the thing now coming toward me through the rainy woods seemed the largest. Certainly he carried the hugest horns. But was he coming toward me? The wet wind was blowing directly into the drive, and from the way he acted I am sure that he had our scent. Through a thicket of young pines he came, to cross our left front at a tangent. I knew where he wanted to go.

Three hundred yards behind us was the beginning of the Big Ocean, one of the greatest natural deer sanctuaries I have ever known. It is a wild sea of greenery, over which giant man-bodied vines riot; the footing is no better than that afforded by a quaking morass. You really can't get into the Ocean; or once in, the chances are against your getting out.

Deer have been hunted in my part of Carolina since long before the Revolution, and hunters have always abandoned a chase if the quarry made his escape into the Ocean. Whenever deer are jumped within two or three miles of this inviolate place, they will likely either head straight for it or else circle and eventually enter this old-time fastness. Our present buck was making for it on a slant.

He was running low, head down and far extended. His great antlers rocked from side to side with every jump. We were in the big open woods, and the huge thicket that the stag wanted to reach was directly behind us. On he came, crossing our front at 150 yards. My hope was that when he cleared the pine thicket he would bear our way, which would bring him within range.

I had my old thirty-inch double gun, with which I had killed many deer up to seventy yards; but beyond that distance, the chances of killing a big buck are slight. One buckshot might bring him down if it were fortunately placed, but several might do him no harm if at that distance they were not fortunately placed. My only chance in this case was to wait in the hope that the great buck might bear toward me. Breathless we waited. This might mean Christmas for Steve, and a record head for me.

The buck never broke his stride. Through the streaming woods he came, this noble old veteran of many an escape. I marked his antlers. He was a ten-pointer, but of no ordinary kind. The beams of his horns were massive and craggy. The architecture was perfect in its symmetry; the color was a rich chestnut-brown. I was sure that he must have a twenty-four-inch spread; and the tines were the longest I had ever seen. Steve was either praying or swearing under his breath—probably both.

At that distance the buck would have been a perfect target for a rifle, and I lamented having left my .250–3000 at home. Steve, I knew, shared my regret, for he had urged me to bring it. He had never quite recovered from his superstitious respect for that rifle since he had seen what it had done to a bull alligator at two hundred yards.

Did the great stag bear toward us? He did not. He had our wind, and he held his tangent course so that at no time did he come nearer than 110 yards. I never put my gun up. It's a shame to shoot at such a creature when you know that your chance of hitting him is slight. Soon he was past us. We turned to watch him go. When well out of danger, he made the turn that I had hoped for earlier, and headed straight into the mysterious borders of the Big Ocean. The huckleberry bushes on the edge of it had been burned, and I will remember how he crashed through these.

"Dat's dat," said Steve.

"If I had only had the rifle!" I said.

"Ain't I done tole you, Cap'n, to bring it? My mind done tell me dat something like dis would sholy happen. If you have a rifle," he went on, "and you want a buck, all you done need is his address."

"You think he's gone for good? Isn't there any chance for us to drive this end of the Ocean where he went in?"

Steve thought deeply. "In a rain like dis," he said, "dat ole buck ain't gwine far. I think I know a chance."

Long years of comradeship with good old Steve in the woods have made me respect his opinion about deer and their ways. I listened carefully. "I will go home and get de rifle," said he: "and when I done come back, you and I gwine take a little scout."

With his swift shuffling gait Steve was off through the pinelands on a five-mile hike. In a little while my drivers came out. They had neither heard nor seen the buck. As they were wet and miserable, I sent them home. By the time Steve returned with the rifle, the wind and rain had let up somewhat, but it was growing colder. Both of us were soggy and chill.

"Cap'n," he asked, "is you know how to get to Buck Ridge?"

I told him that I did. It is a long strip of high sandy ground dividing the east end of the Ocean from the main body of it.

"You must go clear round de place where he went in," Steve told me. "Den when you get on de Ridge, come back to me to dem three big pines what we does call de Three Sisters. Dat is de stand. If he done stop between here and de Ridge, he will cross by de Sisters. But you have to take up three stands. Dat's why I say we must have de rifle. I gwine wait here till I think you is to de place; den I gwine come through to you. It might so happen dat we will have a good luck."

Northward through the blear woods I went for a half mile, then bore west. Following a game trail in the Ocean, I bogged and scuffled and tore my way through that wild chaos of greenery. Three times I started deer from their beds; but these were not our deer. At last, dripping and exhausted, I came out on Buck Ridge. By this time the sun, which was now trying to break through the rolling and massive clouds, was almost down. There was little wind, and the rain had ceased altogether.

Down the ridge I went until I came to the Three Sisters. Noble yellow pines they were that by growing in the Ocean had escaped the lumberman. Steve had said there were three stands, but that I must stay by the pines. A giant fallen pine afforded me a good watching place. I got all set, but I did not have much hope that Steve's little plan would work out.

A little breeze whispered in the pine-tops; the rain-drenched forest glittered in the fitful sunlight. I suppose there is hardly a lonelier place in the world; not that it is far from human habitation, but that it is accepted as an inviolate region. It surprised me, indeed, that Steve should have proposed our coming here, for he has his share of superstition. But when it comes to hunting deer, he forgets all else.

There was so wide a murmuring of the woods, with the wakening and dying wind and the dripping of the wet trees, that it was not easy to hear anything approaching. The thicket through which Steve was heading was a wild tangle of young pines, bay-bushes, high-bush huckleberries—all of these smothered by smilax and swamp-brier vines. I hardly saw how a deer could get through, let alone Steve himself. But I waited and watched, while the sun sank and twilight birds began to call.

I was almost ready to give the whole thing up and call Steve to me, my chief concern now being that the Negro was lost, when I heard a stealthy footfall on the sandy ridge behind me. It was Steve, his face dominated by an expression which told me that something great was on his mind. He put his hand over his mouth for silence.

When he was close, he whispered, "I done seen him. Come with me very quick, Cap'n."

Back down the ridge he led me in a little fox-trot for two hundred yards. Then he paused and pointed to the left where a huge savanna glimmered in the sundown light. Wild it looked and primeval, a fit harbor for the great stag we were seeking.

"You jumped three deer, Cap'n?"

"Yes."

"Well, sah, dey done joined de old buck, and all is done gone in dat savanna. When I come out behind dem, dey were standing by dat big cypress yonder. Dey were not scared, and maybe we can get a shot."

Let me confess that I have not stalked many deer; most of mine have been driven to me. There is about stalking an old whitetail stag, absolutely wild and free in the wilderness, a peculiar thrill that hardly any other kind of sport affords. And when the odds are against the hunter, as they were here, the sport is stepped up considerably in excitement.

"What is your plan, Steve?" I whispered. "The light is leaving us fast."

"De wind is to us," he answered softly.

"We must follow, and try to get a sight of dem. He's a much bigger buck dan I thought for, Cap'n. And you done got de rifle, thank God!"

Mists were rising in the dripping twilight woods as we stepped forward toward the forbidden heart of the Ocean. The greenery was at this point waist-high and as dense as a continuous hedge; but through it ran game trails that had been used for countless centuries. We made fair time, and our approach was almost noiseless. Underfoot, deep sphagnum moss muffled our footsteps.

"We ought to keep below de bushes." Steve admonished in a voice hardly audible; "and when we get to dat big bay-tree ahead, we must stop to look."

It was almost a certainty that we must now be within range of the superb stag; the only question was: could we make him out? In that dense underbrush I doubted if we could see more than his head and neck. Even if he were visible, we might not see him. All deer hunters know what I mean by that. For the wild deer is a singularly spectral creature. Against a forest background, a few trees or bushes camouflage him admirably; and he not only has sense enough to dash away at full speed when man approaches, but he likewise (and this takes more sense) knows how to stand almost without breathing, watching the hunter and craftily calculating whether it is wiser to make a break for it or to take a chance on the hunter's not seeing him. A wiser wild creature there may be, but I have never hunted any wiser.

We came to the bay-tree, a huge thing fifty feet high, from the shelter of which Steve had suggested that we take a scout. As soon as we reached it my Negro did a touching thing. He bent himself over almost double beside the tree.

"Stan' on me," he said. And his tone, though whispered, was an order. This was Steve's hunt.

Holding the tree with one hand and my rifle in the other, I stepped up on Steve's broad back. Good old Steve. He was as steady as a stump.

From my curious point of vantage I looked over the gently rolling sea of greenery before me, the long undulations of which were caused by the wonderful growth of evergreen vines that festooned the bushes. It was as if a wide expanse of water, with green waves rolling and deep hollows between glimmering, had suddenly been stayed by some magic hand. It was in this kind of country that I was looking for my stag.

For a minute or so I saw absolutely nothing but the lonely landscape. Then, out of gunshot but clearly visible, a doe stole out of the brush and began to nibble some huckleberry buds. Another one joined her. Just at that moment the sun, half-way down over the rim of the horizon, broke through the clouds and sent a last shaft through the jeweled woods. Suffusing the tall pines with soft radiance, these sunset rays lighted up other things as well. I had been looking for a telltale glinting of horns, and now I saw it. Then the whole buck came into view, striding in lordly fashion behind the does. Only for an instant did I see his whole body as he walked clear of the bushes; then he faded as he stepped forward, soundlessly vanishing in the misty bushes. I said that these deer were out of gunshot—but not rifle-shot. The distance was about 125 yards.

It was evident that these fugitives had not quite recovered from their fright. While deer at all times seem to live in an atmosphere of alertness and while, when feeding, they often keep moving as if nervous, these seemed to be heading for somewhere—and that place was probably far beyond where they were now tarrying.

I forgot that I was standing on Steve; I tried to forget the treacherous shimmer and the faint fog over the brush country—the low visibility, so to speak. I got my rifle up, steadying it against the trunk of the bay-tree. Holding for the broad base of the neck, where it joins the shoulder but not too low down, just as the old stag paused on a tussock I let drive. I knew there would be no chance for a second shot, and made no attempt to follow up the first. But I did try to mark the exact spot where the buck had been standing when I saluted him.

There were sounds of crashing through the far thickets; then all was still. I did not know whether it had been a clean miss or a clean kill. I was still listening for some possible telltale sounds of struggle when I felt my underpinning begin to move. I stepped down.

Steve and I looked at each other. Somehow we never try to pretend.

"You done kill him?" he asked.

"I don't know. Let's go and see."

Through the reeking bushes we went; and when we came to three tall sweetgums, we began to look about. This was the place. Steve did a thing that you will hardly believe, yet it is true. It was very dusky. Twilight had come, Steve began to smell about.

"I can always smell a deer," he said, "at dis time of day, when de bushes is wet."

I myself have smelled deer, but I don't undertake to find them that way.

Steve left me for five, ten, twenty yards. Then I saw him straighten up and raise his hand high. When I joined him, there lay the great stag which had escaped me once that day, but not this time. It had been a clean kill after a peculiar but thrilling stalk.

"You done had his address," muttered Steve in subdued triumph.

After some two hours' toil we got the old stag home. When we got him out of the woods and to the road, we made a sled of pine boughs and hauled him over the soft sand.

"Steve," I asked, "what's Amnesia going to say to you for coming home about five hours late tonight?"

"Cap'n," answered the Negro after a few moments of thoughtful silence, "I gwine be just like dat mule you wouldn't let me buy."

Steve's meaning made me stop hauling the deer to stop and laugh. Several years before I had gone with him to help him buy a mule. The forlorn creature was led out of the barn, and immediately proceeded to walk head on into the barnyard fence. Backing off groggily, it next ran face foremost into a tree. Steve and I watched these performances with misgiving.

"Dat mule blin'," Steve muttered.

"No man," said the Negro owner, with magnificent sales poise. "He ain't blin'; he just don't give a durn."

The thing had become a standing joke with us; so that when I asked Steve how he was going to appease his wife for coming home after hours, he felt that the thrill of killing the old stag had taken out of his heart even the dread of 260-pound Amnesia; had given him new manhood, and a certain superior indifference to his aforetime master and ruler. And it is a fact that our stalk of this master buck did, for a time, restore Steve to a position of domestic ascendancy. But it couldn't last. It never does.

The Lady in Green

◡⁚◠

Originally published in the October 1941 issue of Field & Stream *(pages 26–27, 68–70), this is one of the best-known Rutledge stories. It appears in* Hunter's Choice *(pages 3–12) and has been included in a number of anthologies, among them* Strayed Shots and Frayed Lines *(pages 135–46), ed. John E. Howard, and*

Last Casts & Stolen Hunts *(pages 147–55), ed. Jim Casada and Chuck Wechsler. Written in an era when women seldom hunted—so much was this the case that Paulina Brandreth, the author of a great book on the sport,* Trails of Enchantment, *used the pseudonym Paul Brandreth—it provides a fine example of Rutledge's ability to take offbeat circumstances and weave a wonderful tale around them. The green-clad lady wipes everyone's eyes, and Steve, the endearing rapscallion who is featured in the previous selection, enjoys the last word at the expense of the man telling the tale.*

"Steve," I asked my good good-for-nothing Negro, "have you ever seen a woman wear pants?"

"I ain't done seen it, Cap'n," he responded, a fervent fire of recollection kindling in his eyes, "but I has done seen some wimmins what act like dey wears dem."

"Has your Amnesia ever worn them?"

"When I is around home," he assured me, "she don't ever wear anything else but."

"Have you two been falling out again, Steve?"

"Cap'n," he answered solemnly, "for yeahs and yeahs we ain't never done fell in."

"I guess she doesn't like your playing around with all these young girls, and leaving her at home."

"I tole her dat woman and cat is to stay home; man and dog is to go abroad. She didn't like dat atall, atall."

"Well," I said, "this is Friday. Monday will be Christmas Day. I know just one way I can get you out of the dog-house where Amnesia has put you. Wouldn't you like to get out for Christmas?"

Steve licked his lips, a sure sign that he is about to take the bait. Besides, as I had beforehand been of assistance to him in the vital matter of domestic reconciliations, he regards me as a kind of magician.

"Tomorrow," I told him, "will be Saturday, the day before Christmas Eve. I will help you, but I expect you to help me." I was testing his loyalty in a large way.

Haunted by a sense of his own helplessness and by the mastery of his huge Amnesia, he appeared pathetically eager to do anything. In fact, such was his yielding mood that I had to be careful what I asked him to do, for he would do it. Steve can resist anything but temptation.

"I'm giving a big deer drive tomorrow," I said. "There will be twenty men and one woman—but I hear she wears pants."

"Great Gawd," was Steve's comment.

"Green ones," I went on.

"Jeedus!"

"Now, Steve, you know that old flathorn buck in the Wambaw Corner—the one that has been dodging us for about five years?"

"You mean him what hab dem yaller horns, flat some like a paddle?"

"He's the one."

"Cap'n, dat's a buck what I knows like I knows the way to another man's watermelon patch," Steve assured me, grinning. "What you want me to do, and how Amnesia suddenly gwine take me back because of what you is planning for me to do?"

"Well," I told him, "You've got a job, all right. I don't want to be unfair to these men, but ordinary bucks will do very well for them. Your business is to get the buck with the palmated horns to run to the lady in green. If you will do this, I will give you a whole haunch of venison, a ham out of my smoke-house, a dollar in cash and a dress for Amnesia. How about it?"

Steve was stunned. When he came to, he said, "Boss, when I gits to heaben, I ain't gwine ask, 'How 'bout it?'"

"Of course," I told him, "I will put her on the Crippled Oak Stand. You know that is the favorite buck run. Just how you are going to get him to run there I don't know, but you probably can figure it out. Oh," I added, "I will not hold you responsible for her killing the buck. Being a woman, she'll probably miss it anyway. But I want you to give her a chance to shoot."

I could see that Steve was already deep in his problem. Knowing the woods like an Indian, so familiar with game that he can almost talk with it, familiar also with the likelihood of big game's acting in ways unpredictable, Steve was pretty well equipped for his task.

"One more thing," I told him: "this lady doesn't shoot a shotgun. She always uses a rifle."

"Cap'n," he sensibly asked, "does you think she knows a deer? If she don't I mustn't get too close to dat rifle."

"I have never seen her," I told him, "and I don't know whether she is a real huntress. All I know about her is what I have been told. But she's the daughter of one of my best friends, a gentleman from Philadelphia. I want her to have a good time. Think of what it would mean if she could kill the crowned king of Wambaw Corner!"

"I sure loves to please wimmins," Steve mused, "but so far I ain't done had too much of luck."

As we parted I kept pounding home his job to him: "Drive the buck with the flat horns to the Crippled Oak Stand. Drive him there if you have to head him off. And remember the haunch and the ham that will be yours if you manage it right."

Not long after daylight the following morning the crowd of Christmas hunters assembled in my plantation yard. As the season was nearing its close, every man I had invited came. And there was the lady in green. When I saw her, I was ashamed of the way in which I had bandied words with Steve about the nature of her attire. She was slender, graceful, and very lovely. She looked like Maid Marian. Clad in Lincoln green, with a jaunty feather in her Robin Hood's cap, she was the attraction of all eyes. I could see that all the men were in love with her, and I didn't feel any too emotionally normal myself. She appeared a strange combination of an elf, a child, and a woman; and though I do not profess to know much about such matters, that particular combination seems especially alluring, perhaps dangerously so.

While my Negro drivers were getting their horses ready, and while stately deer hounds, woolly dogs, and curs of low degree gathered from far and near on account of the general air of festivity and the promise of some break in the general hunger situation, I got everybody together and told them that we planned to drive the Wambaw Corner; that we had standers enough to take care of the whole place, we had drivers and dogs, we had deer. The great, and really the only, question was, Can anybody hit anything? That is often a pertinent question in hunting.

Wambaw Corner is peculiarly situated. A tract of nearly a thousand acres, it is bounded on two sides by the wide and deep Wambaw Creek. On one side is the famous Lucas Reserve, an immense backwater, formerly used for water-power, and now chiefly for bass and bream. In shape this place is a long and comparatively narrow peninsula, with water on three sides. On the south runs a wide road, along which I usually post my standers; but when I have enough (or too many), I post them along the creek. The chance there is excellent, for if a buck is suspicious there's nothing he'll do quicker than dodge back and swim the creek.

With the woods still sparkling with dew, and fragrant with the aromas from myrtles and pines, I posted all my standers. I had sent my drivers far down on the tip of the peninsula, to drive it out to the road. I had also had a last word with Steve.

"Only one mistake you might be can is makin', Cap'n," he told me: "I donno how 'bout wid a gun, but with a rollin'-pin or a skillet or a hatchet a woman don't eber seem to miss. Anyhow," he particularized, "dey don't neber miss me!"

"Have you got your plan made?" I asked him. "You've got five other boys to drive. That just about sets you free to do what you want to."

"I got my plan," he said. "And," he added darkly, "if so happen it be dat I don't come out with de other drivers, you will onnerstan'."

In a place like Wambaw Corner there are at times a great many deer. They love its remote quiet, its pine hills, its abundant food, its watery edges. I have seen as many as six fine bucks run out of there on a single drive, a flock of wild turkeys, and heaven knows how many does. I have likewise seen wild boars emerge from that wilderness—huge hulking brutes, built like oversize hyenas, and they are ugly customers to handle.

I knew that there was sure to be a good deal of shooting on this drive, certain to be some missing, and possibly to be some killing. Everybody seemed keyed just right for the sport. I had men with me who had hunted all over the world, grizzled backwoodsmen who had never hunted more than twenty miles from their homes, pure amateurs, some insatiable hunters but rotten shots—and I had the lady in green.

After I had posted the men, there being no stand for me, or perhaps for a more romantic reason, I decided to stand with my Maid Marian. She seemed like such a child to shoot down a big buck, yet she was jaunty and serene. When I had explained to certain of the standers as I posted them just how an old stag would come up to them, I could see, from the way they began to sweat and blink, that they were in the incipient stages of nervous breakdowns. But not so my Sherwood Forest girl.

Her stand, by the famous Crippled Oak, was on a high bank in the pinelands. Before her and behind her was a dense cypress swamp, in the dark fastness of which it was almost impossible to get a shot at a deer. If the buck came, she would have to shoot him when he broke across the bank, and likely on the full run—climbing it, soaring across it, or launching himself down the farther bank. All this I carefully explained to her. She listened intently and intelligently.

She appeared concerned over my concern. "You need not worry," she assured me, for my comfort. "If he comes, I will kill him."

"Have you killed deer before?" I asked.

"No," she admitted lightly but undaunted. "I never even saw one."

My heart failed me. "This one," I told her, hoping that Steve's maneuvering would be effective, "is likely to have big yellow horns. He's an old wildwood hero. I hope you get him."

About that time I heard the drivers put in, and I mean they did. A Christmas hunt on a Carolina plantation brings out everything a Negro has in the way of vocal eminence. Far back near the river they whooped and shouted, yelled and sang. Then I heard the hounds begin to tune up.

Maid Marian was listening, with her little head pertly tipped to one side. "What is all that noise?" she asked with devastating imbecility.

Tediously I explained that the deer were lying down, that the Negroes and the dogs roused them, and that by good fortune an old rough-shod stag might come our way.

"I understand," she nodded brightly. But I was sure she didn't.

Another thing disconcerted me; I could hear the voice of Prince, of Sam'l, of Will, and of Precinct; Evergreen's voice was loud on the still air. But not once did I hear the hound-dog whoop of Steve. However, his silence did indicate that he was about some mysterious business.

In a few minutes a perfect bedlam in one of the deep corners showed that a stag had been roused. The wild clamor headed northward, toward the creek, and soon I heard a gun blare twice. But the pack did not stop. There was a swift veering southward. Before long I heard shots from that direction, but whoever tried must have failed.

The pack headed northeast, toward the road on which we were standing, but far from us. I somehow felt, from his wily maneuvers, that this was the buck with the palmated horns. Ordinary bucks would do no such dodging, and the fact that he had been twice missed would indicate that the standers had seen something very disconcerting.

Watching the lady in green for any telltale sign of a break in nerves, I could discover none. She just seemed to be taking a childish delight in all the excitement. She was enjoying it without getting excited herself.

About that time I heard the stander at the far eastern end of the road shoot; a minute later he shot again. He was a good man, a deliberate shot. Perhaps he had done what I wanted Maid Marian to do. But no. The pack now turned toward us.

Judging from the speed of the hounds, there was nothing the matter with the deer; judging by their direction, they were running parallel to the road, at a little over a hundred yards from it. It was a favorite buck run, and at any moment he might flare across the road to one of the standers at the critical crossings. Ours was the last stand on the extreme west. It seemed very unlikely that he would pass all those crossings and come to us. Now the hounds were running closer to the road. It sounded as if the buck were about to cross.

It is now just fifty years since I shot my first buck, and I have hunted deer every year since that initial adventure. But never in all my experience as a deer hunter have I heard what I then heard on that road, on which I had twelve standers. Judging from the shots, the buck must have come within easy sight, if not within range, of every stander. The bombardment was continuous. Together with the shots, as the circus came nearer, I could hear wild and angry shouts; I thought I heard some heavy profanity, and I hoped the lady in green missed this.

She was leaning against the Crippled Oak, cool as a frosted apple. I was behind the tree, pretty nervous for her sake.

"Look out now," I whispered. "He may cross here at any minute."

My eyes kept searching for the buck to break cover. Suddenly, directly in front of the stander next to us, I saw what I took to be the flash of a white tail. The stander fired both barrels. Then I saw him dash his hat to the ground and jump on it in a kind of frenzy that hardly indicated joy and triumph and all that kind of thing.

The next thing I knew, the little rifle of the lady in green was up. I did not even see the deer. The rifle spoke. The clamoring pack, now almost upon us, began a wild milling. Then they hushed.

"All right," said Maid Marian serenely, "I killed him."

Gentlemen, she spoke the truth, and the stag she killed was the buck with the palmated horns. At sixty yards, in a full run, he had been drilled through the heart. On several occasions I had seen his horns, but I had not dreamed that they were so fine—perfect, ten-point, golden in color, with the palmation a full two inches. A massive and beautiful trophy they were, of a kind that many a good sportsman spends a lifetime seeking, and often spends it in vain.

However, mingled with my pride and satisfaction there was a certain sense of guilt; yet I was trying to justify myself with the noble old sentiment, "Women and children first." I had told Steve to drive this buck to my lady in green. He had done it—heaven knows how. But his plan had worked. But now came the critical phase of the whole proceeding. Standers and drivers began to gather, and afar off I could hear many deep oaths. These, I felt sure, would subside in the presence of Maid Marian. They did, but not the anger and the protests.

There seemed to be one general question, asked in such a way that it would be well for the person referred to to keep his distance. "Where's that driver?" I heard on all sides. "I mean the big, black slue-footed driver. I believe you call him Steve. I had a good mind to shoot him."

"I'd have killed that buck if he hadn't got in the way."

"What was that flag he was waving? Looked to me like he was trying to turn the buck from us."

"He was coming right on me when that gorilla jumped out of a bush and started waving that flag."

"Well, after all, gentlemen," I said, "here's the buck, and I must say the lady made a grand shot. Wouldn't you rather have her kill him than do so yourselves?"

Everybody had now gathered but Steve. When questioned, the other drivers disclaimed all knowledge of his whereabouts or his peculiar behavior. But they knew perfectly of both. One artfully sidetracked the whole painful discussion by saying, "Steve ain't neber been no good deer driver nohow."

Tyler Somerset, a prince of backwoodsmen, drew me aside. "Say," he said, "I know what went on back there. You can't fool me. That's the smartest darky I ever did see. More than once he outran that buck. And he sure can dodge buckshot. I wonder where he got that red and white flag he used to turn that old buck?"

We made several other drives that day. Five more stags were slain. But the buck and the shot of the lady in green remained the records. On those later drives Steve put in no appearance.

When my friends were safely gone, Steve shambled out of hiding to claim his just reward. I loaded him down with Christmas.

"By the way," I said, "some of the standers told me that you headed that buck with a red and white flag. Where did you get that?"

Steve grinned with massive shyness, as he does only when anything feminine comes to his mind. "Dat's de biggest chance I took—wusser dan dodging buckshot. Dat was Amnesia's Sunday petticoat."

"Huh," I muttered with gloomy foreboding. "If she ever finds that one out, I'll have to take you to the hospital."

"Cap'n, I done arrange it," he told me—the old schemer! "I did tore seven holes in it with all that wavin'; but I tole Amnesia I was ashamed to have my gal wear a raggety petticoat, and you was gwine give me a dollar, and I was gwine give it to her to buy a new one for Christmas."

That Christmas Eve Stag

This piece appears in An American Hunter *(pages 398–406). It is one of many Rutledge tales recounting experiences with Prince Alston, his friend since boyhood whom he deemed "a companion to my heart." The Rutledge boys are involved as well, and ultimately fortune shines on their hunt, even if it doesn't really bring full and final resolution to a problem Prince faced back on the home front.*

Nearly all hunting in the Northern states closes before the middle of December. Having been abroad on several zero days near the end of the season, I have heartily wished that it had closed earlier. But in the South some seasons for hunting are open until late in the winter; and on the great plantations venison and wild turkey for Christmas and New Year are standard fare. Not to have a stag hanging up on Christmas Eve is to confess a certain degree of enfeebled manhood—almost a social disgrace.

When I met my Negro driver Prince on the morning of that famous Christmas Eve, I could tell from his mien and general attitude that something was heavy on his mind. A thought of any kind on a Negro's mind—barring the joyous fundamentals of eating and sleeping—is likely to be depressing.

*"Old Buckshot," Rutledge's son
Archibald Rutledge Jr. From
the Elise Rutledge Bradford
Collection*

"What's the matter, Prince?" I asked. "Did you tie your horse last night with a slip-knot round his neck?"

"Not this time," the good Negro assured me. "But I was just thinkin', Cap'n, that all these years we been huntin' deer together we ain't neber yet done hang up a buck on Christmas Eve."

"Well, let's do it to-day."

"We can try, Cap'n. But my wife done say we ought to be gwine to church 'stead of hunt."

"I see," I said, understanding his difficulty. "You think we are on the down-grade when we hunt on Christmas Eve?"

A gleam of humor came into Prince's eyes. "Cap'n, it ain't that; but we must use this day to show my woman that Christmas is a good time to hunt. If we can't bring nothin' back to-night, she gwine say, 'Ain't I done tole you, you tri-flin' sinner?'"

Prince had put it over to me that we must prove our moral soundness by bringing home a buck. I had never hunted deer before for this especial reason; but as I intended hunting anyway, I didn't mind that reason tagging along with me. Yet so long and so well had Prince hunted with me that whatever affected him had its influence on me. And as that day in the woods advanced, the taunt of Prince's wife seemed to have more and more in it. Eleven deer we started—six of them full-antlered bucks—but my three boys and I didn't get a shingle shot. It was a day on which all breaks broke the other way. Perhaps the most extraordinary escape of a stag is a matter worth recording.

For several seasons we had seen a huge creature that we had christened the Blackhorn Buck. He was one of those oversize men of the woods, and his antlers were massive, craggy, and swarthy. The buck seemed to have a body as big as a swell-front barrel.

Well, after posting us at Fox Bay, Prince was riding back to the tail of the drive when he rode up this old monster. Of course, the deer headed the wrong way. Mounted on a fleet and sure-footed pony, Prince undertook to race the stag to turn him. Helped somewhat by a header that the old buck took over a fallen log, the Negro actually got ahead of the deer. Both stopped, some twenty feet apart, horse panting and buck panting, looking at each other curiously.

But it's a darn hard thing to make a deer right-about-face, especially if he has a notion that he is the object of herding tactics. The Blackhorn estimated his chances, saw a stretch of fallen timber marking the wake of a summer storm, and lithely rocked away over the obstructions. The horse could not follow.

"If I done had a rope," Prince declared to me, his honest face glistening with the perspiration of his effort to give us sport, "or just a sling-shot, we might've had him."

"Or if it hadn't been Christmas Eve," I reminded him soberly.

By the time this deer escaped us, the sun was burning low in the crests of the yellow pines, and we knew that we might as well turn homeward. Our party divided. Some took a short cut through the woods to the house; but my two older boys, Prince, and I traveled the road.

Now I'm ready to tell you about this Christmas Eve buck. We got into the highway by the Brick Church. Before us lay a straight stretch of broad road three miles long—a stretch that was used as a race-track in Revolutionary days. The last rays of the setting sun were glinting in the forest, and the wildwoods as far as we could see were suffused with a rosy light. But despite the beauty of it all, our hearts were dejected. We were going home on Christmas Eve without a thing to show for our long day's hunt.

We had come a half mile down the road in our complaining little car, with Prince's walking horse almost able to keep up with us. I saw something skulk across the road about two hundred yards ahead of us, heading for Montgomery Branch, a dense thicket of pine and bays just off the road to the right.

"Turkeys!" I said, jamming on the brake so suddenly that the tiny car tried to stand on her nose.

Violently I waved for Prince to come up. The three of us piled out of the car and began loading our guns with turkey-shot.

Prince was with us in a moment. In another he had the whole situation straight. "I'll ride ahead and around," he said.

"You go across the branch. Put one boy in the thicket and leave the other on this side. Christmas Eve ain't done over yet!" he added with twinkling eyes.

I left my Gunnerman, as I call my second boy, in a tiny patch of bays a hundred yards on the near side of Montgomery—just half-way between the road and the branch. My eldest boy I posted in the branch itself, while I stole quickly forward into the open country beyond.

Just as I was emerging from the fringes of the dewy thicket, I heard a sound ahead. Then I saw a tall white flag! If I hadn't had turkey-shot in my gun, I might have let drive at him. In a moment he was lost in a thicket of young pines.

Creeping forward, I took a stand for the turkeys. At any moment they might come through the broomsedge in their swift, jerky fashion. But nary a turkey did I see or hear. The sun set. The woods seemed full of shadows. I could hear Prince riding down the thicket toward us. There seemed to be no game in front of him. When it comes to giving the hunter the slip, wild turkeys must always be given an A No. 1 rating.

I turned back toward the thicket, and was half-way through it when I heard my eldest son call out. All I could catch was "A buck!" At the same moment I heard something split the bay-bushes wide open. I dashed forward to get into the open for a shot, at the same time changing my turkey-shot for buckshot. By the time I had cleared the branch, the buck had done the same thing.

The scene that followed is imprinted on my memory as vividly as any recollection I have of the wildwoods during nearly forty years of roaming in them. The buck broke the thicket about seventy yards to my right, running as if he had just turned into the home stretch of a quarter mile Olympic race. Directly ahead of me stood my little Gunner. He had heard his brother call. He saw what I saw.

I was afraid to shout to him; besides, he appeared to be taking in the situation. Yet he was in acute distress. His gun was in his left hand, unbreeched. He had the turkey-shot shells out. His right hand was jammed in the tight pocket of his corduroy trousers, from which he was trying to pull out the buckshot shells. He could get his hand out, but not his hand and the shells too.

Meanwhile the buck, running on a curious arc, was coming for him, apparently gaining momentum at every leap. I have seen many a deer run in my time, and certainly they have showed me some breezy capers. But I do not think I ever saw a deer run like this one. I believe that deer feel unusually frisky at twilight, and they often frolic then just for the fun of the thing. Are they not limbering themselves after a long day's rest, and do they not feel the glamour of the twilight, just as we do—or at least to some degree?

I remember roaming the pine-lands after sunset one January day and coming upon a stag that had just begun to feed. He did some fancy jumping that I have never seen another deer do—cavorting over high bushes, blowing through his nose, and then making a few more spectacular leaps, just like a pony that plays with you and won't let you catch him.

But the deer that was headed for my Gunner was not putting on any flourishes. He was just plain scared, and was running as a ringneck does when he means to get away and doesn't care to take wing. Wildly this buck ran, low to the ground, skimming over the bushes and the logs like an incredibly swift hurdler doing his stuff. He seemed to glimmer between the trees. The fading light emphasized the speed at which he was going. Probably he knew that he was in the same fix as were the chargers of the Light Brigade, who, as we learned back yonder in school days, had

Cannon to right of them,
Cannon to left of them.

When he thinks he is cornered, that is the time a deer is going to show you how to get out of a corner in a hurry. Indeed, in one sense, you can't corner a deer.

I could see from the course he was taking that the buck would run about thirty yards from my boy, crossing his front. I could see that the stander now had the breech of his gun closed. He was awaiting the moment. Between him and the deer, as the fugitive got directly in front of him, there would be a tiny pine about four feet high—a young yellow pine with a bushy top. I wondered how the Gunner would manage that obstruction. I didn't have long to wonder. The twilight hurricane was upon him. The buck looked very curious. His tail was down, his head and neck far outstretched. He was in the utmost extremity of speed.

Up went the gun with steady precision. A second later came one barrel. I saw two things distinctly: the top of the little pine was shot away, and the stag flinched, changing his stride. Such a bit of behavior is said to indicate that a deer is certainly hit. But it seems to me that a deer will sometimes flinch from the sound of a gun, if it is close to him—just as he will sometimes execute a dodging maneuver after the first shot has been fired at him. Many a hunter has claimed to have shot down a deer, when, as a matter of fact, the crafty stag has only dodged.

Whether struck or not, this buck gave no evidence of having any difficulty in getting away. I wondered why my Gunner did not salute him with the second barrel. Straight toward the sunset ran the stag, far through the rosy woods— a beautiful but heartbreaking sight. My chief feeling was one of pity for my Gunner. I knew how he would mind this. Yet that flinching of the deer. Had he really been missed?

A full three hundred yards I watched the fleeing stag. Then he vanished in a tall growth of weeds by an old abandoned sawmill.

In another moment I was with my boy. "I think you struck him," I said. "How about the second barrel?"

"My pocket was so tight," he said, "that I couldn't pull out both shells at once, and I didn't have time to pull them out one by one."

He looked peaked and miserable, as a hunter will look after missing a fair shot at a stag.

With my hand on his shoulder, he and I started to look for any signs of blood, but the light was so bad that we couldn't see a thing to encourage us. My elder boy meanwhile came up, and Prince rode up expectantly. What he saw in my face confirmed the superstition that had haunted us both all day.

"'Bout five turkey done fly up and gone back," he announced.

"Well," I told him, "at least one buck flew by there and has gone ahead."

The dusk of Christmas Eve was fast settling down—on the world and in our hearts.

"Prince," I said, "this deer flinched at the crack of the gun."

He grinned good-humoredly. "If anybody would shoot at me, Cap'n, I would flinch too. He was so close," he went on, taking on the tone of the professional hunter, "he would sure have come down."

"Well, anyhow," I told him, "ride down yonder by the old camp and see if you can see any sign at all."

My boys searched about disconsolately for blood-signs while Prince rode down the glimmering ridge. He was out of my mind for a few moments until I heard the whoop of whoops. Looking toward the far-off camp, I could barely see him, his hand raised high in ecstatic triumph, while the wildwoods rang with his superb shouts of victory.

"Gunner," I said to my young huntsman, "you killed that buck. Prince has him now."

Together the three of us ran through the darkening woods. When we came to the place, the Negro was on the ground beside the fallen stag. A beauty he was—in his prime, with good antlers. He lay just within the shelter of the tall dead weeds into which I had seem him vanish.

A joyous home-coming we had that Christmas Eve. On the plantation the Negroes take the killing of a fine deer as an occasion for much festive hilarity, and certainly the white hunter has in his heart rejoicings of his own. In state we hung up the Gunner's buck, and then went in to a wild turkey dinner and an hour of perfect peace, yarning before the great open fireside.

I must add that when the stag was dressed we found that one of the three buckshot that struck him had passed straight through his heart. I examined it very carefully to be certain of the fact. Yet he had run nearly a quarter of a mile at top speed without a hesitation or a blunder. The vitality of wild game is a thing almost incredible.

After a day that ended so happily, I had to have a little talk with Prince before saying good-night to him. "Well," I asked, "what does your wife have to say now about our hunting on Christmas Eve? Doesn't this deer prove to her that she was wrong?"

"Cap'n," said Prince soberly, "I ain't never can't prove nothin' to a woman what she ain't want to believe. She done say this luck was a acci-dent."

And the more I think of Sue's description of our good fortune, the more inclined am I to believe that she was right.

That Christmas Buck

Originally published in the January 1920 issue of Field & Stream *(pages 833–35), replete with an illustration from noted wildlife artist Hy Watson, this piece was subsequently included in* Plantation Game Trails *(pages 216–25). Its thrust, involving a full ration of frustration succeeded by one crowning moment of glorious success, is one with which any serious hunter can surely identify.*

*W*hen I am at large in deer country there is no need for friends to try to lure me off the fascinating following of the whitetail by promises of more abundant sport with smaller game. Quail and ducks and woodcock and the like do not look very good when a man feels that an old buck with majestic antlers is waiting in the woods for someone to talk business to him. I admit that the game of deer-hunting is sometimes tedious and the shooting of the occasional variety; yet my experience has been that the great chance does come to the faithful, and that to make good on it is to drink one of Life's rarest juleps, the memory of whose flavor is a delight for years.

It may be that this love of deer-hunting was not only born in me—the men of my family always having been sportsmen—but was made ingrowing by a curious happening that occurred when I was not a year old. One day I was left alone in a large room in the plantation house where first I saw the light of day. Lying thus in my crib, what should come roaming in but a pet buck that we had. My mother, in the greatest dismay, found him bending over me, while, if we may believe the account, I had hold of the old boy's horns and was crowing with delight. I have always felt sure that the old stag (since he knew that his own hide was safe) passed me the mystic word concerning the rarest sport on earth. He put it across to me, all right; and I am going to do my best here to hand on the glad tidings. I want to tell about a deer-hunt we had on Christmas not long past.

Things on the plantation had been going badly with me. There were plenty of deer about, and a most unusual number of very large bucks; but our hunting-party had achieved nothing of a nature worth recording. We had been at the business nearly a week, and we were still eating pork instead of venison. That's humiliating; indeed, in a sense, degrading. On a certain Wednesday (we had begun to hunt on the Thursday previous) I took our Negro driver aside. It was just after we had made three unsuccessful drives, and just after some of the hunters had given me a look that, interpreted, seemed to mean that I could easily be sold to a sideshow as the only real fakir in captivity. In the lee of a great pine I addressed my partner in crime.

"Prince," I said, drawing a flask from my pocket, "as deer-hunters you and I aren't worth a Continental damn." (This term, as my readers know, is a good one, sound and true, having been the name of a coin minted before the Revolution.)

"Dat's so, sah, suttinly so," Prince admitted, his eyes glued to the flask, his tongue moistening his lips.

"Now," I went on, "we are going to drive this Little Horseshoe. Tell me where to stand so that we can quit this fooling."

The flask sobered Prince marvelously, as I knew it would. To a Negro there is no tragedy like seeing a drink without getting it; and the possibility of such a disaster made the good-natured Prince grave.

"Dis summer," he said, "I done see where an able buck done used to navigate regular by the little gum-tree pond. Dat must be he social walk," he further explained; "and dat may be he regular run. You stop there, Cap'n, and if he is home, you will bline he eye."

That sounded good to me. Therefore, the calamity that Prince dreaded might happen did not occur for we parted in high spirits, and with high spirits in at least one of us. But there must have been a prohibition jinx prowling about, for what happened shortly thereafter appeared like the work of an evil fate.

As I was posting the three standers, the man who had already missed four deer took a fancy to the stand by the gum-tree pond. I tried politely to suggest that there was a far better place, for him, but he remained obdurate. I therefore let him stay at what Prince had described as the critical place. And it was not five minutes later that Prince's far-resounding shout told me that a stag was afoot. Feeling sure that the buck would run for the pond, I stood up on a log, and from that elevation I watched him do it. He was a bright, cherry-red buck, and his horns would have made an armchair for ex-President Taft. He ran as if he had it in his crafty mind to run over the stander by the pond and trample him. He, poor fellow, missed the buck with both barrels. His roaring ten-gauge gun made enough noise to have stunned the buck; but the red-coated monarch serenely continued his march. All this happened near sundown, and it was the end of a perfectly doleful day. Prince laid the blame for the bull on me when he said, in mild rebuke:

"How, Cap'n, make you didn't put a true gunnerman to the critical place?"

The next day—the seventh straight that we had been hunting—it was an uncle of mine who got the shot. And this thing happened not a quarter of a mile from where the other business had come off. My uncle and I were hardly a hundred yards apart in the open, level, sun-shiny pine-woods. Before us was a wide thicket of bays about five feet high. The whole stretch covered about ten acres. Prince was riding through it, whistling on the hounds. Suddenly I heard a great bound in the bays. Prince's voice rang out—but a second shout was stifled by him designedly. A splendid buck had been roused. He made just about three bounds and then stopped. He knew very well that he was cornered, and he was evidently wondering how to cut the corners. The deer was broadside to my uncle and only about fifty yards off. I saw him carefully level his gun. At the shot the buck, tall antlers and all, collapsed under the bay-bushes.

Then the lucky hunter, though he is a good woodsman, did a wrong thing. Leaning his gun against a pine, he began to run forward toward his quarry, dragging out his hunting-knife as he ran. When he was within ten yards of the buck the thing happened. The stunned stag (tall horns and all) leaped clear of danger, and away he went rocking through the pine-lands. Believing that the wound might be a fatal one, we followed the buck a long way. Finally, meeting a Negro woodsman who declared that the buck had passed him "running like the wind," we abandoned the chase. A buckshot had probably struck the animal on the spine, at the base of the skull, or on a horn. Perhaps the buck simply dodged under cover at the shot; I have known a deer so to sink into tall broom-sedge.

That night our hunting-party broke up. Only Prince and I were left on the plantation. Before we parted that evening I said:

"You and I are going out to-morrow. And we'll take one hound. We'll walk it."

The next day, to our astonishment, we found a light snow on the ground—a rare phenomenon in the Carolina woods. We knew that it would hardly last for the day; but it might help us for a while.

In the first thicket that we walked through a buck fawn came my way. He was a handsome little fellow, dark in color and chunky in build. It is possible to distinguish the sex of a fawn even when the lithe creature is on the fly, for the doe invariably has a longer and sharper head and gives evidence of a slenderer, more delicate build. I told the bucklet that I would revisit him when he had something manly on his head.

Prince and I next circled Fawn Pond, a peculiar pond fringed by bays. Our hound seemed to think that somebody was at home here. And we did see tracks in the snow that entered the thicket; however, on the farther side we discerned them departing. But they looked so big and so fresh that we decided to follow them. Though the snow was melting fast I thought the tracks looked as if two bucks had made them. Deer in our part of the Carolinas are so unused to snow that its presence makes them very uncomfortable, and they do much wandering about in daylight when it is on the ground.

Distant from Fawn Pond a quarter of a mile through the open woods was Black Tongue Branch, a splendid thicket, so named because once there had been found on its borders a great buck that had died of that plague of the deer family—the black tongue, or anthrax. Deciding to stay on the windward side (for a roused deer loves to run up the wind), I sent Prince down to the borders of the branch, telling him to cross it, when together the two of us would flank it out. The tracks of the deer seemed to lead toward Black Tongue, but we lost them before we came to the place itself. While I waited for Prince and the leashed hound to cross the end of the narrow thicket, I sat on a pine-lot and wondered whether our luck that day was to change. Suddenly, from the green edges of the day I was aware of Prince beckoning violently for me to come to him. I sprang up. But we were too slow. From a deep head of bays and myrtles, not twenty steps from where the Negro was standing, out there rocked into the open woods as splendid a buck as it has ever been my fortune to see. He had no sooner cleared the bushes than he was followed by his companion, a creature fit to be his mate. They were two old comrades of many a danger. Their haunches looked as broad as the tops of hogsheads. Their flags were spectacular. They were just about two hundred yards from me, and, of course, out of gunshot. Had I been with Prince at that moment (as I had been up to that fatal time) I should have had a grand chance—a chance such as does not come even to a hardened hunter more than a few times in a hundred years or so. The bucks held a steady course straight away from me; and their pace was a rocking, rhythmic, leisurely one. Speechless, I watched them go for half a mile; my heart was pretty nearly broken. As for Prince—when I came up to him, I found him quite miserable and unnerved.

"Oh, Cap'n, if you had only been where I been just now!" was all he could say.

From the direction that the two great animals had taken the Negro and I thought that we knew just where they were going. Telling him to hold the hound for about fifteen minutes, I took a long circle in the woods, passing several fine thickets where the old boys might well have paused, and came at last to a famous stand on a lonely road. Soon I heard the lone hound open on the track, and you can imagine with what eagerness I awaited the coming of what was before him.

The dog came straight for me; but when he broke through the last screen of bays he was alone. The deer had gone on. It was not hard to find where they had crossed the road some ten yards from where I had been standing. Judging from the easy way in which they were running, they were not in the least worried. And from that crossing onward they had a perfect right not to be concerned; for beyond the old road lay a wild region of swamp and morass into which the hunter can with no wisdom or profit go.

I did not stop the dog, deciding that by mere chance the bucks might, if run right, dodge back and forth, and so give me the opportunity for which I was looking. The old hound did his best; and the wary antlered creatures, never pushed hard, did some cunning dodging before him. Once again I saw them far away through the woodlands, but a glimpse of their distant beauty was all the comfort afforded me. After a two-hour chase the hound gave them up. Prince and I had to confess that we had been outwitted, and in a crestfallen mood we quitted the hunt for the day.

The next day was my last one at home; and every hunter is surely familiar with the feeling of the man who, up until the last day, has not brought his coveted game to bag. I felt that we should have luck on our side or else be beaten. I told Prince as much, and he promised to be on hand at daybreak.

Before dawn I was awakened by the sound of steady winter rain softly roaring on the shingle roof of the old plantation house. It was discouraging, to be sure; but I did not forget that the rain ushered in my last day. By the time I was dressed Prince had come up. He was wet and cold. He reported that the wind was blowing from the northeast. Conditions were anything but promising. However, we had hot coffee, corncakes deftly turned by Prince, and a cheering smoke. After such reinforcement weather can be hanged. By the time that the dim day had broadened we ventured forth into the stormy pine-lands, where the towering trees were rocking continuously, and where the rain seemed able to search us out, however we tried to keep to the leeward of every sheltering object. The two dogs that we had compelled to come with us were wet and discouraged. Their heads, I knew, were full of happy visions of the warm plantation fireside that they had been forced to leave. Besides, it was by no means their last day, and their spirit was utterly lacking in all the elements of enthusiasm.

After about four barren drives, when Prince and I were soaked quite through and were beginning to shiver despite precautions that we took (in Southern deer-hunting a "precaution" means only one thing), I said:

"Now Hunterman, this next drive is our last. We'll try the Little Corner, and hope for the best."

Two miles through the rainy woods I plodded to take up my stand. All the while I took to do this Prince waited, his back against a pine, and with the sharp, cold rain searching him out. The wind made the great pines rock and sigh. Even if the dogs should break into full chorus I thought I could never hear them coming. At last I reached my stand. A lonely place it was, four miles from home, and in a region of virgin forest. So much of the wide woodland through which I had come looked so identical that it hardly seemed reasonable to believe that a deer, jumped two miles back in a thicket, would run to this particular place. But men who know deer nature know what a deer will do. I backed up against an old sweet-gum tree, waiting in that solitary, almost savage place. I thought that in about a half-hour my good driver, bedraggled and weary, would come into sight, and that then we two disillusioned ones would go home sloshing through the drizzle.

But wonderful things happen to men in the big woods. Their apparently insane faith is not infrequently rewarded. Hardly had I settled myself against the big tree for shelter when, far off, in a momentary lulling of the grieving wind, I heard the voice of a hound. One of the dogs had a deep bass note, and it was this that I heard. Sweet music it was to my ears, you may well believe! From where I was standing I could see a good half-mile toward the thickets whence had come the hound's mellow, rain-softened note. And now, as I looked searchingly in that direction, I saw the deer, heading my way, and coming at a wild and breakneck pace. At that distance I took the fugitive for a doe. It was running desperately, with head low, and lithe, powerful legs eating up the pine-land spaces. If it held its course it would pass fifty yards to the left of me. I turned and ran crouchingly until I thought I had reached a place directly in the oncoming deer's pathway. I was in a slight hollow; and the easy rise of ground in front of me hid for a few moments the approaching racer. I fully expected a big doe to bound over the rise and to run slightly on my left. I had a slight suspicion that the deer might be an old buck, with small, poor horns that on my first and distant view had not been visible. But it was not so.

Hardly had I reached my new stand when over the gentle swell of ground, grown in low broom grass, there came a mighty rack of horns forty yards away to my right. Then the whole buck came full into view. There were a good many fallen logs just there, and these he was maneuvering with a certainty and a grace and a strength that it was a sight to behold. But I was there for more than just "for to admire."

As he was clearing a high obstruction I gave him the right barrel. I distinctly saw two buckshot strike him high up—too high. He never winced or broke his stride. Throwing the gun for his shoulder, I fired. This brought him down—but by no means headlong, though, as I afterwards ascertained that twelve buckshot from the choke barrel had gone home. The buck seemed crouching on the ground, his grand crowned head held high, and never in wild nature have I seen a more anciently crafty expression than that on his face. I think he had not seen me before I shot; and even now he turned his head warily from side to side, his mighty horns rocking with the motion. He was looking for his enemy. I have had a good many experiences with the behavior of wounded bucks; therefore I reloaded my gun and with some circumspection approached the fallen monarch. But my caution was needless. The old chieftain's last race was over. By the time I reached him that proud head was lowered and the fight was done.

Mingled were my feelings as I stood looking down on that perfect specimen of the deer family. He was in his full prime. Though somewhat lean and rangy because this was toward the close of the mating season, his condition was splendid. The hair on his neck and about the back of his haunches was thick and long and dark. His hoofs were very large, but as yet unbroken. His antlers were, considering all points of excellence, very fine. They bore ten points.

My short reverie was interrupted by the clamorous arrival of the two hounds. These I caught and tied up. Looking back toward the drive, I saw Prince coming, running full speed. The dogs had not had much on him in the race. When he came up and saw what had happened, wide was the happy smile that broke like dawn on his dusky face.

"Did you see him in the drive, Prince?" I asked. "He surely is a beauty."

"See him?" the Negro ejaculated in joyous excitement. "Cap'n dat ole thing been lyin' so close that when he done jump up he throw sand in my eye! I done reach for he big tail to ketch him! But I done know," he ended, "dat somebody else been waitin' to ketch him."

I sent Prince home for a horse on which we could get the buck out of the woods. While he was gone I had a good chance to look over the prone monarch. He satisfied me. And the chief element in that satisfaction was the feeling that, after weary days, mayhap, and after adverse experiences, the great chance will come. For my part that Christmas hunt taught me that it is worthwhile to spend some empty days for a day brimmed with sport. And one of the lasting memories of my life is the recollection of that cold, rainy day in the Southern pinelands—my last day for that hunting trip—and my best.

All of a Christmas Morning

This piece first appeared in the January 1931 issue of Outdoor Life *(pages12–13, 67) and subsequently in the book many consider Rutledge's finest,* An American Hunter *(pages 251–60). There were appreciable revisions in the latter version; the one published here is the original. While there is no indication of the precise year in which this hunt took place, it was during Rutledge's earlier years at Mercersburg*

Academy, when his three boys were youngsters. Since he indicates he had been hunting whitetails "exactly forty years," Rutledge was likely a tad shy of fifty years of age. That places the hunt around 1929 or 1930. It represents Rutledge at his best as a storyteller, showing a real flair for setting a scene. Knowledgeable deer hunters will readily recognize the depth of woodsman's skills manifested in this piece.

*A*ccording to an old English custom, instead of going to church on Christmas morning, we went deer hunting. As the whole affair was typical of this type of Southern sport, yet unique in its thrilling details, an account of it seems worth recording. If any other man is as daft as I am about following stags, he will realize that this pastime can be a sort of religious rite; and that therefore its performance on December 25 is not at all out of keeping with the season.

Because of a series of mishaps, my pack of hounds on this memorable occasion had been reduced to a single beagle puppy, aged six months. She had been bred in the North, and was now for the first time to be tried on deer. Yet little Bing was to show me that, to a blooded hound, game is game; for she transferred her interest from bunnies to bucks as naturally as if there were no essential difference between them.

Our hunt assembled at "Hampton," our plantation on the Santee, in South Carolina, at seven o'clock in the morning. We had six Negro drivers, all on foot; and most of them literally, for shoes come high in that hinterland. These men are good woodsmen, and they have become good deer hunters. Gabe, Steve, Will, Prince, Sammy, and Lewis composed our band of dusky henchmen. My three boys and I were the standers.

Wherever the whitetail is hunted, the general conditions are much the same, regardless of the character of the country or the method of the hunt. The big idea is to get a good shot at a stag; and a buck of the southern pinelands is the same superb, wary strategist that he is in Michigan, in Texas, in the Adirondacks—wherever he may be followed.

While occasionally a hunter may get a dead-easy shot at one, as a rule, to kill a fine buck fairly is a genuine achievement; and those who have hunted deer longest realize most deeply the truth of such a statement. And in proportion to the arduousness of the sport is the joy of bringing to bag one of these sagacious old veterans, than which there is no nobler wild creature in America, and, all things considered, in creation.

Immediately in front of the plantation house I have about a hundred acres of fields, in which the deer feed freely during the summer months; and throughout the winter they wander back there in search of remnants of what once so satisfied their hunger. Three miles from home there is an immense and inviolate swamp known as "The Ocean," and it is the best natural sanctuary for deer that

I have ever seen. Neither dog nor man can safely follow a deer into that wilderness of morasses and gloomy, snake-haunted thickets. Harboring in "The Ocean," the deer at night troop forth, to roam the pinelands and the plantations adjacent to the river. They usually return to their fastness about dawn, but occasionally they lie out in the river thickets and the great broomsedge fields in the woods. It is with these outliers that we always have our sport.

Beyond our fields, and to the eastward down the margins of the river, we have an ancient shrubbery, some eighty acres in extent. Here giant pines and massive live oaks tower over the dense greenery of the copses; and here both wild turkeys and deer delight to roam. When they decide to bed for the day in this "Pasture," as we call this wilderness of sweet greenery, and we start them out of it, they nearly always head toward "The Ocean"; and making, as all deer are accustomed to do, pretty regular runs, we can generally intercept them at the stands. The river is behind them; and they will not take that, as a rule, unless they are wounded.

I took the first stand at the bend of the plantation road; my youngest son was second; my eldest boy, third, and my second son I sent far down on the last stand. He is exceedingly woodwise, and is active; and as a result he was stationed at a critical spot.

As the morning was warm and still, with the dew glinting on the pine needles and the world half-asleep, we could hear the drivers when they put in next to the river, three-quarters of a mile to the north of us. They were stretched in a line, and were about two hundred yards apart.

Our experience is that deer behave very differently in the matter of getting up to the whoops of drivers. They dread the scent of a man, but they are by no means so timorous of the human voice. Repeatedly I have known a stag to keep his bed until a driver, whooping as if prohibition had been repealed, had come within twenty yards of him. As a matter of fact, he probably does not associate whooping with essential danger. Negroes range the woods all year, driving turpentine wagons, shouting at their mules; and all these noises deer are accustomed to. Many a time deer are passed by drivers who are giving all they have in the way of things vocal. They are somewhat indifferent also to the voices of trailing hounds. They may become alert, but they commonly do not rouse themselves until the dogs are upon them. I once heard a Negro driver say: "Dat ole buck wouldn't git up till Trigger done git *in de bed* wid him!"

We have our drivers trained so that when they start something, they "step on her" as far as the shouting is concerned, giving, in their aboriginal but most effective fashion, the ancient "view halloo."

I stood looking toward the misty greenery of the "Pasture"; hearing robins beginning to feed in the tall tupelos; seeing fox squirrels angling in the big pine cones for mast; listening to the sibilant sliding of the dew from the aromatic leaves of the myrtle and the bay. But I heard no excitement among our drivers, and I heard not a sound from little Bing—our pack.

Bing's brother I had given to a friend; well, you know about these gift dogs! The man to whom I had presented the puppy told me that he had taken the youngster into the woods to try him on deer. An old doe ambled out of her bed in the broom grass in front of them, whereupon my friend took Buck to let him get the hot scent. The morning being rather frosty, and the pup none too enthusiastic, he turned around in the bed, found it warm, and promptly lay down there and went fast asleep!

In about ten minutes Steve came whooping up to my stand, and there was nothing ahead of him except his voice. Steve is a good driver because he is always vastly hungry, and a deer means a dinner to him. As he came up to me, I joined him, and together we started down the road toward the other standers. The other drivers were almost out to them, and I felt that I at least would get no chance in that drive.

"Didn't see a thing?" I asked.

"No, sah, and I don't know how cum either, 'caze I done wash my feet las' night."

For some reason Steve has always attached good luck to this rare ceremony of his.

"Who is that way back by the river?" I asked.

"Dat's Prince," he said; "he done gone down deep in that river corner with Bing."

"He's a long way behind you all," I said.

"I dream 'bout a buck las' night," Steve said earnestly. "We gwine hang one up today."

At that instant I heard Irvine, my youngest son, shoot. He was about a hundred yards down the road from us. Almost immediately came two other barrels. Then I heard the voice of Bing—a high pitched, infant treble—"Yipe, yip, yap, yipe!"

Then there were sounds of confused yelling, and running, and calling of the tiny hound.

"Three shots," I said to Steve, as we began to run forward. "They call for three deer."

"But sometimes, Cap'n" he sagely answered, "we call for more than we git."

When Steve and I reached Irvine's stand, the entire Hampton Hunt was there gathered; and nobody seemed to know exactly what had happened, or how much had been done. As far as execution was concerned, there was no evidence of any.

Prince, it seems, had started a splendid buck down by the river, and it had come straight out, with Bing after it. Before it reached Irvine, seeing him in the road, it had flared to the right. He had taken a long drag at it, but without apparent effect. By great good chance, my second son, Middleton, who had had the last stand, thinking the drive was over, had moved up between his brothers; and as the old buck sailed off to the right, he offered this boy of mine a right-hand quartering shot—always a mean one, I think. He gave the stag both barrels.

"He went down when I first shot," Middleton told me, "but I just took a snap at him the second time when he got up. I never saw a deer run so in all my life. Here's where he crossed the road."

"No blood?" I asked.

"Ain't a blood," old Gabe lamented.

But I have long since learned that a mortally wounded deer, shot with buckshot, may at first throw no blood. And I have also learned that if a deer runs as if demented after he is fired upon, he is probably badly hit. If he "changes his stride," he is certainly hit.

Into a long pine thicket flanked by a wild watercourse of bays and gall berries, the stag had gone. What should we do? Bing seemed the only member of our entire hunt who was not crushed and crestfallen and all that. She was all eagerness to be up and after the fascinating gentleman with the heavy scent that she had made bound from his bed in the little pines by the old pond.

"Steve," I said, "it looks to me as if something is wrong with your religion. You dreamed about a buck, and you washed your feet, and now the buck gets away."

Sammy and Lewis began to snicker over Steve's responsibility and his chagrin.

"Maybe," Sammy suggested, "Steve ain't wash but *one* foot."

Steve protested volubly, but all of us drowned him out, leaving him with the impression that he was a sad backslider.

Stooping down once more to examine the buck's tracks, I noticed that, where he had hit the road, the hoof marks were sprawled out amazingly. Of course, the ground being fairly hard and the deer on a dead run, such sprawling was to be expected; yet there was something about these tracks that made me think the stag had lost control of himself. His desperate run was only swift staggering. So I hoped. Therefore I turned to the hunt and said, "Middleton shot the buck down; Bing is rarin' to go. Let's have a race."

But little did I think of what a sudden and dramatic end that race would have!

In following deer with hounds, in the case of a wounded stag it is always a question whether the dogs should be permitted to run him, or whether to break them off. Much depends on the apparent nature of his wounds. And, though I have hunted deer exactly forty years, and have always tried to watch carefully their reaction to a wound received, I confess that it is almost impossible to tell how far one will go. I have often seen a deer go headlong at a shot, apparently dead; yet scuffle up, gain momentum, and eventually get clear away. And I have seen deer go off after a shot as if the sound of the gun cheered them on to show some real style in running, yet drop dead after a superb display of what seemed to be physical perfection. But, after all, it is much the same with everything else that is hunted. In shooting deer with buckshot, a common experience is to "crease" one; that is, to tip his backbone with a shot, at which he will drop as if struck by lightning only to be up and away in a moment, as sound as ever.

The danger of letting your pack go on a wounded deer is that the dogs may run him for hours, clear out of your hunting territory; and that your hunt for the day will therefore be disorganized. In fact, it may be a week before you recapture some of your hounds.

But as our pack on this occasion was a strictly nursery affair, and, as the buck had behaved as if he were really wounded, I thought it wise to let Bing go.

She needed no encouragement; I think she smelt blood. At any rate, away she dashed after the lordly stag, a white midget not much bigger than an under-sized rabbit. I thought that any one of my Negro drivers could catch her at any time in her mad pursuit.

We followed in a kind of mock-hilarious fashion, with not much "real faith or hope in our hearts." But it did us good to see the puppy streak away under the pines, her infant voice waking the old wildwoods. It was then just after sun-rise on Christmas morning, and the whole world was softly reddened by the warm and glorious sunlight.

Suddenly my eldest son, who was in the lead, gave a wild shout; this was echoed by the driver nearest him. The next thing I knew, I had caught sight of little Bing trying to hold down one of the biggest stags I have ever seen in the woods. In fact, he was down, but was struggling to rise; but Bing had nailed him in the haunch, and even her puny strength he could not resist. Up we crowded, an excited and happy lot of Christmas hunters, gathered about this fallen monarch of the great pinelands and the lonely swamps. His race was run. He needed no *coup de grace*. By the time the Steve reached us, the stag was dead.

Upon examining his wounds, I found that four buckshot had struck him broadside, high up. The fatal shot must have injured his spine, a fact that accounted for his falling. Then, his prodigious run had literally broken his back; for when we dressed him, his backbone was severed. I have seen larger horns and more handsome horns; but seldom have I ever seen a head with more gallantry in it—with that rakish jauntiness that so well expresses the character of such a cavalier of the wilderness, such a patrician of the waste lands.

Our Christmas hunt ended at eight o'clock, when we returned in triumph to the plantation house, to a breakfast of hominy, cold wild turkey, corn bread, and coffee. And as long as we live, not one of us will ever forget our hunt that Christmas morning.

A Christmas Hunt

Christmas Day hunts, often followed by sumptuous feasts, have long been a holiday tradition in the South. In my boyhood home, as was the case at Hampton Plantation, such outings were as much a part of the family celebration as the opening of gifts. Often whitetail hunts in the South Carolina Low Country involved scores of standers, a dozen or more drivers, and a mighty pack of hounds. In this piece from Those Were the Days *(pages 349–56), Rutledge opens with an overview of the typical holiday deer hunt and then turns to events associated with one that took place in Wambaw Corner, a wild, desolate tract of some eight hundred acres frequently mentioned in his hunting tales. At hunt's end there were six bucks to be dressed and shared, hearty appetites all around, and smiles on the faces of the drivers, who knew "the solid satisfaction of the assurance of plenty of venison for them and their families."*

On the old plantations of the Deep South, many of which are still in operation, and still in the hands of their original owners, there is an old tradition of having a big deer hunt on Christmas Day. In these ancient estates Christmas is probably as picturesquely celebrated as it is anywhere in the world. The Christmas found there has an old English flavor; it is the jovial Christmas of Shakespeare, of the Cavaliers, of Dickens. There are manifest the high spirit, the boisterous but wholesome cheer, the holly, the mistletoe, the smilax in wreaths, the roaring fires of oak and pine; the songs, the laughter, the happy games, and all the other festive enjoyments of the days of long ago. Whatever else may be said of those who settled the South from the court of King Charles I, who, according to Edmund Burke, "had as much pride as virtue in them," they certainly knew how to make themselves happy at Christmas; and this fortunate characteristic they have bequeathed to their far descendants. While their rollicking spirit may not be so nearly akin to that of the original Christmas as the stern joy of the sober-hearted Puritans, their hearts were warmer, and their homes were full of laughter and of light. The Puritan had the lilies and the snow and

Archibald Rutledge, attired as he usually was in high-top boots and riding pants, standing before the steps at Hampton Plantation, circa 1948

the wintry starlight of mystic love and devotion; the Cavalier had the roses, the red wine, and the ruddy fireside of human affection.

Quaintly, and very humanly, the chief business on Christmas Day on an old Southern plantation is not going to church. While the women naturally think religion should come first, they do not greatly demur when their husbands, brothers, and lovers, like the attractively boyish barbarians men always really are, decide to take to the woods.

While there is a proverb in the South that Christmas is hard on a hunter's aim, yet that is no deterrent to the annual gathering. Friends and neighbors will meet on Christmas morning at one of the great plantations—some coming in cars, and some on horseback; and behind the latter will be trailing their deer-hounds in the order of their enthusiasm. On such an occasion all the packs of the countryside hunt together. I have known as many as eighty hounds to be used on one such hunt. The presence at one of these gatherings of some plantation owners who hunt on Christmas only, and who have never been known to hit anything, offers the wags of the party a rarer sport than deer could afford. About such a holiday company there is a spirit of wholesome irresponsibility, of genial laxity, that Southern hunters, who usually take their sport with gravity, almost as if it were a religious rite, do not usually manifest.

As the wildwoods into which they are going is too rough for cars, all the hunters and the Negro deer drivers are mounted, though it must be confessed that many of them ride mules and horses that are hardly fit for the plow. But what is lacking in the elegance of equipage is compensated for by good cheer—by Christmas cheer, which is unique, wherever it is found. As the hunters ride away, to the winding of horns and the soulful yowling of the deerhounds, they appear like some cavalcade of old, riding away into the shadows of the past.

Since I have mentioned the hounds, and since they form so integral a part of the Christmas hunt, I think it well to make some remarks about them. The deerhounds of the South, usually Walkers or else Redbones, are really foxhounds trained to hunt deer. Such is the density of the cover in the rural South, even in midwinter, with gray moss shrouding the impenetrable jungles; and where, even on higher ground, evergreens such as the scrub pines, sweet bay, cane, and gallberry prevail, that deer stalking such as is practiced in the North and West is never possible. The hunter is compelled to use hounds.

I love a hound. He is the philosopher among dogs. He has a profound and genuine distrust of the general scheme of things in this life. Melancholy of an ancient and appealing sort is his. What makes his pessimism worthy of regard is the fact that it has its source in remarkable sagacity. His honest and steadfast refusal to be optimistic not only lends to his character a noble severity but also gives to his philosophy the serene charm of truth. He invariably seems to me to belong to an older and wiser generation which regards the behavior of all other living things as an exceedingly juvenile performance. A hound is the only dog that can make me conscious of my own shortcomings. Fixed by his grave appraising eyes, I shrink into my true stature. A sensitive and reflective soul, his spirit has a savor of astute meditation.

The hunters, drivers, and hounds having gathered, it must be decided what drive to take. Shall it be Boggy Bay, or the Long Corner, or the wilds of Peachtree along the South Santee River, or the Huckleberry Branch? Usually the master of the hunt makes the momentous decision. The Negro drivers, knowing these wildwoods better than white men, know exactly where to go and what to do. And with them go the hounds. They all circle until they get to the back of the drive; then they start toward the standers.

These, meanwhile, have been posted on crossings or stands. These are regular runs that deer have made since long before the Revolution. The master of the hunt will post each stander; and if he is at all strange to the country, will carefully describe a buck's usual direction of approach. If a stander is familiar with the drive, he will merely be told, "Take the Laurel Tree Stand," or "The Crippled Oak," or "The Three Sisters."

It is rather wonderful but it is true that both birds and animals steer their course through the air and through the forest by natural objects of the landscape. I have often observed that wild ducks will pass directly over certain solitary pines and cypresses that stand in the marshlands; they fly right over my house, though they have to leave the line of the river to do so. Such objects must be landmarks to them. All over the pineland forests of the South are flat-topped mounds, standing about three feet above the floor of the forest. These are ancient tar kilns, dating back to colonial days. I never knew a tar kiln that was not a good deer stand.

There's tradition and some romance about the old names of deer stands in the Deep South. Thus we have the Doeboy Stand, named long ago for a hunter who forgot or disregarded the buck law; the Shirttail Stand, named for a major miss executed there; the Savanna Stand, taking its name from the character of the swampy landscape there; the Ten-Master Stand, where a famous buck was killed far back about 1840; the Handkerchief Stand, where an unfortunate old gentleman, hearing the hounds starting his way, and finding his glasses a little misty, took them off to wipe them, and shook out his handkerchief almost in the faces of two eight-point bucks that had come up to him without his knowing that they were near! And there's the Green Lady Stand, honoring a Diana who, long ago but within my memory, all dressed in Lincoln green like Maid Marian, killed a noble buck with a rifle, the buck being on a dead run, after seven male standers had shot at him with their shotguns and had missed him.

I remember one Christmas Day when it was my turn to entertain all the nimrods of the neighborhood, I decided to drive the great Wambaw Corner, an eight-hundred-acre tract of pure wilderness, surrounded on three sides by creeks, and a place famous for its bucks. I did not have so great a crowd of hunters with me—just eighteen. I do not care for a huge pack of hounds; among so many dogs there will be some notable liars that will start the others off on false trails; there is difficulty and there is confusion in handling a yowling multitude; then, at the very beginning of the hunt, a doe or a yearling may be started, and the whole pack may get away on it. I therefore left at home about two-thirds of the hounds that had been brought to this meet, and selected twelve tried and true hounds to do the work. Among these were at least three that would run nothing but a buck; it is not generally known, I think, that there is a difference between the scent of the sexes in white-tail deer, and perhaps in all animals of the wilds, and perhaps those that are domesticated as well.

I had four Negro drivers: Prince Alston, my plantation foreman and my best deer hunter; Will, his brother; Steve, who made up in enthusiasm for a piece of Christmas venison for what he lacked in wildwood sagacity; and Old Testament, an ancient crafty Negro, to whom the secrets of nature are like an open book.

Having sent these men with the hounds to the other end of the drive, far back to the lonely edges of the Santee River, I posted by standers on such famous places as the Forked Dogwood, the Gum Tree, the Savanna, the Mossy Oak, the Rattlesnake Stand. This last took its name from the fact that a hunter of the long ago, posted there, had come to him, not a buck but a huge diamondback rattlesnake. It goes without saying that the hounds were not running it!

In about twenty minutes the drive started. The drivers spread out across the big peninsula began to whoop as if they had found religion or a cache of liquor. The dogs began to tune up. While they were still a mile away, I heard one of the standers shoot. I know what this meant: a wary old buck had slipped out ahead of the hounds. While does and yearlings will rarely leave their beds until actually routed out, a wary old stag will attempt to steal away at the first whoop of a driver or voice of a dog; and he does so with a noiseless stealth peculiar to him. I have often known a stander to lose a shot because he had not loaded his gun the minute he was posted.

When one is familiar with his hounds, if weather conditions are favorable, he can recognize, even at a great distance, the voice of each one. I remember trying to describe the music of a pack of deerhounds in these lines:

> There's a short low tenor,
> And a yipping kiji;
> There is a bell-mouth ringing
> That a buck has got to die.
> There's a dingdong chop-mouth
> Always in the noise;
> There's a bass with no bottom,
> And a rolling gong voice;
> There's a bugle with a scream;
> And a high wailing tenor
> Like a trumpet in a dream.

It is not only the dogs that tell us when a fine stag has started; for the drivers make the wildwoods ring with their natively melodious voices—sometimes chanting admonitions such as "'Tis the Old Man comin'! For God's sake don't miss him!"

Now we hear the pack divide: that means two or more deer are afoot. One buck heads for the creek, but from the swing that the hounds make, I can tell that Prince has turned the buck; and now he is heading straight for the standers. The other dogs begin to circle, but Old Testament gallantly takes care of that situation. Later he told me that he had turned two bucks by throwing pine knots at them, "and by jumping high in the air," he added. And he's close to eighty years old.

In such a situation, any other deer lying between the two oncoming packs and the standers would be roused, and would likely come our way, I knew. But quite often a wary old stag will object to being driven, and will race back through drivers and hounds. Once when I protested to a driver that he had failed to drive a buck out to me, but had let the deer almost run over and trample him, he said, "An old buck, he gwine where he gwine."

As the clamoring hounds got within three hundred years of the road, the shooting began. I think in all there were some twenty-one shots fired. Some dogs got away after bucks that had been missed. But as yet no man knew what any other man had done; for there is a stern rule that a hunter must never leave his stand until the master of the hunt winds his horn, signaling that the hunt is over. And the signal may not be given for some time; for it is just like a buck that has passed the line of standers and is followed by hounds to circle right back into gunshot.

On this occasion, however, no deer turned back; and the dogs went out of hearing. When, therefore, the drivers had come out to us, I blew my horn. Then we gathered to report what had been done. I found the usual number of glad faces and red faces. The very first man who shot had killed a nine-point buck as he was stealing out far ahead of the drivers. There were five other bucks killed, one a huge twelve-pointer that had been known to harbor in that drive for years, a regular hart royal that we had always called the Bushmaster.

To get all these deer tied behind saddles, and to round up all the hounds by blowing for them takes time. And of course every successful hunter wanted to tell about his buck; those who had missed were not too keen about going into details.

Our return to the plantation was in the nature of a triumph; but I think the sternest joy was felt by our drivers, not only for the part they had so well played, but because of the solid satisfaction of the assurance of plenty of venison for them and for their families. Steve especially rejoiced; for he has an indefinite number of children—about fourteen, I think.

We gather in the backyard of the plantation, which overlooks the river, and rehunt the whole drive, and other drives as well, as the drivers dress the deer. Prince is delegated to feed the hounds. He had on the ground a long cypress board, and this was, at least in his own mind, divided into spaces, one of which was assigned to each ravenous hound. Bringing forth the pot of steaming food, I remember that he addressed his famished army about like this:

"How come you can't find your place, Music? Ain't you know you have a place at table between Buck and Ringwood? Don't you dare cross that line, Check. You stay away from Mate's dinner. Gambler, you ain't gwine to get a thing if you edge up on me. Red Liquor, if I ever bat you with this big spoon, your jaw will ache until New Year's Day."

During this admonitory address, Prince would be ladling the food on the big board, a portion for each hound; and he had them so trained that, until the banquet was properly spread, not a dog would dare to begin, though certain lean melancholy faces would loll forward languishingly.

With the sharing of the venison, the Christmas Hunt is over; and I say good-bye to my rural friends and neighbors. After this parting, I stroll toward the river, where I see a yellow jasmine blooming, and where a mockingbird is singing. In a patch of warm sunlight I come upon Bugle, an old hound too old now to hunt, fast asleep. Yet his feet are errantly moving, and joyous muffled barks proclaim that even in slumber he is running a buck. Dreams will never let him be, especially when plantation hunting comes to its climax on Christmas Day. I know his memory is full of noble images of stags that he has sped across the river's tide—stags that now for him are swimming forever and forever.

Blue's Buck

◡:◡

This piece originally appeared in the January 1939 issue of Field & Stream *(pages 22–23, 62—complete with a fine illustration by Lynn Bogue Hunt). It was reprinted in* Hunter's Choice *(pages 129–35). Strictly a family affair, with two of Rutledge's brothers, two of his sons, and two of his favorite "huntermen," Steve and Prince, involved, the hunt has a fair share of irony and useful insights on several of the key factors involved in successful drives. Blue, the faithful hound from which the title comes, gets his signals a bit crossed, but all ends well with young Irvine taking a "noble buck."*

Well, old-timers, you know how it is when you have your two brothers visiting you for a Christmas hunt and two of your sons also—all keen woodsmen, and all covetous of a crown worn by an able buck. And you know how it must be, with such a crowd to handle, when the deer drive has only four stands. So it was with me, even so. I put the four where I thought any one of them might shoot, and where someone was bound to shoot; and as for me, I got up on a rise out of the drive and elevated above it in order to watch the thing come off. And, believe me, something did come off, but not what I expected. Indeed, when does anything in the big woods happen just as you anticipate it will?

Right here, boys, let me side-track you to say that I don't believe any of us give enough attention to the details concerning a hunt. Why, if a man would make mental note of all the various happenings on a hunt, his memories would be tremendously enriched. I think, too, that by watching every little incident a man learns more about the woods, about the habits of wild game, and about the high art of hunting. Of course, with me deer hunting is a kind of religion, and I have worshipped at this shrine ever since a grown oak was an acorn.

Anyway, it was still dark on the morning of the day before Christmas when we sallied forth into the great pinelands of my Carolina plantation. In that country you do not wake up at Christmas time to the snuffing of a wolfish blizzard-wind at your window-sills, and you don't hear the trees creaking in their ice sheathing. You are likely to be wakened by the singing of the cardinal and the Carolina wren; you may come out into genial warmth and even more genial sunshine. And there will be a spicy fragrance about the woods such as the Northern forests have in October.

As we were going down the dusky plantation avenue my good deer-driver, Prince, drew me aside and whispered to me that he was sure we were going to have good luck, and that it was coming from Steve. Now, the best way for me to describe Steve is to say that he was born a thousand years too late. He is by no means a hunter; but he always shambles along on our hunts in the hope of plunder at the day's end. To him, a buck's neck represents the last word in epicurean taste. Slow, shuffling, as boisterous in the early morning as a flat tire, so dumb that he thinks Sing Sing is a lullaby, Steve nevertheless has some good points. One of these is the business of forecasting luck. He augurs.

I asked Prince what Steve had done this time to make him hopeful, whereupon Prince said gravely that Steve had washed his feet. He never does that unless he expects to bring about some great happening.

"Well," I told Prince, "if we don't kill an old master on this first drive, we'll make Steve wash all over."

"Dat would kill him," Prince answered, and I caught an amiable grin on his face.

I elected to drive the famous Smallpox Corner, an old deserted plantation that runs back to the Santee. It is full of ideal deer cover and deer feed; bucks come for miles to eat the mushrooms there and the sweet black acorns of the live-oak and the tender browse along the marshes that border the rice-fields. I have known many a fine stag to be missed there, and many a fine one to be killed.

There are but four stands to this drive, and in my country we always christen a stand by name. They were: the Parsonage, a clump of live-oaks where a minister long ago had his house; the Canebrake, which is on the brow of a hill overlooking the fringes of the swamp, heavily grown to canes, wild briers, and elders; the Clay Hill, which is on one side of the branch leading into the drive;

and the Jam, which is on the other. This last is in a deep corner, and toward it several deer-runs converge. It's a tight place, and it takes a good man to cover it.

My son Middleton I left at the Parsonage; one of my brothers at the Cane-brake; and the other at the Clay Hill. My youngest son, Irvine, I stood at the Jam. Although at the time he was just of age, he was an experienced deer hunter. I started him when he was eight years old, and by the time he was twenty-one he had killed fourteen stags. He rolls his own.

As I have hinted, there were not enough stands to go round. I therefore moseyed up on a rise overlooking the Jam. Though I could not see the stander there, I was just out of gunshot from him. Sitting down on a log, I awaited the music. While I was not exactly expecting an elephant or a brontosaurus to come out of the Smallpox Corner, you can never tell what will bust out of a thicket like that. I remember we once ran a whole herd of Negroes out of there; they had been tending a still, and they thought the law was after them. Gentlemen, to see all speed records broken, put a ghost or the law after a plantation Negro.

Steve and Prince and the other drivers must have been talking scandal or religion, for they were a long time in starting to drive. Finally, however, I heard a far-off whoop way down by the river—a full mile from where we were standing. Then I heard Spot and then Red Liquor begin to bawl on a cold trail. But I never get especially excited when I hear either one of these two hounds, good though they are. The reason is that they will run any deer.

With old Blue, the case is different, Blue isn't a deerhound; he is a buck-hound. In some way not known to me, he can distinguish the trail of a buck from that of a doe; and he seems also to know that we do not shoot does. When his voice blares forth, I always open my gun to see if my shells are right; then I give this great hound's broadcast all my attention, for he is probably on a buck.

It's never any trouble to hear Blue. Spot's voice or Red's may be lost in the distance or hushed by the denseness of the brush through which he is traveling; but when Blue opens up, he makes the wildwoods ring. When he bawls, he bawls—reminding me of the Negro widow who insisted to the dry-goods clerk that she had to have not only black shoes, dress, veil, and hat for her mourning outfit, but black under things as well. "You see," she explained, "when ah mou'ns, ah mou'ns."

Without paying any especial notice to the other dogs, I heeded Blue. He had the town news. He was telling the world that no later than last night an old buck had been parading around the Smallpox, and I knew Blue would follow that trail until he jumped the king with the craggy crown. There might be two sovereigns; indeed, in that same drive, the year before, we started a herd of five mature bucks. As they chose to swim the river, we never even got a shot at them.

After about five minutes I heard Spot go out of the drive far below me. He had a fox or a yearling doe, I thought. Red Liquor had quit entirely. He may have been after a swamp rabbit, which probably had swum the lazy creek that meanders through the old rice-fields. But Blue was coming, his deep voice making the wide and lonely forest ring. He had not really opened up but he was steadily warming on the trail. But from the way he was traveling, I knew that old stag must have done some mighty mazy wandering.

The voice of Spot was now lost in the woods to the northward; Red hadn't found anything more. Prince and Steve and Richard seemed perfunctory in their whooping. Only old Blue was taking the business in deadly earnest. He knew what he was after, and he knew his game couldn't be far ahead.

The day broadened; the sun rose; the dewdrops slipped in glittering silence from the pine needles; in the swamps the robins awakened to warble. And old Blue kept singing what was now a sunrise song. He took the track clear down to the river, up toward Romney, back toward Peafield, round and round in the Smallpox Corner; but now he was definitely coming our way. Something would surely happen before long.

Immediately below me, and immediately in front of the Jam, is a dense thicket of young pines. It is just one of those places. It is the kind of place in which, if you'd jump a grouse, you'd never see him. Deer love it. Deer hunters don't love it so well because it is right up against the stands; and when a buck is jumped in such a place, you think a locomotive or two are headed your way.

Listening to Blue, I now made sure that he was coming for the pine thicket; and I also felt sure that the buck was bedded down right there. It is the kind of place that a wary stag will not pass when he is looking for a good safe harbor in which to spend the day, and lying in such a place, a wise old deer is likely to stay right where he is until he is literally run out of his bed.

On account of the position of the pine thicket, I figured that whatever was in there would come to Irvine, at the Jam; and I had a mind to tiptoe down to warn him. But to do so might botch things. Besides, he is the type of woodsman who does not need a warning. But there is one trouble about the critical place where he was standing; if a deer comes out there, he is not only likely to come helling, but he is likely to run too close. There is something about the lay of the land between the pine thicket and the stand that just naturally draws a deer right to you. For my part, I don't like this business of having to put the muzzle of my gun against a buck and pull the trigger.

Except for Blue's chiming, the woods were still. The drivers were far behind the hound; and they might have found a still, for they did not seem to be making any progress. Steve might have been asleep, for all the whooping he did. On came the lone trailer, and he now entered the fragrant darkness of the pine thicket. Suddenly he whooped it up, and I knew he had the buck on his feet.

Satisfied that he was not coming to me, I just listened for the gun. Nor did I listen long.

Just below me in the Jam I heard my son shoot; a moment later there was a second barrel. Hearing the gun, Blue came on a dead run out of the pines, passed the stand, and kept right on. I don't like to hear dogs keep on, after a man has shot at a buck. It may be all right, but it makes the listener suspicious that all is not well.

On went Blue. I heard another shot from one of my brothers across the swamp. The dog went out of the drive; he crossed the road, and soon his voice was diminished by distance. The deer he was after could not have much the matter with him.

For five minutes I sat still; then I rose and eased down toward the Jam. I saw the black pine stump where Irvine had been standing, but I saw no stander and no deer. A little anxious, I reached the stump, and there my anxiety increased, as, just beyond it, the grass and bushes were streaming with blood. I had never seen so much blood-sign at one place before. How a deer that had lost that much blood could go more than ten steps, I could not understand.

To add to my bewilderment, there was an ominous silence. Blue, I was sure, had gone out of hearing. I had expected to come on a crowd of happy standers, jubilant over a fallen stag, but the pineland glimmered away, with nothing to be seen or heard.

Taking up the blood-trail, which was almost a yard wide, I walked slowly toward the road. Suddenly, over a little rise ahead, I heard a shout. Then Irvine came running toward me; his right arm high in the air, and red with blood from the elbow down. In a moment he had joined me; and as we walked forward to what he had to show me this is what he said:

"About the time old Blue got in the pine thicket I heard something coming out of my end of it, and straight for me came a doe and a spike buck. They were not running to pass me; they were running to trample me. If I had not been behind the stump, they surely would have knocked me down. As it was, they passed within two feet of me. I had a mind to shoot the little buck, but you know how an old buck will often send out the women and children first.

"As they brushed past me I saw the old man himself coming, dead on their heels. He was running low to the ground, with his head stretched far out in front of him. I didn't know just when to shoot or just how to shoot him, as he had his head right in line with his breast. While I was trying to make up my mind he was broadside and almost within touching distance.

"I shot, and practically missed him. You will see where two buckshot went through that stretch of skin just forward of his haunch. My next barrel practically blew his heart out. Yet he went on over this hill, but couldn't make it to the road. Somebody must have shot at the little buck on the other side of the swamp."

When we reached the fallen stag, I found that he had run fully two hundred yards, despite the wound that should instantly have been mortal. He was indeed a noble buck, an eight-pointer, heavy in the beam and heavy in the haunches. Here was the case of a deer that had almost escaped because he ran too close to the stander. Irvine said the buck came so near that he could actually hear him breathing heavily, and at the first barrel he had not in the least swerved from his course. A buck on a full run is not likely to change direction, even for a stander. As Steve says, "He gwine where he gwine."

When the other standers came up, we learned that a long but fruitless drag had been taken at the spike buck that Blue had followed out of hearing. At the sound of the gun the drivers came to life and soon were on the buck, which they carried to the road, singing a weird improvised song of triumph, purely African in its spirit. As for Steve, he took the whole thing complacently, solemnly vowing that the good luck was all due to his having washed those huge derelict tugboats that he uses as feet.

From an experience like this there are several lessons to be learned about deer hunting. The first is that if you are posted at a deer stand or crossing— I mean a place that a buck is likely actually to run over—it is better to stand a little to the right of it, facing the drive. Then if the old tactician runs true to form, you have an easy left-hand shot instead of one of these disconcerting head-on encounters. The second is that a deer may have a hole shot clear through him in a vital place, yet with incredible vitality appear to escape. Don't give him up just because he runs out of sight. The third is that if you see a little buck and a doe come out, or two does, the one you want is probably holding back to let them take the shot. And finally we learn that, in a great many cases, even so good a hound as Blue may, when trails become confused, follow the unwounded deer. I have lost more than one fine stag by trouble of that sort.

Because he had trailed him alone for more than an hour, and because he had delivered him to the spot, we always called that Christmas Eve stag Blue's Buck. As for Blue, when he returned to us, as he did before long, and discovered what he had overrun, he was as shamefaced as a man is when his wife has to remind him that it is their wedding anniversary.

The Gray Stag of Bowman's Bank

This piece from early in Rutledge's career appeared in the December 1920 issue of Field & Stream *(pages 752–53). Bowman's Bank was the local name for one of the*

*many wild patches of swamp country that formed regular hunting haunts for Old
Flintlock. He killed the deer at an extraordinary distance for buckshot—a measured eighty-nine yards—and his luck doubled on itself when his sisters happened
to drive by at just the right time, thereby saving him considerable labor in getting
the buck back to Hampton.*

This title sounds as if a story is to follow; and I suppose this narrative might
be dignified by calling it a story. But distinctly it is not fiction. It is just a
matter-of-fact account of a rather unusual deer-hunt that I was fortunate enough
to enjoy during the Christmas season of 1919. The circumstances surrounding
it were somewhat romantic, perhaps; and there was a coincidence involved that
seldom occurs, even in the big woods, where almost anything unexpected is
likely to happen.

The time was the thirty-first of December, and the place the pinelands near
the mouth of the Santee. I had been at home on the plantation for a week and
had had some successful hunting, but most of my time had been spent in fight-
ing a far-reaching forest fire that threatened destruction to everything inflam-
mable in the great coastal plain of Carolina. I know for a fact that this fire
burned over a territory forty miles deep by more than a hundred miles long. Of
course, here and there it was cut off; but for the most part it made a clean sweep.
The wild life of the countryside suffered less in this conflagration than might
have been expected; and more than once I saw deer which seemed not in the
least dismayed by the roaring flames near them. Finally the fire passed us, and
then I took to the woods as usual with my gun.

On several successive trips I hunted deer near a place called Bowman's
Bank, a wild and solitary stretch of swampy country about four miles from
home. In the old sandy road that dipped down from the wild pinelands, I had
seen a track that showed the maker to be a stag worth following. It was, indeed,
I suspected, the track of a very old friend of mine—one who on a certain occasion had played me a kind of a mean trick. He got the thing off in the manner
I now describe.

Early one October morning, two years before this, a party of us had been
hunting near Bowman's Bank. In the big main road we had come upon a track
so large and so fresh that we had decided to let the hounds take it; but before we
slipped them from the leash, four of us tiptoed a half mile through the dewy
morning woods and took up the well-known stands at the head of the bank.
Within a few minutes we heard the dogs open as they were loosed, and they lost
no time in coming our way. From the manner in which they kept bearing hard
toward the left, I felt sure that the buck would come out to me. The hounds
surely were bringing glad tidings in my direction. They clamored through the
deep bay-thicket ahead of me; they were so close that I saw them. But no deer

appeared. He must have dodged, thought I, and I listened for the gun of one of my partners. Suddenly the hounds broke out of the branch and headed straight up the easy hill toward me. They came flying on the trail, and straight at me; yet not a sign of what they were running could I see. With some difficulty I stopped them and tied them up. Then I examined the ground. A big running track had come head-on over my stand. The buck must have heard us coming, and made off over my crossing about a minute before I reached it! The thing hurt me, for I had the crazy idea that a hunter sometimes gets that a certain old stag belongs to him by rights, despite a clever getaway and other significant facts. I felt no better when our party had gathered, and when the stander next to me said: "I saw the deer. I was up on a little ridge when you were in a hollow, Arch; and he went out about a hundred yards ahead of you. He surely was a beauty—and a peculiar-looking buck, too. He seemed an iron-gray color to me; and his horns were enough to give him the headache."

Well, ever since that day I had had a leaning toward Bowman's Bank which was nothing but my hankering after another sight of the gray stag that had played me so heartless a trick. And the track that I had begun to pick up in the vicinity of the bank gave me reasonable hope that my wish might be fulfilled. Although several expeditions into the section of the woods had yielded me only a spike buck, I had a feeling that something else was waiting for me there. That instinct in hunting is not a bad thing to follow; for while I have small faith in premonitions and the like, I do believe in anything that exacts patience from a hunter. In fact, it has been my experience that a man in the woods gets the chance he wants if he keeps in the game long enough.

One afternoon after dinner, which on a Southern plantation means about three o'clock, I got on a horse and turned his head toward the Bowman's Bank region. In many places in the pine forest the woods were still smoldering, and as the afternoon was still and warm, the smoke hung low. Occasionally a smoking mass of debris of some kind would suddenly burst into flame. So prevalent was the smoke that I saw myself coming home within an hour or two with nothing to show for my afternoon's ride.

Turning off from the main road, I made my horse circle a small pond fringed with bays. From the farther side of the pond I was suddenly aware of a deer slipping silently out. It was too far for a shot; and it melted with astonishing quickness into the haze that now was hanging everywhere. Had I been on foot, I might have come much closer on that deer, I thought. Therefore, I dismounted and tied my horse on a strip of burnt ground, where, I knew, whatever fire happened to spring up near him could not cross to reach him. I went forward then on foot toward Bowman's Bank, taking the identical route that I had followed that October morning two years before when the gray stag had outwitted me. The sun was now taking a last red and glaring look through the smoke.

152

The aspect of the forest was weird and anything but inviting. But in hunting, a man has to take the rough with the easy; and not infrequently it is the poor-looking chance which yields the luck.

On account of the smoke, and because the sun was now going down, I knew that I had but a short while in which to do what I was going to do. There would be no long and dewy twilight, with an afterglow in which a man can see to shoot. Night and the pall of smoke would soon shut out the world from human vision. Prospects were discouraging, but I trudged onward.

Perhaps it will not be amiss for me to say that the kind of deer-hunting I was now doing is of the type that I have long enjoyed and found successful. Because the pinelands are interlaced at almost regular intervals with narrow bay-branches, which are small watercourses grown to low underbrush, it is possible for a man to walk these out and get about as many and as sporty chances at deer as he can have in any other way. It approaches stalking as nearly as any hunting in the Southern woods can approach it. I sometimes go thus alone, and sometimes with a friend; and I have had as much luck hunting without a hound as with one. A man gets his money's worth when, in this type of still-hunting, he bounces an old stag out of his bed, and has to hail him for business reasons within the range commanded by a shotgun. I find that a Parker twelve-gauge, with thirty-inch barrels, gives good results when loaded with this shell, which is the best I have ever seen used on deer: U.M.C. steel-lined Arrow, high-base; $2\frac{3}{4}$ inches long; 28 grains Infallible smokeless; $1\frac{1}{8}$ ounces of buckshot. The second size of buckshot is preferred to the big ones, the very best being those that chamber sixteen to a shell. I was loaded with two of these shells on that smoky twilight that will live in my memory as long as memory and such things last.

I had come to a certain wide arm of swampy growth that stretched out from the dim sanctuary of Bowman's Bank, and was undecided as to whether I should cross it or pass round its edges. I decided on the former course. My way was none too easy. Smoke worried my eyes. A fire of some four years previous had left the swamp full of black snags. There were slippery hummocks of sphagnum moss and sudden pools of black water. It is a hard thing for a man to watch his footing when he is intent on looking for something else. Yet his footing is a vital matter; for if he misses it at the critical moment, his chance may be gone.

About halfway across the melancholy morass into which I had ventured I felt as if I might just as well turn back. If anything did get up, there was hardly enough light for a shot—certainly not enough light for a decent chance. Besides, off to the left a terrible fire had suddenly begun to rage, and it appeared unreasonable to suppose that any wild life would be lying serenely so close to that withering sweep of destruction. But strange are the ways of nature, and strange are the things that sometimes happen to a woodsman.

As I was toiling on in a half-hearted way, suddenly above the dull roar and the sharp crackle of the fire I heard a familiar sound. It was the "rip" of a deer out of bay-bushes. I located the sound before I saw the deer. A buck with big antlers had jumped some thirty yards ahead of me, a little to my right. He had been lying on the very edge of the swampy arm, and on the farther side from the point at which I had entered it. I saw his horns first, and they were good to look upon. They gleamed high in the smoke. For the first twenty yards or so he ran like a fiend, in one of those peculiar crouching runs that a buck assumes when he wants to make a speedy start. He hardly had his tail up at all. My gun was at my shoulder, but because of a dense screen of black gum and tupelo trees, I had no chance to put anything on him. And he was getting away on all six cylinders! But he was bearing a little to the left—to run over the regular stand. It was the identical stand where the buck had escaped me before. Into the gap between two trees I threw my sight. By the time the stag reached it, he thought he was clear; for the rabbit-like contortions through which he had gone at his start had given place now to regulation long leaps, with a great show of snowy tail. Indeed, that tail was the thing on which I laid my gun. But the shot seemed hopelessly far. Just beyond the stand that the buck was about to cross was a thicket of young pines. I must shoot before he reached that. Holding on the regimental flag as accurately as I could, I fired. The second barrel was ready to let go, but not a sign of a deer could be seen. "He is gone," thought I; "He's gone into that pine thicket. It was too far, and too smoky."

I crossed the remaining part of the swamp and made my way slowly up the sandy hill. A huge pine marks the stand there. To my amazement, stretched beside the pine lay the stag, stone dead. He lay exactly where I had stood two years before. And he was iron-gray in color! Had I been one of the Ouija-board people, I suppose I would have run. But I just stood there in the twilight admiring the splendid old stag, and wondering over my absolutely dumb luck in getting him, and over the strange coincidence that I had killed him precisely where he had once escaped me. For there was no doubt in my mind that this was the same old buck. Every hunter knows how a stag will take possession of a certain territory and remain in it for many years. As to his color, I suppose that he had some strain of albinism in him. I have seen other gray deer in that part of the country; and, within twenty miles, several pure albinos have been killed.

That my luck was extraordinary I did not fully appreciate until the buck was dressed, when I discovered that the buckshot had struck him in a peculiarly vital manner. Two shots only reached him. Both of these entered the small of the back just forward of the left haunch, and ranged forward through the body, through the neck, and lodged behind the jaw. It was no wonder that he came down without any preliminary flourishes. Had he not been going up a slight rise from me those shots probably would have taken him in the haunches and he might have kept right on. More than once I have taken old buckshot out of a deer's haunches, and the deer themselves appeared to be in prime condition.

Leaving the stag, I walked down into the swamp, carefully pacing off the distance. This I found to be eighty-nine steps. It was too long a shot; but the break had come my way. The question now was how to get my stag out of the woods. But here, too, luck favored me.

I walked toward the main road, hoping to meet a Negro. To meet a Negro in the pinelands is the easiest thing a man has to do. I met one within a few hundred yards. He and I managed to get the old buck out to the road. It happened that two sisters of mine had driven down in a spring-wagon for the mail, the post-office being some five miles from home. As I reached the road, I saw the wagon approaching in the dusk.

"Do you have much mail?" I asked my sisters; "I have a little package here I'd like you to take home for me."

The Surprise of My Life

This piece, supported by two Lynn Bogue Hunt drawings, appeared in the April 1942 issue of Field & Stream *(pages 20–21, 72). The scene, Wambaw Corner, is one of Rutledge's favorite haunts, and he hopes for his boys to get a buck. Fate decides otherwise, thanks to one of those unusual circumstances so often encountered in deer hunting.*

There are two or three deer drives on my Carolina plantation that I usually save for special friends. One of these, the famous Wambaw Corner, is about as certain a place for an old buck as any I know; and when a friend of mine is badly in need of slaying a stag, I usually take him there. But one should not make the mistake of supposing that the laying low of one of these rough-shod veterans is merely a matter of killing a deer. Its consequences are likely to be far-reaching. I have known a beautiful, wavering girl to marry a man for having proved his woodland valor by bringing home a twelve-point buck, and I have known many a husband to emerge from the domestic dog house when he filled the ice-box with venison.

Of course, to assure a friend a shot at a big buck is one of the hardest of all promises to fulfill. In the first place, the buck doesn't want to co-operate, even if the plan were made clear to him. Then, time and again, he will run to a stander to whom killing a deer is an old story. Finally, an old buck is full of stratagems of his own, and you can't kill him mathematically. I mean, he is a highly intelligent big-game animal, a born dodger and skulker; and what he is going to do is usually unpredictable.

During last Christmas holidays, two of my sons were hunting with me. As I had already killed four bucks that season (our limit is five) and as they had not had a shot, I naturally was eager to give them some sport. They had only a few days at home, and we had to hunt intelligently if we were to do something.

Early one morning we started for the Wambaw Corner, a long peninsula with deep water on three sides of it. Our plan was to send the drivers far down toward the river and drive it out to the road. At the head of this drive, on the old broad, sandy county road, there are really only two stands, and both of them are buck stands. You know, every drive has its stands, but some of them cover favorite buck runs. Does and fawns will come out to any stand, and often to no stands at all; but a buck, true to his warier nature, has his decided preferences every time.

It has been my experience that when a buck goes into a corner such as the one we were about to drive he is likely to come out exactly where he went in. I once knew a buck to enter such a drive by going under a bridge. Not believing that when he came out, with drivers and hounds in full pursuit, he would go under the bridge again, I stood on a rise some distance away, a rise on which there is a regular crossing. But that deer sailed right under that bridge and got clean away!

My drivers with the hounds had gone silently deep into Wambaw Corner, and I then proceeded to post my sons on the two famous crossings known as the Ground Bridge and the Dogwood Twins. At the latter stand I saw where a master buck had walked in over this place the night before. He wore a No. 16 shoe. Here I posted my youngest son, Irvine; my son Middleton I put at the Bridge.

Then I wandered off into the drive, but clear of the runways, so that the boys could shoot. I was not ahead of them, but off to one side. On the slope of a little hill about a half mile from where they were standing I sat down on a pine stump just to wait until the bombardment was over. The drive was off to my right. The hill on which I was sitting sloped downward toward the drive and then upward for a long distance; but, like all so-called hills in my part of the country, the rise was gentle. Over this long slope the woods were open with just a few big pines standing here and there. I could see for a long way.

Possibly I had been on my stand for fifteen minutes when things began to happen. I had not heard a sound from the drivers or the hounds, but as I looked far ahead and to my right I saw something coming. During the course of forty-nine years of deer hunting I have seen thousands of deer in the woods, and most of them were running; but never before had I seen a truly great buck running for so long a distance within plain view. From the time he first came into sight until he disappeared toward the standers on the road, he must have run a full half mile.

Motionless on my stump, I watched him. He had been startled, but he did not seem worried; he was not running hard, but was steadily covering the ground with a kind of cautious haste. When he was broadside, he was within 150 yards of me. That distance is no good for a shotgun; it would have been a perfect rifle shot. But I did not want the chance. I was only too happy that he was heading straight for my boys. I barely turned my head to watch him pass, and not until he was out of sight did I move around on the stump to locate the sound of the gun so that I would know which son had killed him.

Whoever got him would, I knew, have a prize, for rarely have I seen in the woods so burly a buck—a true swamp stag, with short heavy legs, barrel-like body, and massive and craggy horns. Indeed, as I watched him pass me a slight feeling of relief came to me, and I was glad that the responsibility of laying him down was not mine. A buck as big as that one, running in that masterly fashion, makes a man lose a little faith in his gun's ability.

As I had been able to see the buck until he was within three hundred yards of the road, I fully expected to hear a gun within three or four minutes. Beyond the road is a famous swamp known as Deertown; it was toward this that he was heading. And he simply had to cross the road at one of the two stands. I listened. I heard no gun, but from the direction from which the sound of the gun should have come I thought I heard laughter. The road is not much traveled; but occasionally Negroes pass along it, and when they do they are always bantering one another. I wondered if what I heard had really been laughter; and if so, if it would be enough to upset all my carefully laid plans.

As you come to understand buck nature, two of his characteristics will impress you as almost paradoxical. One is that he is one of the hardest animals in the world to turn. I mean that if he has really made up his mind that he is going to a certain place, why, that's where he's going. My Negroes put it succinctly where they say, "He gwine where he gwine."

On the other hand, if a buck is "feeling" his way out of a drive, nothing else in the world is so easy to turn. This buck that had passed me had some definite sanctuary in mind, but he had not fully committed himself to the course he was taking. A buck that hasn't gone all out for a certain run is the old boy you have to watch. The slightest hint of danger ahead will suffice to make him change his course radically and suddenly.

Well, here I was, sitting on that stump, waiting for somebody's gun and for somebody's wild war-whoop of triumph. But I heard nothing.

"The old devil has stopped short of the road," I said. "Those boys aren't expecting anything, but I hope they aren't moving."

The very best way to fail to get a shot at a buck is to move around when you are covering a crossing. The motionless, self-effacing hunter is the one who gets the big chances. Even to smoke or to fidget on a stand may be fatal. Do what you please when it's all over; but as long as you are the guardian of a crossing, be as still as King Tut, who has been dead three thousand years, I believe. Not only that your approaching buck will infallibly see movement of any kind, but you can't listen properly if you are restless.

Often a moment's warning is enough to afford the deer hunter a chance to get ready, and he is not likely to hear that warning unless he is still and listening. What I mean by a warning is that shuffling of the dead leaves, that stealthy cracking of a dry twig—any sound not in consonance with the prevailing sounds of the forest. A hunter, and sometimes a good hunter, is likely to miss a deer if it takes him completely by surprise. Always surprise your buck; try never to let him surprise you.

So there I sat on a stump, facing the standers and facing the place where I had last seen the buck, which was running straight for them. As they had not shot, I felt certain that he had stopped to reconnoiter. Unless a deer is hard pushed, he is almost sure to do that very same thing when he comes to a road. My gun lay across my knees. It was not my old long deer gun, either. That being temporarily out of commission. I had borrowed this one, and my faith in it was none too strong.

When I had last seen the stag, he was disappearing into a dense growth of sweet-bay and myrtle that fringed the road deeply. Now I saw some of those bushes jarred into movement. Something was not going through them, but was coming through them! The old buck was heading back my way. There was no time to consider just why he had so radically changed his course; my immediate business was to shoot him. He was not coming straight for me, but was coursing off to my right, to pass me at about sixty yards. Making for the river, he was running through bushes that almost hid him. Honestly, he looked so big that the gun in my hands felt insignificant.

I didn't move, letting him come as close as he would. When first he had been roused from his bed and had made that long run to the road, he was decidedly uneasy; he was getting out of that country. But now he was really scared. I have seen deer run faster, but never with more purpose and power. Just as he came in sight, I heard the hounds take his trail from his bed, nearly a mile away in the drive.

Considering his speed, the distance he was away from me, and the angle, I gave him the choke barrel, drawing six inches in front of his burly neck. At the crack of the gun he literally tore the thicket open. He got away so fast and so low that I had no chance for a second shot. The last I saw of him was just the tips of his great chestnut horns sliding through the bush-tops. While I was satisfied that I had hit him, I never hoped to see him again. Neither coming to me, nor going from me, he had had his tail up.

Some hunters claim that if a buck is running with his flag up, and you hit him, he will flatten it down. Yet I have seen mortally wounded bucks sail off with their tails as high as they could get them. But here is one infallible sign of a wounded buck: if at your shot he changes his stride, you have done something to him; how much will remain to be seen. In the case of this buck, I had no chance of seeing a change in stride; but from the way he ripped out, he was evidently aware of something more than the sound of the gun.

On came the hounds in full run. Soon they were in sight, running my buck's trail. They went almost to the road, just as he had done. Now they came back toward me. When they struck the place where I had shot at this old man of the woods, their clamor suddenly increased.

"That means blood," I said to myself.

Within a minute their wild chase ceased, and I could distinctly hear Red Liquor growling. He claims every dead deer for his own.

I walked over where they were, and there lay my buck, and I mean he was truly one of them. He had gone only sixty or seventy yards; and if the woods had been open, I could have seen him fall. I had put only three buckshot in him; my own gun would have put about seven. But one of these three had gone through his heart.

There was then a happy gathering of drivers and dogs and standers about this fallen monarch of the deep river swamps. An idea of his size may be had when I say that when fully dressed, with hide and head off, he weighed 178 pounds.

"Boys," I asked of my sons, "who was that laughing in the road? That laugh cost one of you this chance."

They told me that, not thinking the drive had even begun, they had been joking with an old Negro who happened to wander by.

I felt less selfish later that same day when my son Middleton killed a fine stag, and my son Irvine killed two great bucks in the same drive. A dad likes to accomplish things in the wilds, but I guess he gets more real pleasure out of having his sons accomplish what he knows is not so easy to do.

The Case of the Elmwood Buck

This piece comes from the January 1929 issue of Outdoor Life *(pages 8–9, 59–60). Later reprinted in* A Treasury of Outdoor Life *(pages 82–85), ed. William Rae, the*

original article was accompanied by a half-dozen photos, including one of Rutledge standing next to a massive oak with a buck at his feet. Long deserted, Elmwood Plantation was situated on the same Santee River Rutledge called home, and credit must be given to Rutledge for sharing a story that, in the strictest sense of ethical hunting that demands the sportsman eat what he kills and do his utmost to recover wounded game, puts him in less than an ideal light.

Tho I have had the rare privilege of following the whitetail deer for a period of more than thirty-five years, and tho, as would be natural under such circumstances, I have had some strange and startling experiences, none had perhaps the same dramatic interest as the case of the stag of Elmwood. This business happened on the morning of Thursday, December 29, 1927, on the old plantation that has been mentioned. It lies some eleven miles from the mouth of the Santee River, in Carolina. Long deserted, it is a good place for deer—if a man can stand the somewhat nerve-racking strain of hunting in dense thickets wherein, at any moment, an old master will rip up under his feet. I used to enjoy greatly the business of bouncing bucks from their beds, but I am beginning to feel the tension of such hunting. A stag so roused makes Lindbergh and other flight artists look like the last rose of summer.

I shall tell this thing as simply as I can.

Five of us took up stands on the ancient avenue leading into Elmwood Plantation. The old roadway is still in good preservation, but the thickets have encroached upon it, so that sweet-smelling bowers of smilax and jasmine overhang it. We stood a few paces in from the road where the woods were a bit clearer. Two hundred yards ahead of us were dense thickets of pine and myrtle, ideal country for deer to bed during the day. Yet it has been my experience, and doubtless it has been shared by many another deer hunter, that in the hunting season old bucks will deliberately avoid dense cover. Of course, no man can lay down rules about the behavior of intelligent wild things, imagining that a really resourceful animal like a stag will always act in the same way. His very variability is a part of his life-insurance. But I have found that old bucks prefer to lie on the thin edges of thickets, in the tops of fallen trees in comparatively open woods, or in low bushes or patches of broomsedge. On a good many occasions, while walking up deer, I have detected one lying down by seeing it crouch below the short bushes or grasses that were not tall enough to conceal it as it lay in a natural position.

The case of this Elmwood stag illustrates this matter of a deer's lying down in the open, and it also illustrates so many other wiles and characteristics of the whitetail that I believe a detailed account of the whole business may be of some interest, especially to those who are as incurable deer-hunters as I am.

After posting my standers, I watched the Negro drivers ride far down the avenue, chatting with that infectious humor characteristic of plantation Negroes. As we were in the heart of the deer-country, all of us, I think, made too much noise; yet what difference did it make? Directly ahead of my stand, and right in the open, with no shelter save that afforded by the bare limbs of a little bush, at that very moment was lying the Elmwood stag.

Instead of going straight to my stand, I turned in somewhat to the left, going thru a thin thicket of young pines. I took this route because we had left one stand uncovered, and I was supposed to straddle two. The forest was silent, hanging with dew, glistening. Fragrant airs moved softly. High overhead I could hear the dreamful mighty pines sighing mystically. My gun was loaded. I was stepping thru the broomsedge cautiously. The place was just like one of those sparse thickets in which a sportsman in the North is likely to flush a ruffed grouse. But I had no premonition of the superb stag lying *not thirty yards away,* off to my right front. But for a few waving tufts of broomsedge, but for a tiny pine, but for a paltry screen of a dry bush, he would have been in ridiculously plain sight. As I discovered later, he had no regular bed; he was lying on the bare damp ground. The day was so warm and still that, after a long night of roaming and browsing, he just luxuriated down by this old road—and here he intended staying unless he was actually kicked out of his "form."

I should have seen the buck before he got up; but I never expected anything so close to the road. My gaze was fixed farther away. Besides, he doubtless flattened himself when I got near. So crouched, if he did not move his antlers, he would be exceedingly hard to discern. At such a time, a buck will draw his feet up under him, take a regular stance for a start, meanwhile "grounding" his head until his lower jaw rests flat on the ground. Once when driving for a party of hunters I saw a buck in that position. Every time I whistled he would flatten his head to the earth; and after a moment or two he would raise it craftily to reconnoiter. He kept performing in this way until I was within easy gunshot of him.

The Elmwood buck must have felt that he was in something like a corner, for he surely had been aware of the general approach and also the separation of our hunting party. He must have had his fears confirmed when he saw me approaching on his left. He might have then sprung up and raced away from me. It seemed the obvious thing to do. But the principle of nearly all wild life strategy is the principle of doing the thing least expected by the pursuer. It is a game of wits. This stag lay still and let me not only approach but pass him—he all the while lying practically in the open. He was a big buck, too, full-antlered. As the time was about eight o'clock in the morning, I am sure that the old stag could not have been couched more than an hour. It is safe therefore to suppose that he had hardly settled himself for the day. I was ready for a shot, for in such woods the hunter must continually be on the alert; but I saw and heard nothing. True, I was on the fringes of a thicket of young pines, and the dew sliding from their needles made a sibilant whisper in the broomsedge below; otherwise I might have seen the Elmwood stag as he roused himself.

It may be that I am making too much of this story and of all its incidents; yet, as I said before, it seems to illustrate almost perfectly many of the traits of behavior that we associate with the most popular of all American big game animals.

I had passed the stag perhaps twenty feet, he being at that time about thirty-five yards off to my right, and partly behind me. He must have crawled from his bed, gently insinuating himself up, elongating himself like a rabbit for a length or two. There was no semblance of the standard "rip"—a sound that has thrilled me in the wildwoods since the time of my first deer hunt, when I was nine years old. What first attracted my attention to the buck was the sudden and amazing sight of him, caught out of the corner of my right eye. My vision was dramatically filled with this superb creature, now on the run dead away from me. I shall never forget how he seemed to prance, turning his head slightly so as to keep a weather-eye on what had startled him. At that moment he was just behind a very thin screen of bare bushes and several small pines, yet there was plenty of opening for a shot. One thing momentarily deterred me, even as I threw my gun up. He was headed straight for the stander next to me. Should I take a chance shot when the man below me on the road might get a perfect one? Little hesitancies of this kind often determine whether a man hits or misses—or perhaps does neither, but just does not shoot.

I had my gun on the Elmwood stag when he executed a master-maneuver, worthy of the ancient craft of the whitetail. In two great bounds he dodged artfully toward a dense thicket bordering the road, making these jumps sharply at right angles. In that final instant that remained for me to do some deciding, I knew that he would not now go near the next stander. I also knew that whatever my own intentions were, I must make them known at once. There was no time for more than one shot. I fired the choke barrel just as the stag took his last leap out of the broom grass savanna toward the friendly darkness of the sheltering thicket. A hunter generally knows when his eye and gun sight and the game have coordinated rightly. It seemed to me that I was holding dead on the buck's shoulder.

Apparently I was right, for at the crack of the gun, much to my surprise (for the distance was not under sixty yards), the Elmwood stag went headlong. I saw him go down, but I could not see him on the ground.

Running forward thru the sparse thicket, I came near where he had been when I shot. He was not there, but near the road I heard a terrific blundering such as is made by a deer that falls, gets up, and falls again. I listened carefully so as to determine by the nature of his struggle whether he would go far. Three times I heard him go down heavily. Then there was silence. I did not know but that he might be lying just across the road.

As soon as I came to where he first fell, I found spatters of blood, then a trail of it; I also could see where the old stag, in his heroic struggle, had fallen, risen again, blundered, yet somehow gone on. In the road and beyond it there were the same telltale signs of the wily and stubborn old creature's hardihood.

He was not lying within sight, nor yet within two hundred yards of where he had first gone down. I therefore blew my horn, summoning the drivers and all the standers.

> *They held a council standing*
> *Before the river-gate;*
> *Short time there was ye well may guess*
> *For musing or debate.*

Thus it was with us. And I then made one of the master-blunders of my life as a hunter. As every word of this story is true, I must not fail to turn the spotlight on my own shortcomings. So confident was I that we could easily overhaul the wounded stag with the seven hounds with which we were hunting—for the whitetail in the South is seldom hunted without hounds—that I suggested that the pack be set to the slot at once. The amount of blood thrown out by the deer and the color of it led me to believe that the chase would be short and swift. Of course, I should have taken the standers a mile or so ahead and posted them in front of the oncoming circus parade. This I failed to do, and it was exceedingly dumb of me not to take this precaution.

As soon as we gave the hounds their heads, they went wild on the hot blood-trail. We followed fast; and I had fond visions of soon hearing them come to bay. It did not seem possible to me that a stag so thrown and so blundering could possibly go far. At a point about a quarter of a mile from where we started we came to an old ditch. Its sides were of clean white sand, and its bottom also, for it was empty. In this the buck had evidently lain down, for there was a pool of blood. Also, the old fellow had had much difficulty in negotiating the farther bank when he had again taken his feet. Over such a ditch he would usually have lithely sailed. Now he had the bank pawed down in his gallant effort. But he had gone on.

The dogs, the mounted riders, and certain standers who are younger than I distanced me. I kept pausing, not only to get my wind but also to listen to the hounds. They were having a great race. At last, in one of my pauses, I heard them divide. That was not so good. They had run into other deer; and in such a case it frequently happens that the hounds will take the wrong trail. I heard some of the dogs bearing far to the southward; others had turned due north, heading toward the creek. Fainter and fainter grew their voices, mingling at last with the soft music from the crests of the mighty pines. Fainter also grew my hope; and the antlers that my eye had coveted seemed farther away than I ever dreamed they could possibly be, after I had seen them go down in the broomsedge.

There were features about the horns that I had carefully noted, even in the fleeting dramatic moment when the stag had been in full sight; tall they were, and gray in color; and either because of foreshortening, or because of actual formation, the left antler looked considerably shorter than the right. He looked to me to be a heavy deer, with antlers not quite up to his size—but good horns of seven or eight points, and decidedly unusual in color and in conformation. Now, as the chiming hounds passed out of hearing, and as I could no longer hear the shots of the following drivers, I wondered if I should ever see those antlers again. If I should, I felt sure of being able to identify them.

It was nearly an hour after the hounds had passed out of hearing before my crestfallen drivers and the chagrined standers returned. The stag had escaped. Some of the dogs had been recovered, but most of them had run off on other deer. I apologized to the assembled crowd for having botched the business; yet the chance had been small for a good shot. The Elmwood buck was gone.

Yet the interesting horns of this stag look down on me now as I write. About a month after I left the plantation, I had a letter from my Negro head-driver somewhat to this effect:

"My Boss, you is done had a good experience with the old buck you done shoot in Elmwood. He run to the Old Mill, turns to the Ocean, and come as far as Pinckney Run. My boy George done hear his little dog barking at something about three days and one Sunday. But that is a fool no-account dog, and loves to bark at nothing. But when I hear the barking, I say to George, 'Son, come with me.' We find your buck. He done been dead about five days, and he been shoot bad. I send you the horns for 'member that day by."

Such is the tale of the Elmwood buck; not much of a story, perhaps, just one of those hunting yarns that sportsmen like to record. I might add that the run of the stag from where I shot to where he fell was about 2 ½ miles; but the route the fugitive evidently took would have caused him to double a great deal, so that he probably traveled more than three miles.

Hunter Come Home

This moving story, recounting a homecoming hunt for Rutledge's youngest son, Irvine, after his service in World War II, first appeared in the February 1948 issue of Field & Stream *(pages 55, 105–6). Subsequently included in* Those Were the

Days (pages 309–14), its setting comes long after the glory days of the Hampton Hunt, but the story's poignancy and the singular success of father and son make it a fitting conclusion to this section of the book.

Y ou might be interested in knowing how a man who lives on a plantation in the wilderness of coastal Carolina gets ready for a deer hunt, especially one which he hopes to give his soldier boy, returning from his long exile from home, the time of his life. I knew that my youngest son would enjoy most a good deer hunt in our own home woods. Long before his arrival, early in December, I began to get ready to give him what I hoped would be a real homecoming.

For two weeks before he came I did no hunting. I kept the woods quiet. It has always been my experience that, while deer will desert their favorite haunts if much disturbed, yet they love their homes and will return to them quickly if they are given a chance.

Almost every day I would walk out the old mazy plantation roads, searching for signs. And I was not looking for ordinary deer tracks. You know how it is; I wanted to find out where some of the old masters had been using. This was not easy to do, for, the mating season being about over, the bucks were not roaming much. As the crops of both pine-mast and acorns had failed, and the deer knew it, their tracks were not plentiful under the great pines and the live-oaks. In fact, I have known certain bucks to resort regularly to such places over

Archibald Rutledge with the rack of his finest whitetail. He was fascinated by antlers and preserved those of every deer killed at Hampton. From the Elise Rutledge Bradford Collection

a long period of time. While I did not find as many signs as I hoped for, there were plenty, and some had been left by old stormers.

The second thing I did, as my boy's coming approached, was to watch the wind and the weather. In my part of the country deer usually lie down all day, and just where they lie depends on the weather. On cold, sunny days they like the broomsedge on high sun-bathed hills. On rainy days I find them in dense cover, and at such times they often change position from time to time.

On days of high wind they lie on the lee slopes, especially where fallen logs afford them additional shelter. On balmy still days they may just drop down anywhere for a siesta. However, like all other wild creatures, deer carry personal and private barometers; and often where they lie may be determined not by what the weather is, but by what the weather is soon to be. Their positively occult information on what's coming makes an ordinary weather man look like the dumbest guesser in all the world.

To further insure sport, I checked over the hounds: Red Liquor, Sambo, Blue Boy, and Big Mike. As far as I could tell, all they needed was to be let out of the yard. Here, however, I want to say that whenever I mention the use of hounds in deer hunting the boys are inclined to ride me.

Well, if I were hunting in strange territory, the very first thing I should do would be to find out how the local nimrods went to work. Some use the rifle and no hounds; some use the rifle and hounds; we use the shotgun and hounds. What causes the difference is the character of the country. In my dense swamp country, jungle-like even in winter, there is no such thing as stalking. We have to use hounds. To use high-powered rifles would be a very dangerous thing in level country; these express bullets, you know, make no local stops.

Besides, I have found that where hounds are not used for deer it is only because their use is forbidden, for good and proper reasons. Yet all normal hunters love to hear a pack run. Imagine the difference between hearing and seeing a fine pack yowling after a fox or rabbit, and the same pack after an old bruiser of a buck. The excitement is bound to be greater because the game is so much nobler.

Finally, when hounds are used, you rarely have the potshots that are so common in still hunting. An old stag, riding the bushes at thirty miles an hour, with a clamoring pack setting your nerves a-tingle, makes no easy target. As far as downright sport is concerned, hunting with hounds has the edge over stalking. Of course, this is only an opinion. Yet this kind of hunting has behind it age-old traditions, and certainly is not the low-down performance that some men who have never tried it think it is.

As a final preparation, I checked my African pack, my drivers. My son arrived safely and on time from his separation center in the North. He had left me a private; he returned a captain. For two years he had been in England,

France, and Germany. Like millions of other boys from our country, he had seen a good deal that was pretty ghastly. But of all this he said nothing. He did not seem to have changed, only to have matured. I guess no one will ever be able to tell just how glad these boys were to get home. Our feelings are nearly always deeper than our power to express them.

After considering the weather and the sign that I had been studying, I decided first to drive what we call Montgomery Branch. This is a mile-long swamp and watercourse, with dense pine and bay thickets. On either hand are open pinelands. As we had but two standers, I thought it wise to stand the two sides of the head of the branch. My son and I would be within long gunshot of each other, directly opposite each other, yet neither could see the other. A perfect jungle intervened between us.

In this kind of hunting the drivers and dogs, of course, put in at one end and the standers shut off the other. I debated with myself a long time before posting my captain. I felt reasonably certain that we could rouse a buck. I had told Prince and Wineglass to hold the center of the drive, while Evergreen, Sam'l, and Steve flanked so as to keep the deer from flaring out at the sides. But if the old master were at home, and if he made a straight run, on which side of head would he break out? Angels and ministers of grace could not have answered that question.

At last I posted Irvine on the south side, while I took up the stand on the north. And no sooner were we in place than things began to happen far down the drive. The morning was cool and quiet, so that one could hear everything that was happening. And when you get a gang of Negro drivers together on a still day, you are going to hear something. As the African Nandi and Masai curse the lion they surround and are going to kill with their assegais, so my Negroes begin driving by amiably blaspheming all bucks. And each one feels it his duty to try to outdo all others in the energy and the picturesqueness of his language.

They had been driving but a few minutes when I heard Big Mike (who by the way, though a Labrador retriever, is a wonderful deer dog) carry a deer far away to the eastward, hopelessly out of the drive. He must have gotten past Steve, for I heard that huge gorilla trying to turn him and the cruel jeers of his fellow drivers advising him that if he could do no better he might as well go home. Now Sambo and Red took a trail on my side of the branch. It was cold and mazy, and they did not seem able to straighten it out properly. I knew that if they stayed with it long enough they would jump the deer, but I was afraid he was not in our drive.

Suddenly I heard little Blue Boy, a beagle, coming straight down the drive toward us. I could hear him all the more clearly because the drivers had eased up on their racket in order to investigate the possibilities of what Red Liquor and Sambo were claiming they had discovered. My Blue Boy I had hunted for three seasons, and had found him to be a quite matchless deer hound. I got him originally in this way. A beagle fancier had him, along with about twenty others. Blue was the very best of the lot. But his owner wanted him for exhibition purposes only; and he told me that, for the class in which he belonged, Blue's tail was a half inch too long! As for me, when it comes to a dog I really want to hunt, give me the nose. I don't worry about tails.

Blue held a straight course, and he was taking something to my son. I could not hear him so well, as he was running in the thickets, but soon he cleared the cover. Immediately I heard Irvine shoot once. It was a tantalizing thing for me to be so near yet not to know what had happened. I figured he must have killed something, or else he would have fired again.

I heard him talking to Blue; then I heard him taking Blue back into the head of the drive. What had happened? Had an old buck started out, been missed or wounded, and turned back? Whatever it was, I knew I had to hold my stand. For a few minutes I heard nothing whatsoever from Blue Boy. However, Wineglass, on my side of the drive and not far ahead of me, began to whoop as if he had been converted. Evidently he had walked up a deer. He had, and here they came to me—two old does and two yearlings, with no dog following. They passed me at a leisurely pace, within twenty yards, and without ever seeing me.

I was very curious over the meaning of Blue's race, the single shot, his being put back into the drive, and his present silence. The drivers were now in full cry again, and coming pretty close. Suddenly I heard Blue, and he was coming my way. Almost before I had time to get my gun up, a beautiful buck sailed out of the thicket ahead of me. He was running on my right, and he was in high gear; moreover, he was kiting through pines that were thicker than a man likes to have them when he is trying not to miss.

Blue was right after this buck, almost under his tail, and the buck was not trying to hide his purpose of getting out of that hot corner with all expedition. At my first barrel he fell flat. Blue was running so fast that he actually ran up on the prone deer's body, whereupon the old stag righted himself, got off the ground, and started away. I had to shoot him again; at least I did so, for when a hunter sees a buck trying to get away, the sensible and the merciful thing to do is to end the business then and there.

I never understand just how it is done; but however far off hounds may have strayed, and however far away Negro drivers may be, at the blast of a gun they all suddenly appear on the scene of action. So it was now, with the bushes breaking in every direction and hounds and drivers emerging.

When I crossed the thicket to Irvine's stand, I found him with a shaggy eight-point buck that Blue had brought straight to him. Beside him was the delightedly smiling Sam'l. We brought this buck over the branch and laid him beside mine. Mine was only six-point, and I had had to shoot him twice. Irvine's was the finer deer, and he had done the task assigned with one shot. But you understand that is as it should have been.

What happened was probably something like this: these two bucks had probably been lying together, and came to the head of the drive together. One came straight out and ran into my sharpshooter's ambush (my son taught sharpshooting in the Army). The other buck dodged back. His intent was probably to make a run straight back for the river, two miles away. But the drivers had pretty effectively closed off that avenue of escape. Providentially, Irvine, instead of tying Blue beside his dead buck, had put him back in the drive, having a hunch, as he told me, that there might be something more in there. Blue did not then open until he got on the second buck, which proceeded to try my side of the drive, with the aforesaid result.

We had taken to the woods at eight o'clock in the morning. By nine we were at home with two fine bucks. Such a thing had never before happened to Irv and me, nor is it likely to happen again—at least not just that way. And that's why it's a hunt really to remember.

IV

The Hampton Hunt
Other Game

A Unique Quail Hunt

This piece first appeared in the August 1920 issue of Field & Stream *and later was included in* Plantation Game Trails *(pages 160–64). At the time quail, those noble little patricians of fence rows and overgrown ditches, patches of broomsedge and unharvested field corners were plentiful. Since then their numbers have declined dramatically, so much so that were Rutledge alive today it would be impossible for him to fulfill his city friend's need for "birds," as everyone in the South called bobwhites. In this instance, though, he finds bevies of birds and comes home with a game bag laden with what another South Carolina writer, Havilah Babcock, described as "five ounces of feathered dynamite."*

We were just about halfway through our plantation Christmas dinner, which is no mean kind of an entertainment, when a Negro bearing a note for me shuffled to the door. I took the letter and read its brief contents. A friend in the city was having a house-party of a dozen guests. As yet they had enjoyed no game. Would it be possible for me to secure and dispatch immediately about twenty-five or thirty quail? The writer assured me that I knew where the birds were, and all that; and that he would not trouble me, but that he knew how much I should enjoy getting the bag for him. But unless they could be put on the mail Christmas night they would arrive too late for the aforesaid purpose. Gentle reader, have you ever had a friend who knew nothing of hunting ask you to get game for him? He thinks he is conferring a privilege on you; for he honestly believes that on a big plantation shooting quail is just like picking cotton, and bagging a wild turkey is just like going out into the garden and cutting off a cabbage—just like that!

But this friend of mine, however uninformed on some matters, is a man whom I like to please, therefore during the remainder of the dinner I was honestly planning how I might accommodate his wishes. To do this would, in the first place, require quick work, for the sun was hardly two hours high. Moreover, to another friend I had lent my only bird-dog for a Christmas-Day hunt. Unless a man has two or three coveys of quail shooed into a coop, and has the lid clamped down over them, how is he going to produce them suddenly at a friend's mere wish? But in hunting as in most things it pays to try.

Leaving the rest of the company discussing juleps and the like, I emerged from the house just before the sun had begun to burn the tall pines to the westward of the plantation. Seeing several little Negro boys who had already had a share of dinner, I impressed them into my service. We crossed the cotton-fields, heading toward a long stretch of broomsedge that bordered the creek. In this dense yellow grass there are always quail, but to find them without a dog would be difficult; yet there were my dusky henchmen to help. Pausing once to look the situation over, I heard, coming from a far edge of the field, where an extraordinary high tide had begun to back the water into the grass, the carrying-on of two coveys of quail that had run into each other. The voluble gossip that they were engaging in was sweet music to my ears. And there was little lost motion in my getting to where the birds were.

Telling my small trailers to stand close behind me so as to give me a chance to shoot, I began walking up the birds. They must have been having for themselves some kind of a Christmas festival or dinner-party, for they were as loath to rise as some friends I had just left had been unwilling to leave the table. I never saw birds rise so scatteringly; not if I live until the League of Nations or the millennium or something like that comes off, do I expect to see more quail in one place. I said that two coveys had come together. That was all wrong. The thing I am telling is a true thing; and when I say that, standing almost in one place, with birds rising almost continuously, I was enabled to kill eleven birds "on the rise," you will understand what kind of a camp-meeting I had invaded. Nor did the birds, even after much shooting, fly wildly. They must have been too deeply engrossed with social engagements to consider me. From the grassy edges where I had flushed them they swung to the left, settling about in the tall broom grass on a little hillock that rose softly from the dead level of the old field.

The little Negroes retrieved all the shot birds, and we now began to walk up the scattered ones. The sun was down behind the pines now; and the brightly lighted sky gave most excellent visibility. To walk up these fine birds and to have them go whirring off toward the fading sunset afforded me as fine an opportunity for quail-shooting as I have ever enjoyed. The crippled birds were gathered in for me by the small boys, who performed very creditably. They also carried the game, so that all I had to do was to flush the birds and shoot.

They were not followed for the third rise, both because they were by that time widely scattered, and because, on pausing to count heads, I discovered, to my surprise, that we had twenty-eight. They would be enough. The house-party would be supplied. Nor, strange to say, had the matter in this instance been much more difficult than picking cotton. I got the birds off on the mail that night, and learned later that they had arrived in time to render festive the occasion for which they had been gathered in.

There remains, perhaps, a word concerning the remarkable size of this bunch of birds that it was my good fortune to encounter. I have seen at other times coveys numbering as many as thirty-five or forty birds, and these undoubtedly consisted of two or more bevies that had come together. My accounting for this particular covey is this: that on account of the very high water prevailing in the creek, which had flooded the marshes and bottomlands, two coveys, possibly three, that had been used to roosting in the marsh, had come late in the afternoon to the broomsedge field, and there had met another covey. They were discussing the situation when I heard them; and the fact that they realized that their regular haunts were flooded kept most of them in the broom grass. In all, the hunt was a unique one, not the least interesting feature of which being my new type of retriever that proved his worth on that memorable occasion.

Fireworks in the Peafield Corner

One of the most popular of all Rutledge's stories, thanks at least in part to his felicitous choice of a title, this piece first appeared in the December 1932 issue of Field & Stream *(pages 24–25, 62–63). It later served as the title piece for an anthology compiled by Rutledge's youngest son, Irvine,* Fireworks in the Peafield Corner *(pages 59–65). In a delightfully serendipitous development, what started out as a deer hunt sees Rutledge and two of his sons take a trio of turkeys for the holiday table.*

A good many sportsmen find their game by going out and looking for it; others depend to some degree on the intelligence brought them by friendly natives. Some of the best sport I have ever enjoyed has been made possible by hints that the human dwellers in the wilderness have given me. Some plantation Negroes have an almost uncanny finesse in locating game; others are just plain liars, who will tell me of giant stags and huge flocks of wild turkeys that are purely hypothetical. As a result, when tidings concerning game are brought to me, I have to discriminate.

The sun had gone down on the last day of the year when I saw old Gabe Myers riding up the plantation avenue on his white horse. As I had said goodbye to him only an hour before, when I had liquidly wished him a Happy New Year, I could account for his return only by supposing that on his way home to

Peafield Corner he had seen game and had come back to report to me. I have hunted deer and turkeys with Gabe for thirty-nine years.

"Well, old hunter," I said, "did you come back for another Happy New Year?"

"I don't never refuse," he admitted, "but what done bring me is big news. My boy George was shootin' squirrel down by de big oaks a little while back, and he run on four able bucks—yes, say four of 'em. Dat old gun he got miss fire, and he say dem deer just stand right there in de old field and look at him. Four bucks," he repeated.

"And you think we can catch them right there in the morning?"

I confess that I wished that the report had come from a more reliable source than "my boy George," one of the most no-account Negroes who ever stole my chickens and watermelons. For years I had tolerated him merely on account of his matchless father. I had serious doubts whether George could distinguish a deer from a squirrel.

"Plenty of acorns is in dat corner," Gabe told me. "I believe we might pen up dem deer if we start at day-clean."

"We'll meet you by the Old Parsonage at daylight. Now don't drink any moonshine tonight, and don't go gallin'. Let's hang up some horns first."

Promising to be moral and immaculate until the hunt was over, my old woodsman rode into the shadows of the December day.

While the great pine forest that surrounds my Carolina home was still dim and dewy the next morning, we gathered at our rendezvous. Gabe led the Negro drivers: Steve and Sammy and Lewis. My three sons and I were the standers. I have raised them to be hunters, believing that every man should not only know how to handle a gun, but be able to get about in the woods, for a man who is not a sportsman never realizes what harmless and spirited joy he misses. I started each one of my boys to hunt with me when he was six years old. While only one is now of age, each has hung up his gobbler and his antlered stag. Each has learned how to roll his own. Besides, we have countless happy memories of our days together in the woods and fields.

Peafield Corner is a heavily wooded triangle between Montgomery Creek and the Santee River. Once a great and prosperous plantation, it is now the haunt of wild game. Old Gabe, who lives there, has a hard time raising any crops on account of the deer, and his turkeys are forever straying off to mate with wild ones. To drive the place, we send the Negroes back along the river, from which they turn and come out to us on the main road, a mile away.

Sending my eldest son, Arch, to the Tar Kiln Stand on the road, I put my youngest at the head of the Doctor's Branch, a famous crossing so named because a physician of old days had let two old bucks slip by him there. My second boy, Middleton, stood in a deep corner next to the Old Parsonage. I stood at the

Crippled Oak. We had the corner blocked off; but it has been my experience that the game that is cornered is often the game that gets away.

For twenty minutes, while the drivers were taking the hounds back by the river, I heard no sound in the woods save the dripping of dew from the needles of the long-leaf pines, the drowsy awakening call of birds, and the music of the wings of wild ducks speeding over the forest toward the delta.

Then the Negroes began to drive. I have taught them not merely to whoop but to sing their spirituals as they do at camp meetings; and if there is any sound more melodious than those pagan voices ringing in the wildwoods at dawn, I have not heard it. Almost simultaneously with the first voice of a driver came the first voice of a dog. We had two with us, Old Horse and Bing; the former a rangy veteran of the Walker strain, and the latter an English beagle with a high-pitched whimper. Both dogs were soon on a hot trail, and the drivers warmed to their work when they heard the pack begin to give tongue.

Driving out to the hunt that morning, I had told my boys all about the four bucks. All of us seemed equally at a loss to know exactly how to handle such embarrassment of riches. I suggested that two extra shells be taken out of the belt and laid handy. But I had no definite recommendations. I have a friend who killed three deer at one shot, and another who missed a herd of eleven. They were coming straight for him, and he shot both barrels at their twinkling legs, thinking to put the whole crowd out of commission. He didn't cut a hair; and it served him right for trying to kill them all. Of course, I was not sure that "my boy George" had seen four razorbacks or four possums. Yet when the dogs began to chime, hope rose in my heart.

From our stands we could see a long way under the great pines back toward Peafield Corner. There was plenty of light to shoot. It was the first day of the new year. We ought to make history.

Every second I expected to see a forest of horns. That the drivers had seen game was evident from the way they were singing out; it sounded as if they had been converted. But not a thing could I see. On came Old Horse and Bing, the deep-toned musician and the wailing baby. They could not be mistaken. I had a cold chill that the deer had already walked out of the drive and that the dogs were running a trail an hour old. But it was not so.

Suddenly I heard Arch, off to my right, let drive. There was only one barrel; he must have killed his buck. Then, deep down to my left, I heard Middleton salute the dawn with both barrels. The dogs were raging now, and the Negroes had gone quite daffy. To them the sound of the gun suggests a certain dinner, and no other thought stirs them quite so soulfully. But there was something queer about all this. If this bombardment had been at the four bucks, I ought to have seen their telltale flags flashing far off through the misty morning woods;

if the bucks had separated, one should have come to me or to my youngest son next to me. But his gun was silent, and nary a deer did I see.

Little Bing, who is white, I made out some two hundred years ahead of me. She was ranging about frantically, but apparently there was nothing ahead of her. I was completely bewildered—so much so that I committed what is in our country one of the cardinal blunders of a deer hunter: I left my stand. Slowly I began edging my way down toward Middleton. Having fired twice, he ought to have two bucks and would therefore need more help than Arch. You know how we think those things out.

Confused as I was, it did not reassure me particularly to hear the voice of "my boy George" join the hunt. It was a discord in the general harmony. Besides, he is the kind of man on whom you can always count to do the wrong thing in the woods. Anybody can drive deer; but a good hunter will drive them to you. George has a system worked out whereby he always drives them away from you.

I had gone perhaps thirty yards from my stand when an intuition made me stop. I leaned against a pine, scanning the open country between the advancing dogs and drivers and myself. In that space there were only a few sparse bushes—hardly enough to hide a rabbit. But you all know that a deer can sometimes make himself mighty small; I do not know a better skulker. That's why I lingered there, not quite convinced that the dogs were playing me false. They were still on a hot trail; and certainly something had gone to the boys.

Suddenly I saw him. But it was not a buck. Why hadn't I guessed ere this critical moment the solution of the mystery of the great outcry of dogs and drivers, the three shots, and nothing seen or heard? My Negroes had run into a flock of turkeys. Here came one now, a noble gobbler. Evidently he was badly scared. He had been running hard, and had all his feathers drawn in so tightly that he hardly looked to be half his natural size. When a wild turkey comes dodging along through bushes, his long, snakelike neck is often the first thing seen. I once told an amateur hunter to look out for this very thing when I left him on a deer stand one day. Not long after I heard his gun blare manfully, after which detonation one of my old hounds set up a mournful yowling. He had come out through some huckleberry bushes to the stander, who had promptly decided that his tail, waving high over the brush, was the neck of a wild turkey. That dog's tail never did lose its crazy list after that.

The minute I sighted my gobbler, I must have made some instinctive movement, for he instantly checked, standing there tall and wary, a beautiful and splendid creature, utterly wild. Both barrels of my gun were loaded with buckshot. I had no chance now to shift to 2's or 4's. The turkey was going straight to the stand I had left. Now he was sixty-five yards away, broadside; and he would come no nearer. At that distance a man is far more likely to miss a turkey with buckshot than to kill him.

I brought my gun up, got the sight on the gobbler's bronze shoulder, and let drive. He instantly flattened out and began to flop heavily. I started to walk toward him. As I did he recovered his feet and began to run in a wobbly fashion toward a bushy watercourse. I carefully marked the exact spot where he entered this cover.

When we left home that morning, I had left the bird dog, Jim. But when we had reached the rendezvous, Jim showed up apologetically behind the car. I had scolded him for coming, but now I thanked my stars that I had him. He was lying out in the road by the car.

About this time the dogs came up on the trail of the gobbler, and I stopped them. Then came the drivers. Then Middleton appeared with a twenty-pound old tom slung over his shoulder. From the other direction came Arch, with a similar trophy. If I could get mine, we'd have three, and the sun was not yet up.

Going out to the road, we ran full into a party of Christmas hunters, twenty-two strong. Most of them apparently were in the woods for the first time. Their excitement at sight of the two great gobblers slung nonchalantly over my sons' shoulders was interesting to watch. They were full of curiosity and questions.

"Jim," I called my setter, "come in here with me."

"What are you going to do now?" one of the visitors asked, giving all of us a survey as if he thought we were miracle workers.

"Oh," I said lightly, "I'm just going in these bushes here to kill another gobbler."

"By golly!" said the man. "Now ain't that sumpin'?"

"He's just kiddin' you," another said.

I went in with Jim. He made a beautiful point on the wounded bird, which got up heavily and flew back toward my audience. When I shot him, they had to scatter to get clear of his ponderous fall.

"Holy snap!" one of them cried out. "Is killin' turkeys as easy as that?"

"Them's tame turkeys," one of the crew suggested.

"Huh," said one of their old grizzled guides. "If them's tame turkeys, I is the Prince o' Whales."

So, after the fireworks in Peafield Corner, we were back home early to a New Year's breakfast.

"How many were in the flock?" I asked Gabe as we planned further fireworks.

"'Bout sixteen, sah."

"We did well," I said; "but what about those four bucks? I was ready and waiting."

"My boy George," Gabe told me, "he done see them. But he been on the wrong side of them, and he run them across the creek."

George would do that.

Joel's Christmas Turkey

This piece appears in Old Plantation Days *(pages 198–212) and in all likelihood was previously published as a magazine article. Although there may have been some factual underpinnings for the story, it is essentially fictional in nature. Also those who are wise in the ways of the wild turkey will raise an eyebrow at the mention of December gobbling, but in fairness this does happen on rare occasions. Perhaps the most interesting aspect of this story is an ending reminiscent of an O. Henry short story.*

J oel's place was the kind that one comes upon suddenly in the pineland wilderness of the Carolinas: the few meager fields and parched pastures leading up to it were unfenced, and appeared to be but an open stretch of the monotonous landscape. There were no groups of whitewashed buildings behind it, nor pleasant vistas of orchards and meadows; for Joel was a poor white woodsman and trapper, and his home was in the great pine barrens of the coast country of South Carolina. The nearest settlement was eight miles away, southward down the lonely, grass-grown road. His cabin, built of rough-hewn, sap-pine logs, already beginning to sag along their length and to be crushed where the weight of the structure caught them, squatted in a rude clearing not much larger than the building itself. Scrub pines and sparse patches of gallberry and low-bush huckleberry bushes grew almost to the door; a weedy path led from the road, along which few travelers ever passed, to the rotted doorstep-block. The reason why Joel's home was so unhomelike was simple: he had never married, and his real home was in the woods.

Joel was accounted the best woodsman in his county; and while he had many rivals, he had no peers. He killed on the average of twenty deer a season, and his record on wild turkeys was even more formidable. Joel always said that he had never been to school long enough to learn to count above the legal number of deer that the law allowed to be taken in a season; besides, his third cousin was game warden. But for all his craft, there was a wild turkey living in the tupelo swamp behind his cabin that had made Joel stretch himself, and so far, stretch himself in vain. It seemed to the hunter that he had used every whit of

Two examples of "Miss Seduction," the turkey call Rutledge made and
sold as one of his countless endeavors to raise money for the
maintenance of Hampton Plantation

his strength, woodcraft, patience, and tireless energy of pursuit in the attempt to win this royal prize; and doubtless the wild gobbler knew something of the relentlessness of Joel as a hunter, and just how wary he had to be to keep his distance from Joel's deadly musket. This turkey could not speak human speech as can some of the creatures about which our fanciful naturalists write. He could not put his finger to his nose and scoff at Joel, saying, "O sad brother, I am the Wise One. Booloo is my friend. I shall meet him at the Council Tree at midnight, and you will never find us any more." He was just a plain turkey; but when that has been said all has been said that need be mentioned; for if a plain wild turkey is not the most intelligent bird afoot or awing, then the dodo isn't dead.

Joel had first seen him one sultry September day, when the pine woods were fervidly hot, when the grass was as sear as tinder, and when the lush-grown swamps were sending up in steaming moisture the little water that the long drought had left in them. There was no wing stirring. The birds, hidden deep in the thickets, were still. Even the wood-cicadas had ceased their dry, insistent shrilling. Joel, coming down a sandy path through the scrub-oak, not far from the west bank of the Santee River, heard a hen-turkey's sudden and startled "put! put!" Joel halted in his tracks, while his keen gray eyes swept the bushy savanna over to his left, whence the sound had come. He did not see the mother, but he saw the young one (there appeared to be but the one) as it came stepping from behind the shelter of a broomsedge tussock. A half-grown wild gobbler he was, remarkably large and well formed. He was so big as to be awkward; but, like all members of his hunted race, he was shy and swift and wonderfully gifted in the woodland art of silently and suddenly effacing himself. For a second he was in Joel's sight; then he vanished. When a wild turkey vanishes, after having seen a man, depend upon it, bank upon it, he's *gone*.

181

Joel came cautiously round the edge of the thicket, looking for others of the brood. But he saw none. Not far away was the sandy road, and toward this the trapper went; for if one cannot see the game itself one can at least have the dubious satisfaction of seeing its tracks. In the damp sand where a summer-dried stream had crossed the road, he found the turkey's tracks. There, lightly and springily set, were those of the hen; while beside them were great, sprawling tracks, with big, wide-spreading toes that mashed the sand.

"Well, now, jest look at that!" muttered Joel as he bent over them; "the young un's feet are bigger than his ma's!"

Then he stood up and looked toward the dark swamp into whose deep recesses the two turkeys had vanished. Knowing the pine woods from the Santee to the Cooper, and from the railroad to the sea, the trapper knew where these turkeys would feed, range, roost. And he felt sure that by Christmas-time the hen and the fine young gobbler would bring him a big price from some epicurean clients of his living down in the village on the nearby coast.

The luxuriance of the summer passed into the mournful beauty of the autumn, and the autumn gave place to the winter; but still Joel had not fulfilled the plan he had made that September day when for the first time he had looked at the turkey-tracks in the road. A score of times he had seen the splendid wild bird; other turkeys fell before his gun; but the big bronzed racer of the pineland always escaped. The winter wore along to the early spring, but Joel was still unsuccessful. Late one March afternoon, on his return through a tupelo swamp after a trip for raccoon, Joel heard the gobbler down in a heavy clump of cypresses gobbling a provoked answer to a rookery of crows that were cawing away in their careless fashion. As soon as he got to his cabin the trapper took down from a smoke-blackened beam a small white bone, the radius of a turkey's wing. He washed it, blew through it, squinted down it; then, placing it to his mouth and hollowing his hands in front of it, he drew forth the soft and pleading notes of a hen turkey.

"That will fetch the old sport," he said to himself; "leastwise I never yet seen the gobbler that wouldn't jest streak it for me when I called."

It was still quite dark when Joel stepped out of his cabin next morning. The vast forest was sleeping under its mantle of mist. In the velvet-purple of the night sky the stars shone beautiful. High in the darkness the crests of the mighty pines murmured and waved. Fragrances of the wild and virgin woods moved subtly across the path down which Joel stepped, and met him also, more deep and rich, in the glimmering road. But the trapper, to whom such influences were too ordinary to be impressive, pushed on rapidly through the mist. Slung under his right arm, with its cap and priming kept dry by the flap of his old coat, was his musket; an ancient weapon, decidedly out of date as far as appearances were concerned, but one which had never yet failed Joel. On the few occasions when he had missed, he had never blamed his musket for it. No good hunter ever blames his gun, when once that gun has proved itself true.

A short walk down the road brought the turkey hunter to a blind sheep path, which an ordinary man would have passed without seeing; but, to him, the woods and their ways were as well known by night as by day. On he tramped through the bush-hung path. The gallberry bushes drenched him with their dew. The cool, misty tops of the bending broomsedge brushed him with a rainy fragrance. There were many odors of the coming spring wafted on the night air. Joel did not walk carelessly; he stepped with the easy stride of a woodsman, yet with caution and alertness. Only a woodsman knows how to be alert without being strained. Through these woods he was traversing there was danger; for on a certain day of that same week he had counted fourteen rattlesnakes, dragging themselves across his path, lying in loose coils between the tussocks of broom-sedge, and sunning themselves beside fallen logs and sheltering stumps.

In half an hour Joel came to an airy ridge in the woods, and here he halted. Behind him lay the darksome forest, still dreaming in its mantling mists; but before him, like the effulgence from some distant fire, there was a living glow in the sky. Slowly the velvet-purple of the heavens changed to a velvet-violet, then to a velvet-blue. Beyond the vast tupelo swamp where he had roosted the gobbler, the red colors brightened and extended themselves along the horizon.

Joel sat down on a log, laid his musket carefully across his knees, took out his turkey call, and sounded tentatively a few trial notes. The sound was clear and sweet, and the atmosphere was just right for carrying it. He hollowed his big bronzed hands and drew luring music from the white bone; plaintive and pleading and feminine were the notes that came forth. In them were the tenderness and glamour of the voices of young love and the early springtime, voices of hope and of promise.

Far away, on his lonely roost in the huge old moss-draped cypress, the gobbler heard the sound. It pierced the solitude with a poignant sweetness that could not be resisted. Loudly and with masculine assurance he gobbled an answer to the yearning call. Then he launched himself out on his powerful wings, and sailed, straight as a quail flies for cover, toward the crouching hunter. The big turkey came to ground on the edge of the swamp; and there, being greeted by a further call, very soft this time, he put his head forward and down and raced for his alluring goal.

Joel had heard him gobble, but he did not see him coming. Had he known that his royal game was so near, he would have gone down on one knee in the grass. But instead of that he did something that was fatal to his success: he took the call from his mouth and shook the moisture out of it. The hunter had a flashing glimpse ahead of him of a broad bronzed back and a darting blue-black head. Before he could throw his musket up the vision was gone. Silently the great swamp, the sanctuary of the hunted, had taken back its own. Into its secure refuge the great wild bird had vanished.

"I knowed better'n that," said Joel disgustedly, still sitting on his log. "I might have knowed he would come a'pokin' up. But now he's gone; and by *gone* I mean he's *cleaned up*, quit the country, maybe quit the world. If a man doesn't shoot a turkey the minute the turkey sees him, it's good-by, Susie. And I could yelp here all day and he wouldn't even stop getting away from me. I reckon he thought I was shaking my finger at him. Gentlemen, he's a sundowner. But I don't deserve to have him."

The pineland hunter rose to his feet, knowing that his game had escaped him, knowing, too, that for a long time it would be practically impossible to get the wary old gobbler to come to his call. But there were other ways of getting this bronzed racer of the wilderness; and to a man like Joel the woods would not long deny another chance at the coveted prize.

But the spring and the summer passed, and he saw no more of his gobbler. But the autumn, with its bared forests and its fallen crop of acorns to attract turkeys to special places, brought Joel once more into distant acquaintanceship with the big bird. Once he had stalked him among sweet live-oak acorns under the giant oaks on a deserted plantation; but the wary monarch had been just a flash too quick for him. Again he thought he had cornered him in a big patch of high blackberry canes in the woods; and if Joel could have made him fly, the turkey would have been his. But the crafty bird refused to rise. After beating about the briars into which he had seen the gobbler skulk, Joel came out into the road, and there he saw the racer's huge tracks—the flying trail left by him in the sandy loam. Joel whistled incredulously as he stood up after measuring the tracks.

"Four inches from tip to tip," he said, "the biggest gobbler that ever ran these woods. And he'll be mine afore long, or my finger never touched trigger!"

But another whole year passed, and yet another, and Joel was still without his prize. His continual hunting of the big turkey had made that splendid creature abandon his old haunts. He no longer fed in the dense bays and gallberry patches of the Little Ocean; he no longer roosted in the tupelo swamp. Out of the pine woods and towards the river swamps Joel had driven him. The hunter did not altogether approve of the turkey's new range, for well he knew that if once the gobbler took a notion to cross the river he would probably take up with other members of his own tribe in the swamps and pinelands on the North Santee side, never to return to his former home. This was especially likely, Joel knew, if he were not hunted beyond the river. During this last year he had been dividing his time among three or four old deserted plantations—Romney, Montgomery, Oldfield, and Fairfield—that bordered on the Santee delta. It was on Romney, one November morning, that Joel had shot at the huge gobbler as he sailed off his roost in a giant short-leaf. But, as he said to himself with grim humor, "I kindled, but he did not curtsey." For a month thereafter he saw nothing of the object of his quest.

The twilight of Christmas Eve was falling as Joel, weary but hopeful, traversed the desolate, sandy field leading from the pine woods to the river bank on Romney Plantation. All day long he had followed the giant gobbler, and even the hardihood of Joel was sorely taxed. But before him in the sand he saw the fresh tracks which had been left by the wonderful bird he was pursuing. At length he came to a fringe of trees marking the bank of the river. Hardly had Joel paused to look and to listen when, from a thickety clump of elders, a hundred yards away, a great bulk rose heavily and beat its way over the marsh. Its flight took it upward, and bore it into a huge moss-shrouded cypress that stood on the very brink of the wide river. There it alighted heavily; clearly against the afterglow in the sky Joel could see its great bulk rock on the limb, lower its weight carefully, and at last settle on its perch. He had roosted the mighty bird! At last, after all those years, he was going to have a fair chance at the largest and craftiest wild gobbler that had ever ranged the Santee country.

For a half-hour, while the light died and the noises from field and fen wakened and were hushed again, Joel sat in the dry grass with his keen eyes riveted on the black mass that never stirred in the ancient gray cypress. At last the real darkness was at hand, and he must make his shot before it would be too late to see his game.

He could not cross the boggy marsh that lay between him and the big cypress. But a short detour, by way of an old check-bank, brought him almost under the vast bulk of the tree. Through the branches, draped with moss, he saw the Christmas stars; and motionless on a stout limb, to Joel's tingling satisfaction, sat the great wild turkey. All the hunter's stalking ended here.

Joel peered this way and that, trying to get his game clear of intervening limbs. It was tense work, as the light was almost gone. Finally, when he dared to step out on the edge of the marsh to get an unimpeded view, he was amazed and bewildered to see *two* black shapes in the cypress, where but one had been visible before. Moreover, they appeared to be of the same size, and they were undoubtedly of the same shape. Joel exclaimed under his breath. His first thought was there were two turkeys in the tree, but then he came to the conclusion that one was his gobbler and the other was a huge bunch of mistletoe.

But which was which? Joel peered and pondered. The light was going so fast that the great tree had taken on a more shadowy outline, and the two dark shapes were fast merging into the blackness of the cypress branches. Which object should he shoot? Which one was the royal bird, and which one was the bunch of Christmas greens? In vain did Joel crane his neck this way and that, straining his good eyes. Not even he could distinguish between the two dim objects so high up in the night.

At last he raised his musket, gripping it strongly with his bronzed hands. It roared out on the twilight. Its detonation rolled far up and down the misty reaches of the river. And Joel saw two things happen: first, a dark bulk launched flight above the river and toward what lay beyond; secondly, another dark shape swayed in the cypress, turned slowly, cracked, and came rushing to the ground. Joel had shot off the bunch of mistletoe. The king of the pineland wilderness had escaped across the river.

But Joel was a game sport. He picked up the bunch of mistletoe and slung it slowly over his shoulder.

"I'll take it home and hang it in the house," he said: "it will 'mind me of Christmas."

Miss Seduction Struts Her Stuff

Among all of the literally thousands of Rutledge stories I have read, this one takes the prize for the most alluring title. He named his turkey call "Miss Seduction," and notwithstanding the fact that it is the male turkey, not the female, that struts, the title is a pure delight. The piece originally appeared in the January 1934 issue of Field & Stream *(pages 22–23, 53). It has been included in several anthologies:* The Field & Stream Reader *(pages 76–81);* Field & Stream Treasury *(pages 265–68), ed. Hugh Grey and Ross McCluskey; and* The Best of Field & Stream *(pages 164–67), ed. J. I. Merritt. As an interesting sidelight, it should be noted that Rutledge sold handmade replicas of Miss Seduction for five dollars (as advertised in the pages of national magazines). Today verifiably authentic box calls of this type bring sums well into four figures from call collectors.*

*F*or many years I have had a positive superstition about luck on the last day—sometimes during the very last hour. A thrilling and possibly dramatic experience that I had on January 2, 1933, has confirmed me in this way of thinking. True, the affair did not happen on the last day of the wild turkey season in South Carolina, for that is February 28; but it was the last day for me, as I was scheduled to leave for the North early on the morning of January 3.

That summer an old wild turkey hen raised a flock of sixteen birds on my plantation. I had had reports of them, and high hopes were mine that they would still be there on my Christmas visit. But certain turkey-minded friends and neighbors anticipated me; and while they killed only one or two of the birds, they succeeded in utterly scattering and demoralizing the flock. All through the holidays I hunted for them. Their tracks were found in the sandy roads. I once heard a hen drowsily calling at daylight; once I saw one about half a mile down an old woodland trail. But nary a shot was mine.

These birds were genuinely wild in every sense of the word: of the ancient pure wild strain, with no admixture of domestic blood—lovely bronze plumage, black heads, pink legs and a general aspect of being tailor-made. They were so keen of sight and hearing as to be able to detect a wink or a whisper at shot-gun range; so silent and canny as to make an attempt at stalking a ludicrous thing. You know the feeling that I had as the precious days passed; that the game was unquestionably there, but that it was too smart to permit me to come up with it.

Finally my last day came. While I had had excellent sport with ducks and deer, it looked as if I were going to be a total washout on the turkeys. However, at about four o'clock that afternoon, with the kindly Southern sun shining genially and with no wind stirring, my three boys and I decided to try the last chance.

Scattered groups of the birds had several times been reported to me by Negroes as crossing an old abandoned road—usually at about five o'clock in the afternoon, evidently on their way to roost in the great river-swamp. I had not been able to discover their bedroom, yet had a fair notion of where it likely was. I posted my boys on the road and then walked a half mile down the river-bank. My idea was to call a little in order to lure any lonely birds toward the standers posted in front of me. It sometimes happens that for weeks at a time wild turkeys will follow the same range, day after day.

At the place where I stopped, two old rice-field banks converged and met the bank of the river. It seemed a strategic spot, though I had never tried it before. All about me were giant cypresses, softly alight in the rays of the setting sun; lonely abandoned rice-fields, grown head-high in marsh; solitary pines, thickets of cane and alder and birch. Except for the firm footing on the leaf-strewn banks, the country was very wet. As I sat down to call I heard a deer tramping round in the marsh across the river, gray squirrels barking and scuttling about on the leaves, wild ducks hurrying toward the delta, and the big owls beginning their weird hooting.

At a moment when some of these sounds abated, I touched my call.

This call is one of many I have made. Most of them have had faults of tone—either squeakiness, of a tone too high-pitched, or sounding more like something else than a turkey, or prone to emit a sudden false note that is always bad news for a turkey hunter. But on account of the depth, certainty, and mellow tone of this particular box, I had christened her Miss Seduction. I have tested her many times, and I have found that she will do almost anything except actually kill my gobbler for me. On several occasions she has embarrassed me by calling up old turkey hunters to me. I like them, but there's a closed season on them.

For many years I have experimented with making box calls for turkeys from all kinds of woods. Red cedar I have rejected on account of the shallowness of its tone and its inclination to squeak; seasoned poplar is excellent, as is Western fir; dried maple and holly are good. I like willow best because of the quality of the wood, the smooth texture and high tension of the grain, and the mellow tone that can be drawn from such a box. Soft chalk is always applied to the calling-lip of the box and is used to cover the slate caller as well. I have made box calls with the shuffling tops, but the other type is handier and has been more effective for me. It seems a general principle that the best tone is to be had from a wood of medium hardness, such as chestnut or willow. If the wood is too hard, the qualities of depth and vibrancy will be absent.

To call a turkey one will perhaps do best if he will put himself in the place of the bird and will call in such a manner that, if he were the bird, he would come. A great many things are to be considered: the time of day (of course, they call best just after and just before roosting); the condition of the atmosphere (a windy day is bad, and a rainy day not so good); the place from which the calling is done, for it should be of such a character that the bird would naturally haunt it; and then the calling itself, which is a thing to be learned rather than told of.

I may say, however, that an amateur will call too often, too loudly, and with too little variation in the tone. A wild turkey is a patrician, and he does not appreciate any member of his tribe's overflowing and drowning him with too much gushing. Of course, in the mating season few birds are more garrulous than wild gobblers. But in the hunting season they are almost as silent and non-committal as they are wary.

During the next twenty minutes I called about seven times. It pays not to be too urgent. Unless I am mistaken, it is the long, sweet pleading quality of the first note that usually does the work. I had had no answer; but, as every experienced hunter knows, a wild turkey will often come silently to a call. Some answer and come. Some answer and do not come. Some do not answer and come. Some never answer and never come. Some come running; some flying; some walking fast; some stealing along furtively. I have had an old gobbler come within thirty yards of me from behind before I detected his approach.

Down went the sun, suffusing the wild, sweet world with a golden afterglow. I had heard no gun from my standers. It looked about all over. But suddenly I heard a great commotion in the marsh across the river. At first I thought it must surely be a deer jumping in to swim across. Yet when I turned quickly to look, there came a splendid gobbler, flying almost straight for my call. I knew that I ought to get my gun up while he was flying; because if a wild turkey is on the ground near you, the matter of getting your gun on him is just one of those critical things that is awfully hard to maneuver. In the two seconds that it takes you to put it on him, he's going to be executing the greatest vanishing act you ever saw.

Fifty yards from the river-bank the glistening king of the swamplands set his wings and sailed, alighting high and dry about thirty-five yards from me. I made a clean kill with 4's. Miss Seduction had done her work. In forty years of hunting this was the first time I had ever called a wild turkey across a river. And any hunter can easily understand the thrill I got out of it—especially since it was sundown on my last day.

It is not usually worthwhile to call from the same place after a shot has been made there. But I love the river and the swamp in those mystic fading lights, and there might be a bare chance for more sport.

Sundown on a plantation has many compensations even if a hunter never shoots his gun. Winter there is kindly and the coming of dusk does not mean a consequent fall in temperature. A man may sit it out without getting chilled. About me were primeval woods, beautiful with the full-foliaged water-oaks and the moss-bannered cypresses. I could see a little way up the river the immense and shaggy live-oaks whose small sweet acorns wild turkeys prefer to all other winter food. Not until they have harvested this crop will they turn to the somewhat bitter acorns of the water-oaks. They also relish hard black seeds of the American lotus, black-gum berries, gall-berries, and the fruits of the wild greenbriar.

In the old days of baiting turkeys before beneficent laws were passed against this practice, the birds would come almost equally well to corn, peas, and rice. I once examined the crop of a wild turkey that had in it a mixture of salted almonds and whole snails! The former he must have gleaned from the waste of some hunter's luncheon; the latter he probably ate, partly for the food value and party for the grit in the shell.

It was now very dusky in the swamp. The river appeared wan and mysterious. Far up the stream I could see the lights of home shining in the twilight. Once more I touched Miss Seduction. It really seemed too late; yet while I have known some wild turkeys to take the roost long before sundown, I have known others to delay their retiring until it was almost too dark to see a limb on which to perch.

On the farther side of the old wooded bank coming down through the middle of the swamp, I had heard a brown thrasher scuffling in the leaves. This sound grew a little loud and unfamiliar. Save for his keen head, this turkey was completely hidden by the bank. But he was only thirty-five yards away, and coming closer. At the range which he had already reached, I would not have been afraid to try a chance at his head alone; but I had no shells save the two in my gun, and they were loaded with buckshot. All my turkey-shot, save the lone

4's I had already fired, I had given to my boys. Now, a man stands a beautiful chance of missing a wild turkey with buckshot, whatever the range; and to shoot at his head with buckshot is almost certainly to miss him.

The gobbler would pass me on my left. The old bank, behind the shelter of which he was walking, was perhaps of more advantage to me than to him, for I waited for him to get his head behind the bank and then got my gun up, leveling it through a small break in the dyke, across the aperture of which his majesty would pass.

The west was barely glimmering with the last streaks of day and the dusk in the swamplands was almost night when the great gobbler suddenly filled the opening in the bank. I could barely discern the white sight of my gun against his dark and splendid form. I touched the trigger, and immediately stood up.

What I saw was a big gobbler with a broken wing running for the tall marsh as if a dozen wildcats were after him on wings. I could not really lay the gun on him right, but I let drive with my last shell in his direction. Silence profound settled over the river and the swamp. It was my last shot of the hunting year.

A few minutes later I found my second gobbler, killed by a single buckshot in the neck. With my two wild turkeys over my shoulder, I was soon on the homeward road, along dim starlit paths, familiar to me since boyhood days, toward the old home that has always been to me a beloved sort of shrine for a thousand memories of the river, the pinelands, the broom-grass fields, the brooding solitary swamps, and all their wonderful inhabitants.

My Hunterman

⌁⁚⌁

Rutledge regularly mentions his "huntermen" and often pays richly deserved tribute to them, but only one of them, Prince Alston, was "my hunterman." He and Rutledge grew up together, and until Prince's death they were "companions to the heart." Additional tributes to Prince appear elsewhere in this work, but this piece describes the essence of his uncanny abilities in woodsmanship. Interestingly he is never mentioned by name. The story originally appeared in the September 1919 issue of Outers' Recreation *(pages 170, 230). It was later included in* Fireworks in the Peafield Corner *(pages 249–52). There is a deeply moving, indeed compelling, account of Prince's death (on August 2, 1928) in Rutledge's* Home by the River. *As Rutledge prepared to return to his teaching duties in Pennsylvania after the Christmas 1927 break, Prince asked him to get out of the car and said: "Please, Cap'n, take off your hat. I just want to look into your face once more." Rutledge was convinced Prince had a premonition that they would not see one another again. For a fuller account of this timeless partnership, see "Prince Alston: God's Special Child," above.*

*A*s the wheezing river-tug drew away from the decrepit wharf, my Hunterman, never losing an opportunity to be near me to the last, was standing on the end of a cypress-log which jutted out farther than the wharf into the swirling current of the muddy Southern river. My last view of him, as the straining tug turned from the river into the tortuous creek whose marsh-grown banks would shut us from sight, was all my heart desired. There he stood, now a mile behind, straining his eyes and waving his hand.

"Earth's single moments are unique," wrote Austin Dobson; and so certainly are earth's single characters. That momentary scene of farewell was unique, vividly so; and unique also is the picturesque personality of my Hunterman. Thirty years ago, we were boys on a South Carolina rice plantation; I the son of the owner of the place, and he the son of the Negro man of all-work. Until I went away to school we were inseparable companions. We were partners in all kinds of plantation escapades and adventures; in deer-hunting by day and in 'coon-hunting by night, in riding saplings in the great pine forest, in catching alligators in the rice-field canals, in trapping birds, in breaking colts, and in doing a thousand other reckless, delightful things. Then at last came the separation. Though I was white and he was black, I was to become bond and he was to remain free. I went away to school and thence to college; then an opportunity for work in the North was offered me. But at Christmastime I go back to the old plantation to hunt—and to be with my Hunterman.

He, during the period when I was being educated, bought four acres of land adjoining the plantation ("so I can always be near you," he said), showed admirable thrift in putting his sparse earnings into a good house, was happily married, and became the head of a household. But, despite certain traits of character which seem to indicate a domestic nature, he is, first of all, a Hunterman, and as such is unique.

He inherits his talents for woodcraft from his grandfather who, before Emancipation, was the professional slave "Hunterman" of the plantation. It is not generally known that certain slaves were given regular work of this nature—work for which they were peculiarly adapted, and to which they brought high powers of skill and abundant enthusiasm. Each plantation of the Far South had its "Hunterman" and also its "Fisherman," whose duty it was to keep the commissary of the estate supplied. These dusky nimrods became experts in their callings, and both they and their fellows took deep pride in their achievements. Nor did they lack just reasons for pride, for to them the wilds of the forest and the deeps of the rivers yielded rich and rare spoils. Thus it is related that the only

191

channel bass ever taken in the Santee River were caught nearly a century ago by the slave fisherman of Hampton Place. Like a true and jealous sportsman, he did not divulge his secret, and it perished with him. Many stories could be told of these adventurous characters who, by good fortune, were permitted to live in America the type of life most nearly resembling the life which they would have led in their native land. But I must return to their descendant, who maintains with honor the talents which they bequeathed.

My Hunterman has features that are clear and regular. His expression is open and pleasant. I cannot say that "beauty born of murmuring sound has passed into his face"; yet surely there is visible on his dark, quiet, mobile countenance a lingering light of airy pine-woods, a sense of wide spaces and vast river-scenes, a knowledge of great nature and of greater human life. In height he is not above the medium. True, his stature is one which would set all the athletic coaches of America agog if they could see it; his chest and arms are leonine, massive. He got those mighty muscles from sawing down yellow-pine timber, ten hours a day every day for six years. Yet, so easy are his movements and so loosely do my coats fit him that one does not guess his strength until one sees him, while calming a fractious mule, pick up a two-hundred-pound buck and lay it carefully on the prancing animal's back. Once, when he was about to return to the logging camp, he remarked that he had a little walk ahead of him that afternoon.

"How far is it?" I asked.

"Thirty miles," he said.

"But you will not get there today?"

"Oh, yes, sah; it will not take me over five hours."

And I have good reason to know that it really did not take him longer.

I suppose that living in a country of "magnificent distances" has taught my Hunterman to disregard them. He thinks nothing of walking fifteen miles for a bag of tobacco and a pound of bacon; the length of the journey not seeming out of proportion to the purpose of it, for he has never known anything else. To get a pair of wild ducks he will paddle six miles down the river at dusk, knowing well that six miles, and night, and ebb-tide will, after his shooting, lie between him and home. This physical adaptability to his circumstances makes it possible for him to abstain, without inconvenience, from regular meals. When I think my Hunterman is starting for the woods with me too early to have had breakfast at home, of course his lack is supplied. But on one occasion I forgot to ask him. We hunted hard all day. At nightfall, on our return, he informed me, with high good humor, that he had had "no breakfast yet."

Come with us—with me and my Hunterman—on one of these hunts. It does not matter about me; for I do not differ materially from the common army of sportsmen who autumnly haunt our woods and fields, trying not so much to bag game as to get back into tune with Nature—big and sane and wholesome that she is! It does not matter about me; but you must see my Hunterman at his best—as deer-driver in vast pinewoods.

As we leave the plantation yard, he is mounted on a little black mule whose perverse nature he alone comprehends. Once I mounted that creature; but I was not permitted to be there long enough to learn aught but that it was no place for me. To a white man, a mule must remain an eternal mystery. With a whistle and a long, mellow whoop, which resembles the blowing of a horn, my Hunterman summons the hounds. They appear in the order of their eagerness; the younger ones yelping and frisking, the older ones reserving their spirits for the ruling passion—the stern business of the chase itself. From the luring scent of fox-trails and raccoon-trails he whistles and cajoles them away; they never mind my whistle and scorn my cajoling, but his speech is in their language and its tone they diligently heed. Leaving the plantation avenue and the sweet-smelling hedges between the fields, we literally take to the woods—the vast and lonely pinewoods, sun-bright and shimmering.

Once in the deer country, we separate, I to take up a stand at the head of a dense thicket of myrtles and sweet-bays, and he to drive through it with the dogs. I wait quietly at the forehead of the dewy evergreen copse. Soon I hear my Hunterman coming toward me. He is varying the camp-meeting tune he is whistling so that it will urge the hounds on. Presently I hear a tremendous bound in the bays; then my Hunterman whoops at the top of his voice, "'Tis the old buck! 'Tis the ole buck! For God's sake, don't miss him!"

Here comes the buck, bounding grandly, his great antlers outreaching his stride. Probably by the kindly intervention of Providence, which my Hunterman had indirectly invoked, I do not miss the buck. He is a fine one, with a ruddy coat and tall chestnut-colored antlers. For me and my Hunterman the cup of sporting joys overflows. After a little discussion of how the whole happy affair transpired, he puts the deer on the mule and we return home.

The next day I say good-bye to my Hunterman—and it must be good-bye for a year. Of course I write to him and send him things; some garden seeds, tobacco, and a little money; also all the clothes which my children cannot wear without shame to kindergarten, but his can wear not without pride in plantation fields.

Another year and we shall be together again! It is a happy prospect. Our companionship may be unusual, even unique; but if it is not genuine, life has failed to teach me the meaning of loving comradeship.

Archibald and Alice Rutledge on the steps of Hampton, late in his life

V

Christmas Verse

Without much question, posterity remembers and honors Rutledge more for his prose than his poetry. Booksellers indicate that his collections of stories are in greater demand than those bringing together poems, although the scarcity of both attests to his enduring popularity. Fine copies of his rarest books, whatever the subject matter, bring prices that sometimes reach into the four-figure range. To me much of his poetry seems dated, whereas the sentiments and subject matter of his stories have an enduring, timeless quality. Therein lies one explanation of why previous anthologies I have edited and compiled, all focusing primarily on hunting and nature, have consciously excluded poems even though Rutledge devoted many lines in his verses to hunting and other outdoor-related topics.

In the present case, however, it seemed appropriate to include at least a small sampling of verse. After all, Rutledge was South Carolina's first poet laureate and held that position for many years. He loved the traditional songs of Christmas as much as he reveled in the Hampton Hunt, holiday feasts, and festive gatherings of family and friends. For him the season fairly rang with song and verse, and not surprisingly in his poems he turned to Yuletide themes quite frequently. The selections making up this section of the book provide some of the finest examples of his literary endeavors along these lines.

Christmas Eve on the Rapidan (1863)

This poem can be found on page 445 of Deep River *(revised edition, 1966) and on pages 16–17 of* Bright Angel and Other Poems *(1956), among other places. The setting and the subject matter, the Civil War in Virginia, form recurrent themes in Rutledge's writing. He took great pride in his father's service during the conflict and had a real knack for looking at the pathos and poignancy to be found amongst tragedy and our nation's most trying time. A good example would be his wonderful story "When the Yankee Band Played Dixie." Here, in a poem with a delightful twist, we join a simple soldier on the banks of the Rapidan River as he finds solace in thoughts of loved ones and his religion.*

Hal looked to the left, and he looked to the right,
And he looked where the sycamore glimmered white.
The night was asleep, and his regiment slept,
While over his comrades a watch he kept.

The Rapidan smiled when, clear of cloud,
The moon poured her orchid love-light proud.
Hal thought of Bess . . . "I believe I can see
To read the little Book she gave to me."

From his grimy knapsack by his side he took
His love-gift copy of the Sacred Book.
"Bess begged me to carry it over my heart,
But it's been in my knapsack from the start."

It was Christmas Eve on the Rapidan,
And Hal stood reading of the Perfect Man;
Of Bethlehem's Star, and of Mary mild;
Of shepherds and angels and the little Christ Child.

From the glimmering tree by the river's shore
A rifle's sight on the sentry bore.
By the selfsame light that let Hal read
A sharpshooter steadied him for his deed.

A dry branch cracked on the ghostly tree,
And a shot rang wildling and instantly.
At the crack of the branch, Hal the Story thrust
Into his bosom, —then writhed to the dust.

The surgeon was musing: "A woman, they say,
Can keep safe her loved one far away . . .
Hal will come around . . . Now who but a lover
Would sew steel stays in a Bible's cover?"

Christmas Song

This poem appears on page 345 of the revised edition of Deep River *(1966). Its message of goodwill goes to the heart of what the season always meant for Rutledge.*

No conquest gained, no glory won,
No honor bought by sword or pen
Has half the beauty or the worth
Of peace on earth, goodwill to men.

Goodwill toward men, and peace on earth:
O there was One who brought this word!
This triumph, down the centuries,
Alone can joyously be heard.

Still golden in the gloom about
This message saves us now, as when
It first arrived; this gentle charge
Of peace on earth, goodwill toward men.

What other message brings us hope?
A master race? Some order new?
Older and nobler is the faith
Men have found beautiful and true.

Of peace life's Caesars give us naught
But ashes . . . Love's unerring ken
Follows the everlasting light
Of peace on earth, goodwill to men.

A family gathering at Hampton Plantation, circa 1960.
From the Elise Rutledge Bradford Collection

VI

Feasting at Hampton
The Culinary Aspects of a Low Country Christmas

Writing in My Colonel and His Lady, *a moving tribute to his parents, Rutledge offered some insight into the kind of fare that was standard for the holidays at Hampton. "I hate," he ventured, "to describe a plantation Christmas dinner if I cannot offer my readers the dinner itself." References to culinary pleasures as an integral and important aspect of Christmastime at Hampton Plantation spice many of Rutledge's pieces on the season. Indeed they offer one ready benchmark to his ability as a writer, for at times his descriptions of dishes and meals are so powerful that they put the reader's salivary glands in overdrive. Any hunter who has risen before dawn on a cold December day can, for example, readily identify with the penultimate sentence in "All of a Christmas Morning," when Rutledge and his sons, along with the six "dusky henchmen" who had served as drivers on a deer hunt, return "in triumph to the plantation house, to a breakfast of hominy, cold wild turkey, corn bread, and coffee." Not exactly gourmet fare, but simple and eminently satisfying provender straight from nature's larder as found in Hampton's cultivated fields and wild woods, as these snippets from his writing suggest.*

And yet I cannot think of it without recalling the snowy pyramids of rice, the brown sweet potatoes with the sugar oozing out of their jackets, the roasted rice-fed mallards, the wild turkey, the venison, the tenderloin of pork fattened on live oak acorns, the pilau, the cardinal pudding!

Festive is a plantation dinner table, with a huge haunch of venison, a wild turkey, snowy pyramids of steaming rice, crisp brown corn breads, and Bahama sweet potatoes, the sugar oozing out of their loose jackets.

Our Christmas breakfast of hominy, venison sausages and corn bread . . .

Here the breakfaster may regale himself on plantation fare: snowy hominy, cold wild turkey, brown crumbly cornbreads, venison sausages, beaten biscuits, steaming coffee, home-made orange marmalade. Unless my observation be at fault, the making of coffee on a plantation is a solemn rite, not to be trusted to any one save the mistress of the house. She loves to make it herself before the ruddy fire in the dining room, its intriguing aroma mingling with the fresh fragrances from the greenery hunt about the walls. She loves to carry coffee-making to the point of a fine art, and to serve it out of a massive silver coffee-pot— the same used when a gentleman named General George Washington visited this home during his Southern tour in those last years of the eighteenth century.

Rutledge offered a quintet of recipes published in the December 1913 issue of Country Life in America *(pp. 106–7). To my knowledge these are the only recipes he ever published, and all of them appear below. In introducing the recipes, he wrote: "It is impossible to speak or write of Southern hospitality or plantation festivities without falling into a discussion of Southern cooking. Many of the recipes have never found their way into cookbooks." He then provided "a few of the recipes that still form a part of the Christmas celebration at Hampton Place."*

Drinks and Cordials

Rutledge occasionally mentions spirits in his writing, and it is clear he enjoyed a comforting libation at day's end and the conclusion of a hard hunt. Similarly he would lift a festive glass to toast visitors or celebrate special occasions such as holiday meals. All the drinks described below are his personal recipes.

Blackberry Cordial

Shakespeare once wished that "reason was as plentiful as blackberries." Certainly the latter were plentiful along the ditch rows and field edges at Hampton, and in the "make do with what you've got" practicality that financial straits mandated through Rutledge's life, blackberries were picked for cobblers, jams, jellies, and canning. They were also used for a flavorful, refreshing libation. Here is what Rutledge offered in that regard, saying, "this has been a beverage long esteemed in the South both because of its rich flavor and because of its medicinal qualities. This cordial will be drunk, not made, at Christmas-time, but the recipe for it is given here."

Select the ripest berries, mash them with a wooden or agate spoon, and squeeze them through a jelly bag. For every quart of juice, allow one pound of sugar, a half ounce of cloves, and a half ounce of cinnamon. Boil the whole to a thin jelly. When this is cold, add one-half pint of brandy to each quart of jelly, stir all well together, then bottle, corking securely. This is not fit for use under three months and improves greatly with age.

Syllabub

Taken from The Carolina Housewife, *written by "a Lady of Charleston" (Sarah "Sally" Rutledge, the spinster daughter of Declaration of Independence signatory Edward Rutledge), this rich drink was a holiday favorite. Rutledge was a great lover of tradition, and a toddy tracing back to his ancestors would have been particularly appealing to him.*

To a quart of cream add a half pint of sweet wine (in which the peel of the lemons used for juice has been steeped) and a half pint of Madeira. Then add the juice of two lemons, finely powdered allspice, and sugar to taste. Whisk all ingredients together, stirring vigorously until a froth rises. Skim away the froth and continue whisking. The froth is placed in glasses partly filled with the liquid mixture to produce syllabub.

Saints' Delight

Quite possibly the name of this Hampton Plantation favorite originated elsewhere, but it carries the ring of Rutledge's way with titles. It was one of his personal favorites and made regular appearances during the Christmas season. The use of mint in midwinter may seem strange, but it should be remembered that the climate in the Low Country approaches being subtropical, and mint's hardiness ensured its being available throughout the year.

This is a Southern beverage that should be mixed in glasses. In each glass put one tablespoon of honey and two of whiskey or brandy. Then fill the glass with rich milk [i.e., milk with the butterfat left in it, which would have been the norm in Rutledge's prime]. Stir well, adding crushed ice and a few leaves of mint. This drink takes its name from the presence in it of the innocent milk.

Golden Moonbeam

For generations the Rutledge family spent the hottest months of the year in the North Carolina high country, doing so to escape the heat, humidity, and insects of the Low Country. Indeed he has grandparents buried in Flat Rock, a favorite retreat for affluent folks from the Charleston area in the nineteenth century. This drink almost certainly owes its name to those who spoke what a noted 2004 book by Michael B. Montgomery and Joseph S. Hall calls, in its title, "Smoky Mountain English." I grew up in the heart of this country and heard terms such as moonshine, snakebite medicine, squeezin's, *and* peartin' juice *used on a regular basis, but* golden moonbeam *is new to me, although I do recall that one of Al Capp's cartoon characters in his* Li'l Abner *comic strip was named Moonbeam McSwine. Yet the connotations of the phrase, redolent of such thoughts as chasing moonbeams or mild inebriation, suggest the term may well have originated with Rutledge. He merely writes that "this is a fanciful name given to a famous drink which originated on the northern slopes of Carolina, where much illicit whiskey is distilled, and where one never mentions a drink by its real name, but by some pseudonym."*

To a wineglass of whiskey or brandy add the juice of half an orange and a teaspoonful of sugar. Add a pinch of red pepper and powdered cinnamon.

Stir into it crushed ice and bits of orange peel. This is one of the drinks that are said to renew one's youth—temporarily.

Starters

Okra Soup

This recipe is offered in the precise fashion Rutledge provided in 1912. Like many soups, it is at least as good warmed over as when served fresh from the stove. Many portions are inexact, as was typical of cookery at the time, but that in no way affects the culinary quality of this hearty fare. At Hampton the soup would be served as an early course, but with home-baked bread or a sandwich made from sliced venison or wild turkey leftovers, it can form a fine and filling midday meal.

One good knuckle or shank of beef or mutton. One soup ladle heaped with dried okra, well washed and cut into small rings [today's cook would want to use frozen okra]. Rather less than half that quantity of canned tomatoes, rubbed through a colander. Dissolve one tablespoonful of sugar in the tomatoes. Boil all together slowly and steadily [i.e., simmer] for at least five hours, with four or five quarts of water being added just before boiling begins. This recipe will make soup sufficient for a large family. Never add water after the soup begins to boil.

Toasted Pecans

Pecan trees, both wild and cultivated ones, were plentiful at Hampton, and the inhabitants used pecans as a ready-to-hand snack, in dressing, and as something to munch with a cocktail or cup of tea.

    4 cups pecan halves
    ⅓–½ cup melted butter
    ½ teaspoon salt

Place pecans in jelly roll pan (do not use a dark-colored pan). Drizzle butter over pecans and stir until nuts are well coated. Sprinkle with salt and bake at 325 degrees for thirty to forty minutes or until lightly toasted. Stir frequently and watch carefully to avoid overbrowning. Place on paper towels to drain. Store in air-tight containers.

Oyster Stew

Hampton was close enough to the Carolina coast to enjoy access to the sea's rich bounty, and oysters roasted, used as stuffing, and offered in other ways were fairly common fare. A steaming bowl of oyster stew was an ideal start to a festive meal or end to a demanding hunt.

> 1 pint shucked oysters
> 3 tablespoons butter
> 1 quart milk
> salt and pepper

Heat oysters slowly in their own juice until edges begin to curl. Season with salt and pepper. Add butter. Combine with scalded milk and serve with crackers. Note: Can be prepared with milk using a double boiler.

Duck Soup

At Hampton no palatable foodstuff was wasted. There were simply too many mouths to feed and too much dependence on nature's bounty for it to be otherwise. This recipe, which utilizes duck carcasses, is a prime example.

> 4 duck carcasses (fillets removed)
> 4 diced carrots
> 3 diced onions
> 6 diced stalks celery
> 1½ teaspoons marjoram
> 1½ teaspoons thyme
> 1 teaspoon oregano
> 1 bay leaf
> dry sherry, 1 ounce per serving
> 4 cups wild or Carolina Gold rice, cooked

Add water to cover carcasses in a large pan, bring to a boil, and simmer for 150 minutes. Cool and strip meat from bones, discarding skin and bones. Skim off most of the fat (easier to do after refrigerating the meat and broth).

Return broth and meat to the heat and add remaining ingredients except the sherry and rice. Bring broth, meat, vegetables, and seasonings to a boil and simmer for twenty minutes. Add salt and pepper to taste. Add the four cups of cooked rice, simmer an additional ten minutes, and remove bay leaf. Pour an ounce of sherry into prewarmed soup bowls, fill with soup, and serve.

Side Dishes

Hoppin' John

Hoppin' John, a dish featuring ingredients that were everyday standards in the Low Country, was traditionally consumed on New Year's Day. It is included here because the Rutledges normally ended their holidays at Hampton by staying through January 1 before beginning the long, somewhat sorrowful trek back to Mercersburg.

1 cup rice
slab of bacon (or fatback)
1 medium onion
salt and pepper
1 cup black-eyed peas
sliced bacon

Soak peas overnight. Cook peas in salt water with bacon slab. When peas are done, cook rice in a steamer with minced onions and sliced bacon, which has been fried separately. Add liquid the peas were cooked in and then add peas. Add additional water if needed. Add salt and pepper to taste.

Herbed Rice

With rice being readily available, easily stored, and highly versatile, it figured prominently in Hampton cuisine.

2 tablespoons butter
1/2 cup chopped onion
1/4–1/2 cup chopped hazelnuts or pecans
1 cup uncooked long-grain rice
2 cups chicken broth
1/2 cup chopped fresh parsley
1/2 teaspoon dried thyme
dash of black pepper
1/4–1/2 teaspoon curry powder
dash of paprika

Melt butter in skillet. Stir in onion, hazelnuts, and uncooked rice. Sauté until onions are tender and nuts and rice are golden. Stir in broth, parsley, thyme, marjoram, curry powder, pepper, and paprika. Mix thoroughly. Bring to a boil, reduce heat, cover, and cook until liquid is absorbed and rice is tender.

Gumbo

Most gumbo-type dishes trace their origins to slave culture, and with black cooks handling kitchen chores at Hampton, okra- and tomato-based dishes were common fare. Interestingly canned tomatoes were used, but the okra often came from dried pieces rather than a canned form.

1 quart okra
½ small onion, chopped
1 pint can tomatoes
Salt and pepper to taste
2 slices bacon
dash of Worcestershire sauce

Broil bacon and add tomatoes, chopped okra, and other ingredients. Simmer slowly for two hours. Typically served over rice.

Candied Sweet Potatoes

Sweet potatoes were standard daily fare at Hampton. Rutledge mentions them frequently, such as when he writes of "a row of baked sweet potatoes, with sugar oozing out on their brown skins," lining the bricks of hearths in black homes in "Christmas in the Castle." Baked sweet potatoes provided a hearty snack or a nice complement to a full meal, and doubtless the habit of carrying one or two cold in the capacious pockets of a Duxbak hunting coat, something I did regularly as a youngster, was commonplace with Rutledge and his sons. A cold sweet potato tastes mighty fine when one gets peckish in the midst of a hunt. Of course sweet potatoes were utilized in more sophisticated fashion, such as this recipe, as well.

3 large sweet potatoes
½ cup water
1 cup brown sugar
4 tablespoons butter
6 pieces orange peel
cinnamon

Boil whole potatoes until done. Take off skin and slice thin. Place in a buttered Pyrex dish, sprinkling each layer of potatoes with sugar, cinnamon, and butter. When dish is full, cover top layer with sugar, butter, cinnamon, and orange peel. Add water and bake at 350 degrees until brown (about thirty minutes).

Breads

✌∴✌

Cornbread

At Hampton, as was almost universally true throughout the South for much of the twentieth century, cornbread figured prominently in daily fare. Throughout my boyhood, for example, we had hot cornbread at dinner (the midday meal) and then leftover cold cornbread crumbled in milk or buttermilk for supper. During the winter months crackling cornbread, using the tasty if cholesterol-laden bits skimmed from lard when we butchered and processed our own hogs, often substituted for meat. One suspects the same approach prevailed with the Rutledges, and mention of cornbread occurs frequently in Old Flintlock's writings.

1 ½ cups sifted cornmeal
¾ teaspoon baking soda
⅓ cup all-purpose flour
1 tablespoon sugar
1 ½ cups buttermilk
1 teaspoon salt
1 egg
4 tablespoons bacon drippings or shortening
1 teaspoon baking powder

Mix dry ingredients in bowl. Add buttermilk mixed with egg. Add two tablespoons drippings last. Heat remaining two tablespoons in a cast-iron pan and pour batter into the pan. Batter should sizzle when hitting the pan. Bake in a 400-degree oven until brown and done. If you want the top to be a golden brown (the bottom will be crusty and dark brown), place under broiler briefly.

Buttermilk Biscuits

When it came to bread, cornbread was standard at Hampton. Biscuits required "store-bought" flour as opposed to the cornmeal that came from grain raised on the plantation's fertile acres. Accordingly big biscuits, sometimes described as "cathead biscuits" because of their whopping size, were served only on special occasions such as Christmas.

2 cups all-purpose flour
3 teaspoon baking powder
1 teaspoon salt
⅛ cup Crisco or solid shortening
¼ teaspoon baking soda
1 cup buttermilk

Sift dry ingredients together, then cut in Crisco and stir in buttermilk. On a floured board, knead lightly about ten times. Roll out, cut biscuits, and place on an ungreased baking sheet. Bake at 450 degrees for twelve to fifteen minutes.

Spoon Bread

Often called batter bread, this was a favorite at Hampton and utilized the cornmeal that was a staple.

1 cup cornmeal
2 cups milk
1 teaspoon salt
2 eggs
1 heaping teaspoon baking powder
1 cup boiling water
1 tablespoon melted butter
1 tablespoon melted lard

Mix meal, salt, and baking powder. Add egg, beaten lightly, sweet milk, and enough boiling water to make a very thin batter. Then add butter and lard. Place in a well-greased baking dish and cook for thirty minutes (or until done) in a 375-degree oven.

Hominy Bread

Hominy, made on the plantation using traditional methods and corn grown on Hampton grounds, was used in many forms. Often leftover hominy would be combined with raw hominy to produce a hearty and unusual (but delicious) bread.

1 cup cooked hominy
1 cup raw washed hominy
1 egg

1 large tablespoon shortening

½ teaspoon salt

Combine cooked hominy, egg, shortening, and salt, rubbing until smooth. Add raw hominy that has been drained fairly dry after washing. Bake at 350 degrees for a half hour or until nicely browned. This can be baked as a "cake" or in muffin rings.

Main Dishes

Venison Roast

Venison was the most important of all the meats served at Hampton during the Christmas holidays. Deer hunting was central to the annual family pilgrimage to the plantation, and deer meat provided fine fare for the family, those in permanent residence at Hampton, and guests. In a typical year several whitetails would be killed, and that meant meat on the table and sumptuous fare for all.

1 venison haunch

1 chopped onion

½ pound sliced bacon

salt and pepper to taste

Wash the venison haunch and dry thoroughly. Mix onion with salt and pepper, cut slits in meat, and stuff with the mixture. Cover the haunch with bacon strips. Place in a large roasting pan. Add one cup of water, cover, and cook in slow oven until done (allow twenty-five minutes per pound). Baste frequently with moisture in pan.

Shrimp-Stuffed Venison Tenderloin

With shrimp and venison being readily available at Hampton, this would have been a delightful dish that ranks right at the top of nature's bounty. It comes from Wild Bounty, *a cookbook written by the editor of this book and his wife.*

1 whole venison backstrap

½–1 cup Italian salad dressing

12 whole medium shrimp, cooked and peeled

1 teaspoon Old Bay seasoning

1 tablespoon butter, melted
2 teaspoons lemon juice
1–2 slices bacon

Cut loin lengthwise to within a quarter inch of bottom, then marinate in Italian dressing for at least four hours. Cook shrimp in water seasoned with Old Bay seasoning and peel. Place shrimp end-to-end inside loin. Melt butter and add lemon juice, then drizzle over shrimp. Close meat around shrimp and secure with toothpicks or string. Place bacon strips over shrimp and secure with toothpicks. Place loin on a rack in broiler pan and roast at 400 degrees for about forty minutes or until rare (do not overcook—an instant-read meat thermometer is very helpful here). Meanwhile, prepare wine sauce (see below).

Wine Sauce

$\frac{1}{2}$ cup butter
$\frac{1}{4}$ cup finely chopped onion
$\frac{1}{2}$ cup sliced mushrooms
1–2 large garlic cloves, minced
$\frac{1}{2}$ cup white wine
$\frac{1}{2}$ teaspoon Worcestershire sauce

Melt butter. Sauté onion, mushrooms, and garlic until tender. Add wine and Worcestershire sauce and simmer slowly to reduce to about half. To serve, slice loin, remove toothpicks, and spoon on wine sauce.

Venison Steak and Potatoes

Hearty food was a must for the Hampton hunters, and a dish of this sort, using the fruits of the chase with homegrown produce, would have formed welcome fare.

1 pound cubed venison steak
2 tablespoons olive oil
1 can (10 $\frac{3}{4}$-ounce) cream of celery soup
$\frac{1}{2}$ cup milk
$\frac{1}{2}$ cup sour cream
$\frac{1}{4}$ teaspoon fresh ground pepper
16 ounces hash brown potatoes
$\frac{1}{2}$ cup shredded cheddar cheese, divided
1 (3-ounce) can French fried onions, divided

Brown steaks in olive oil in a skillet and set aside. Combine soup, milk, sour cream, and pepper. Stir in cooked hash browns, $\frac{1}{3}$ cup cheese, and

½ can onions. Spoon mixture into nine-by-thirteen-inch baking dish. Arrange steaks over potatoes. Bake, covered, at 350 degrees for forty-five to fifty minutes. Top with remaining cheese and onions and bake, uncovered, for an additional five to ten minutes.

Roast Wild Turkey

Unlike the situation over most of the country, wild turkeys never vanished or even became exceptionally scarce at Hampton. Second only to deer, they figure most prominently in Rutledge's writings, and wild turkey and venison were considered the essential centerpieces of Christmas feasts at the plantation, with the gustatory delights they provided being a close second to the thrills of the chase.

Weigh the dressed bird and multiply its weight by twelve to get the cooking time (a ten-pound bird would require two hours). Place the bird in a shallow roasting pan and cover its breast with bacon strips. Roast in an oven preheated to 350 degrees for the allotted time. Internal temperature, which should be 140–150 degrees, can be checked with a meat thermometer. It is important to remove the bird from the oven when it reaches 150 degrees. Let it rest for ten to fifteen minutes. It will continue cooking during that time. Overcooking is not merely a mistake; it is a cardinal sin. You can prepare stuffing using the giblets or make a separate dressing if desired. Note: While wild turkey breast is moist, tasty, and more than holds its own with a domestic bird, the dark meat will be coarse, stringy, and tough. It is best suited to making pâté or using in sandwiches.

Wild Duck and Mushrooms

Rutledge frequently mentions ducks (usually calling them "wildfowl") as an integral part of holiday feasts at Hampton. The rice fields and wetlands around the plantation formed an ideal habitat for waterfowl, and he wrote a number of pieces about hunting ducks. Most of this hunting was done from a flat-bottomed boat, poled by Prince Alston or others of his "huntermen."

1 duck
1 cup fresh mushrooms, sliced
1 onion, sliced
2 tablespoons flour
salt and pepper to taste
¼ teaspoon thyme
2 cups water
1 bay leaf
½ cup butter or drippings

Clean and disjoint duck, then brown with onion and fat. Add salt and pepper with two cups of water and a bay leaf. Cook slowly for ninety minutes. Sauté mushrooms, then add flour and thyme. Add to duck and cook an additional thirty minutes. Serve flanked by wild rice and venison sausage.

Shrimp and Hominy

Hominy seems, in today's culinary world, to have given way in large measure to its cousin, grits. Yet this dish, featuring two standards of Low Country fare, was, according to Two Hundred Years of Charleston Cooking, *"served in almost every house in Charleston during shrimp season." It was primarily a breakfast dish and would have provided hearty fare, when accompanied by venison sausage, eggs, and biscuits, for a prehunt meal.*

> 1 pound raw shrimp
> ½ cup butter
> salt and pepper to taste
> 2 cups cooked hominy

Shell the shrimp, place in a saucepan in which the butter has been melted, add salt and pepper, and stir until the shrimp turn pink. Serve with piping hot hominy.

Duck Gumbo

Although his literary output on waterfowling was relatively sparse, Rutledge did his fair share of duck hunting in a place and time when they were comparatively plentiful. More to the point, he regularly refers to ducks as a standard item of holiday fare at Hampton.

> 2 mallards or 3 wood ducks
> 3 chopped medium onions
> 3 large Irish potatoes or rice
> 8 chopped celery stalks
> salt and pepper to taste

Clean ducks and boil in a covered pot until meat falls from the bones. Remove meat, saving stock, and cut it into chunks. Cool the stock and remove the fats and oil. Add salt and pepper and enough water to cook the potatoes or rice (with celery). Cook over medium heat until a firm done is reached. Add meat and cook just long enough to reheat.

Quail Hash atop Buttered Wild Rice

The heyday of bobwhite quail, universally known simply as "birds" to Southern hunters, has long passed. Yet the agricultural practices and rural living conditions of Rutledge's prime were perfect for quail. They thrived in the pea field corners and fence rows, and tenants kept the numbers of their many enemies—snakes, raptors, 'coons, possums, and foxes—at a minimum. There were no coyotes or fire ants in the Low Country at the time. As a result bevies of bobwhites abounded, and Rutledge mentions hunting and eating them quite often.

12 quail, cleaned
1 medium onion, sliced
5 stalks celery, cut
½ cup light cream
1 ½ cups uncooked wild rice

Place quail in a large saucepan, add two cups of water along with the onion and celery. Simmer gently (covered) for fifteen to twenty minutes. Remove and allow to cool. Reserve the liquid, removing the onion and celery, and then boil until reduced to one cup. Add the light cream and set aside.

Once quail have cooled, debone and julienne into strips. While quail are being prepared, the wild rice can be cooking. Place in a large saucepan with four to five cups of water. Bring to a boil, then lower the heat and simmer for fifteen minutes. Strain, rinse rice, and start again. Repeat the process a third time (total cooking time of forty-five minutes). After about ten minutes in the final cooking period, watch rice to see if the jackets have burst. When this happens, the wild rice is done, and overcooking will make it mushy. Drain and keep warm (leave in sieve over simmering water) while preparing sauce.

Quail Hash Sauce

3 tablespoons butter
3 tablespoons potato or rice flour
1 ½ cups liquid (1 cup reduced poaching liquid plus
    ½ cup light cream) heated
4 minced shallots
1 minced celery stalk
12 cups minced parsley
1 teaspoon chervil

1 teaspoon salt

¼ teaspoon ground nutmeg

While the rice is boiling, melt three tablespoons of butter in a large saucepan. Add three tablespoons potato or rice flour and let bubble gently for three minutes over medium heat. Heat the poaching liquid and pour it into the flour and butter, whisking constantly until thick and creaming. Set aside over hot but not boiling water in a double boiler.

Sauté the parsley, shallots, and celery over medium heat until soft. Add salt and pepper to taste. Grate the nutmeg into the sauce and add the julienned quail meat. Mix thoroughly and heat long enough to be hot. Serve over the boiled and buttered wild rice. Make sure not to overcook the quail, a tip that holds true for almost any wild game dish (and which is the most common mistake in dealing with such dishes).

Hampton Plantation Smothered Chicken

This recipe comes from the fine cookbook Charleston Receipts *and is credited to a Miss Caroline Rutledge. Caroline, who never married, was Archibald's oldest sister.*

Cut chicken in pieces. Place gizzard, neck, and tips of wings in saucepan. Cover well with water. Add chopped celery, onion, and salt. Simmer about twenty minutes. Then put grease in frying pan, using a good tablespoon or more. When hot, though not too hot, add chicken, which has been salted and rolled in flour. Cover and cook about twenty-five minutes over medium flame. Turn pieces several times. Pour off grease, add the simmered gravy, cover closely, and cook on a very low heat for five to ten minutes.

Hampton Plantation Shrimp Pilau

Presumably, given its title, this was a dish served regularly at Hampton. Certainly it features ingredients regularly used in the Low Country, and it comes from Mrs. Paul Seabrook (Rutledge's sister, née Harriott Horry Rutledge), who provided it for a popular cookbook, Charleston Receipts.

4 slices bacon

2 tablespoons chopped bell pepper

1 cup rice

salt and pepper to taste

2 tablespoons butter

1 teaspoon Worcestershire sauce

½ cup finely chopped celery

1 tablespoon flour

2 cups peeled shrimp

Fry bacon until crisp and set aside. Add bacon grease to water to be used to cook rice. In a second pot, melt butter, then add celery and bell pepper. Cook for a few minutes and then add shrimp, which have been sprinkled with Worcestershire sauce and dredged in flour. Stir and simmer until flour is cooked. Season with salt and pepper. Now add cooked rice and mix until rice is "buttery and shrimpy." It may be necessary to add more butter. Finally, stir in the crisp bacon, crumbled, and serve hot.

Low Country Shrimp Boil

Seafood looms large in Southern cooking, and this dish from the Carolina coast is hearty, easily prepared, and ideally suited for consumption in an outdoor setting such as a midday hunt meal. Since most of Rutledge's life predated the advent of home freezers, he would not have included corn in a shrimp boil.

  3 pounds smoke venison sausage kielbasa, cut into 2-inch pieces
  3 ribs celery, cut into 1-inch pieces
  4 tablespoons Old Bay seasoning
  8 potatoes, cut into 2-inch pieces
  10–12 ears corn, halved
  3 onions, cut into 2-inch pieces
  5 pounds headed shrimp
  3–4 pounds crab legs (optional)

Fill a large pot half full of water and bring to a boil over medium-high heat. Cook sausage, potatoes, onions, celery, and Old Bay seasoning thirty minutes or until potatoes are fork tender. Add corn, shrimp, and crab legs and let simmer for three or four minutes or until shrimp turn pink. Drain and serve immediately on large platters.

Desserts

Cardinal Pudding

This was one of Rutledge's personal favorites, standard fare at Hampton when Christmas came around. Rich and flavorful, it took the place of fruitcake (and contained many of the same ingredients).

Put a layer of simple sponge cake in the bottom of a deep pudding dish. Dampen with sherry, and stick the cake full of raisins, citron, and blanched almonds. Cover with boiled custard seasoned with wine. Then put on another layer of cake treated in the same way, and pour over the rest of the custard.

Plantation Persimmon Pudding

Beloved by deer and a whole host of other creatures when ripe, persimmons were also a favorite tool for country kids who wished to fool their city slicker cousins. When unripe a persimmon redefines pucker power thanks to its astringent, alum-like taste. Persimmons were plentiful along dusty roads and field edges at Hampton Plantation, and they formed the essential item for a rich, divine pudding.

  2 cups persimmon pulp
  2 cups packed brown sugar
  ¼ cup butter, melted
  1 teaspoon vanilla
  1 ½ cups self-rising flour
  ½ cup light cream
  ½ teaspoon cinnamon
  ½ cup raisins or pecan meats (optional)

Combine all ingredients and beat just until well mixed. Pour into a greased nine-by-thirteen-inch pan and bake at 350 degrees for thirty to thirty-five minutes or until golden brown and just beginning to pull away from the sides. Remove from oven and cool slightly. Cover with foil or plastic wrap. Cut into squares and serve with whipped topping. Note: Persimmons have a subtle but sublime flavor. You can add a tablespoon of bourbon for flavoring if desired.

Raspberry Mousse

This recipe, taken from Charleston Receipts, *originated with Rutledge's sister Caroline.*

  2 eggs
  2 ½ tablespoons gelatin
  1 quart cream
  1 quart milk
  1 pint raspberry jam
  ½ cup cold water

Beat eggs into cream and jam. Soften gelatin in cold water and then dissolve in hot milk. After that cools, pour in the mixture and put in refrigerator until set.

Bread Pudding

    12 slices bread
    ¾ stick butter
    1 egg
    milk (enough to cover bread)
    2 tablespoons sugar
    cinnamon

Break up bread into medium-size crumbs. Place in a casserole dish. Bring milk and butter to a boil. When cool add beaten egg and sugar to milk and butter. Pour over bread crumbs (just to cover), sprinkle top with cinnamon, and add a bit of sugar to top. Bake uncovered in oven at 350 degrees for about forty minutes or until top is brown. Note: Raisins or other fruits can be added to the bread crumbs prior to baking, and it is common to cover individual servings with a hard sauce or custard (see below).

Boiled Custard

Milk and eggs were plentiful at Hampton Plantation, as would have been true for any large household in rural South Carolina in the first half of the twentieth century. Accordingly custard was a favorite, frequently offered dessert, either by itself as a topping.

    1 pint sweet milk
    ¼ cup sugar
    2 eggs
    ½ teaspoon vanilla

Heat milk in top of a double boiler. Beat eggs and add sugar. Pour a small portion of milk into egg mixture. Add more gradually, stirring constantly. Heat mixture in top boiler, stirring constantly until it will coat the spoon. Remove from heat and add vanilla. Can be served hot over bread pudding or other desserts or allowed to cool and eaten by itself.

Plantation Plum Pudding

Plum pudding traces its origins to England, and it was a festive dish likely to be served on Christmas Day. Many households would include a coin or small piece of jewelry in the pudding, which contained no plums despite its name, with the lucky "finder" feeling especially blessed. Extremely rich, plum pudding kept well, with a bit of wine being added to keep the pudding moist. It was often served with a hard sauce.

1 pint bread crumbs
1 pint brown sugar
1 pint finely chopped suet
2 pounds seeded raisins
1 pound currants
¼ pound grated or finely cut citron
5 eggs
2 wineglasses of brandy
1 teaspoon powdered cloves
1 teaspoon nutmeg
1 teaspoon cinnamon
1 teaspoon soda
½ pint flour
¼ pound chopped almonds

Sift flour on fruit, beat eggs and brown sugar together, and add other ingredients. Place in four one-pound coffee cans (this was the way it was cooked at Hampton, although other receptacles will work), tie on gauze covers with string, and steam for three hours on a rack in a large pot holding water to a level just below the rack.

Pumpkin Pie

Although more commonly associated with Thanksgiving, pumpkin pie would have been a part of the dessert offerings at a Hampton Christmas. Easy to grow and resistant to rot for months after harvesting, pumpkins and other types of winter squash, such as cushaws, were eaten by folks living on the plantation and also used to fatten hogs.

1 cup stewed pumpkin
1 cup brown sugar
1 teaspoon ground ginger
1 teaspoon ground cinnamon
¼ teaspoon salt
2 eggs
2 cups milk
2 tablespoons melted butter
pastry

Add the sugar and seasonings to the pumpkin and mix well. Then add the slightly beaten eggs and the milk and lastly stir in the melted butter. Turn into a pie plate lined with pastry and bake in a 425-degree oven for five minutes. Then lower the heat to 350 degrees and bake until the filling is set. The pie should be allowed to cool prior to serving.

Orange Jelly

Rutledge mentions oranges a number of times in his writing, with orange marmalade apparently having been one of his personal favorites. This recipe, originally published in the enduring classic Miss Rutledge's Cook Book, *might well have been used by generations of Hampton cooks. It is somewhat complex, but the end results justify every bit of the preparation and cooking time and trouble required.*

This jelly, so beloved by Rutledge (who clearly had a sweet tooth), would have given a Hampton Plantation biscuit a college education or served as a fine glaze for duck breasts.

Take the juice of eight oranges and six lemons, then grate the peel of half of the citrus fruits and cover it with a pint of cold water. After it has soaked long enough to extract the flavor, strain and mix the water with the juice. Add a cup of melted sugar, a package of melted gelatin, and the beaten whites of seven eggs. Place everything in a saucepan and stir until boiling. Let boil for a few minutes, then place in a mold or in glass containers. Place in a refrigerator until set, when it is ready to serve.

About the Editor

JIM CASADA, a retired history professor, is one of the country's most widely published outdoor writers. He has written or edited more than forty books, contributed to many others, and authored some five thousand magazine articles. A longtime student of Archibald Rutledge, Casada has edited four previous Rutledge anthologies—*Hunting and Home in the Southern Heartland; Tales of Whitetails; America's Greatest Game Bird;* and *Bird Dog Days, Wingshooting Ways.* Casada has been honored with more than 150 regional and national awards for his writing, including the Federation of Fly Fishermen's Arnold Gingrich Memorial Award, the National Wild Turkey Federation's Communicator of the Year Award, and the South Carolina Wildlife Federation's Harry R. E. Hampton Memorial Award. A past president of the South Carolina Outdoor Writers Association, the Southeastern Outdoor Press Association, and the Outdoor Writers Association of America, he serves as editor at large for *Sporting Classics* and *Turkey & Turkey Hunting* magazines. Casada lives in Rock Hill, South Carolina